Management
Stripped Bare

THIRD EDITION

Management Stripped Bare

What they don't teach you at business school

JO OWEN

KoganPage

LONDON PHILADELPHIA NEW DELHI

First published in Great Britain and the United States in 2002 by Kogan Page Limited
Second edition 2006
Third edition 2012

120 Pentonville Road
London N1 9JN
United Kingdom
www.koganpage.com

1518 Walnut Street, Suite 1100
Philadelphia PA 19102
USA

4737/23 Ansari Road
Daryaganj
New Delhi 110002
India

ISBN   978 0 7494 6476 9
E-ISBN   978 0 7494 6477 6

British Library Cataloguing-in-Publication Data

A CIP record for this book is available from the British Library.

Library of Congress Cataloging-in-Publication Data

Owen, Jo.
    Management stripped bare : what they don't teach you at business school / Jo Owen. – 3rd ed.
        p. cm.
    Includes bibliographical references.
    ISBN 978-0-7494-6476-9 – ISBN 978-0-7494-6477-6   1. Management.   I. Title.
    HD31.O846 2012
    658.003–dc23
                                                          2011045411

Typeset by Graphicraft Ltd, Hong Kong
Printed production managed by Jellyfish
Printed and bound by CPI Group (UK) Ltd, Croydon, CR0 4YY

Contents

Introduction

Managers the world over face the same problems. Bad meetings, boring presentations, political intrigue, difficult bosses and unhelpful staff plague them. They are caught in the crossfire of unreasonable goals with inadequate resources, complex organizations and an uncertain and changing outside world. Somehow managers are meant to make sense of this.

And yet, there is no training or guidance on how to deal with the problems that managers face. It is simply assumed that they know instinctively how to run good meetings, how to write well, how to deal with the thousand tricky situations that crop up in the managerial year.

In the end, managers serve an informal apprenticeship where they learn from the successes and failures of all those around them. After some years, they land up with a model of how they think their world works and how they can survive in it.

The good news is that those patterns of success and failure are common to all managers in all industries. There is no single rule of success. Instead, there are a thousand small things that a manager can do right or wrong every day.

In the 10 years since *Management Stripped Bare* was first published, the world has changed dramatically. China has come from being nowhere to the cusp of global domination. The dot.com bomb was merely the prelude to a world that is increasingly being lived online. And we have had a global financial crisis from which we are still recovering. But the essence of management has not changed. Managers still face tough targets, ambiguous demands, uncertain markets, stroppy customers and awkward colleagues. And these are precisely the sorts of things an MBA does not address.

This third edition includes over 30 new sections. Some are profound, such as why the capital asset pricing model is no longer fit for purpose in the wake of the financial crisis. Others appear light, such as the art of flattery. But there is a serious purpose to each section: to show how practising managers can practise better in big ways and small.

Management Stripped Bare is unlike other management books. **This is not about management as it should be. It is about management as it is.** As you read the book, it should describe a world you recognize, because it draws on over 2,000 interviews and 30 years' experience of serving different industries across the world to map out what consistently does, and does not, work in the situations managers face. It is not a grand theory of management. It is a practical guide to survival in the managerial world.

You can read *Management Stripped Bare* any way you like: from start to end, back to front, from the middle out or just dip in and out. And the book assumes you are smart: it is not a textbook that lays out exactly what you have to do in every situation, because the world is not a textbook – it is messy. Each section lays out a simple issue and offers a simple way of dealing with it: you can figure out how to apply the idea in practice to your daily work.

TABLE 0.1

Accenture	Chase Group	Mitsubishi Chemicals	SABIC
AEGON	Citibank	Monsanto	San Miguel
AGM	Cognitas	National Air Traffic Services	SDP
American Express	Dow Chemical		Start Up
ANZ bank	Future Leaders	NatWest	SWIFT
Apple		Nordea	Symantec
Armstrong Industries	Hallmark Cards	Norwegian Dairy Association	Teach First
Aviva	HCA	Philips	Teaching Leaders
Barclays	HMRC	Playtex	Thorn Rental
BT	ItoChu	Procter & Gamble	UBS
Cap Gemini	Lloyds Bank	Qualcomm	Zeneca
Central Bank of Indonesia	MAC Group	RHM	Zurich Financial Services
	MetLife	Royal Sun Alliance	

Ultimately, we all learn from experience. This book condenses thousands of years of hard-won experience from managers around the world into a few pages. It will help you accelerate your learning. But I have only been able to write this book because of the experience I have gained working with others: this includes over 100 of the best, and one or two of the worst, organizations on our planet. From some I have learned good lessons, from others I have learned what not to do. Table 0.1 shows some of the many organizations I have worked with, and I would like to thank them all.

Inevitably, this book would not have got off the ground without an army of people to make it happen. So my thanks go to Frances Kelly, my agent, for having faith in this project from the outset and to Jon Finch and the team at Kogan Page for turning the idea into reality. And finally, my thanks to all those managers and organizations that let me work with them: I hope they got something out of it as well.

Summary

This is not a universal theory of management. It is not a simple formula for instant management success. And that is, perhaps, the most important lesson: you have an infinite number of ways to succeed and fail. Do not trust or follow one simplistic management theory.

The challenges managers face on a daily basis are consistent around the world and across industries. They are the familiar challenges of inadequate resources, wasted meetings, difficult bosses and staff, mountains of administrivia. Just as the challenges are the same the world over, so too are the patterns of managerial success and failure. The most important of these are:

- *Understand the rules of the game.* Every industry and every company has different rules by which competition is played out. There are, however, different attitudes to risk taking, career progression, hierarchy, dress codes and even use of language. These rules are rarely written. If you understand the rules by which you are expected to play, you can decide if a particular company and industry represents a good fit with how you like to live and work. And, once you understand the rules of the game, you will know when you can profitably break the rules. Breaking the rules is a vital part of the rules.
- *Get the basics right.* All managers spend a large amount of time in meetings, and preparing or reviewing documents and presentations.

This is common to all industries and all managers, and yet very little training or guidance is available on how to do these things well. Not surprisingly, most management documents, meetings and presentations are deadly dull. This gives power to those managers who stand out from the mediocrity around them. **Do not search for excellence, search for competence** if you want to stand out against your peers.

- *Manage people, not things*. Management is about human nature, and human nature is not always rational. People and management are naturally political. That means that core management skills have to include politics such as building and using alliances to secure the support or resources you require. People are also emotional. They crave recognition, they normally dislike risk. Understanding and managing this requires being able to see the world through their eyes, not yours. Most training focuses on technical skills such as accounting, IT or marketing. These are important at the start of your career. As you gain seniority, the people skills become more important relative to the technical skills. But, if there is any training on managing people, politics or emotions it is normally some flaky psycho-babble.

- *Focus on what's important, not just what is necessary*. Most of your time is likely to be spent dealing with the necessary: the flood of daily e-mails, routine meetings, preparing reports. This administration is more or less necessary to keep the business ticking over. But it does not move the business forward. If you are to make a mark, you have to move the business forward. You have to make a difference.

Nearly all of this is common sense. This is a commodity that is in short supply. Little common sense is available through training; it is assumed that either you have it or that you pick it up by some magic form of osmosis. And you will certainly not find any of this taught at business schools, although common sense is what you need to survive in business.

An age of ambiguity

It used to be so simple: managers managed, workers worked. Thinking and doing were separate. People may not have liked it, but at least they knew where they were. Now, no one knows where they stand. We work in a high commitment but family-friendly environment. Passion is in, but loyalty is out. We have gigabytes of data, but no useful information. Organizations are flat, but we are matrixed to two bosses where the old hierarchy gave us just one. We are meant to be empowered, but we have more reporting than ever. We are meant to be entrepreneurial, but are not meant to fail. It's not even clear what we are meant to wear. Conformity of the suit has been replaced by confusion of choice. The gurus have all the answers, but all the answers are different. No one knows the problem.

For the brave, ambiguity is great. It creates opportunities to ignore the rules, break the rules, change the rules as it suits. **The brave enjoy career acceleration: they succeed fast or fail fast.** For the rest of us, we are left searching for the few rocks of certainty and stability that we can call our own as the revolution gathers around us. This book is a survival guide to the revolution.

Agreement and argument

Agreement is easy, and dangerous. Excessive agreement is positively unhealthy. Human nature dislikes conflict. Managers often pretend to agree even when they disagree. Agreement is safe, disagreement is dangerous. The disagreement only becomes apparent after the meeting when people are chatting around the coffee machine. This is the wrong time to start the disagreement. Excessive agreement is dangerous because:

- *It rarely represents the best solution.* When everyone agrees without discussion, this normally shows deference to the hierarchy or lack of interest, rather than enthusiastic support.

- *It fosters cynicism.* The real discussion and disagreement starts outside the meeting.

- *It wastes time:* if the real opposition and discussion start outside the meeting, then huge effort has to be displaced to round up all the dissident ideas and deal with them.

- *It reinforces hierarchy:* that bosses tell and staff do, which may have worked 50 years ago, but not today. An effective organization is one in which **bosses do not have to pretend to have a monopoly of wisdom**.

- *It represents a post-dated cheque for someone.* Once something is agreed, it normally implies a next step or outcome for someone else. If it's you, be ready to have the cheque cashed.

Clearly, some organizations are more prone to the plague of agreement than others. Traditional, hierarchical organizations such as government agencies and insurance companies are the worst. In creative industries, some staff could start an argument in an empty room.

The main challenge is how to encourage positive discussion in which disagreement is seen as helpful, rather than disloyal. Both boss and staff are responsible for changing behaviour. The boss has to signal that discussion is good, and to reinforce those signals both in private and in public.

For the staff member, the challenge is to frame the disagreement positively, so that it is not an objection but is supportive. Two habits help. First, state benefits (what you like about the idea) before concerns. This helps show you have listened to and understood the idea. Then, state the concerns as 'how to'. Instead of: 'That's really stupid, we can't afford it' try 'How do we build the financial case for this?' The same concern, but at least in the second case you are hinting that you could be part of the solution, not just part of the problem.

Alliances

From the day we start our careers, we are forming alliances. A large part of the art of middle management is alliance building: successful managers know instinctively how to build, sustain and leverage alliances across the organization.

Alliance building becomes more important as organizations become more complex, more matrixed and less hierarchical. This means that most middle managers do not have the resources or authority to achieve their goals. And you cannot rely on the hierarchy to force other parts of the organization into cooperation.

In building alliances you are always either creating personal equity (helping someone else) or using personal equity (receiving help from someone else). It is worthwhile trying to keep a reasonably positive balance of equity: someone who always needs help and never gives it is a pain in the backside.

Ultimately, alliances rely on trust. There is a simple formula for thinking about trust: $T = (S + C)/R$ where:

- **T = Trust.**
- **S = Shared goals and interests.** The more you have common interests, the more likely you are to be able to collaborate.
- **C = Credibility.** This is the credibility and the ability of both alliance partners to deliver on their commitments. There is no point in allying with someone who shares your goals, talks a great talk, but never delivers.
- **R = Risk.** The greater the risk, the more difficult it is to gain someone else's trust. Most alliances build up slowly through mutual help on small things. Where this has not happened before, working hard at taking away the risk, the time and the effort that your proposed alliance partner has to expend makes all the difference between getting cooperation or not.

Never mistake alliances for friendship. Remember Lord Palmerston's dictum of British foreign policy when Britannia ruled the waves: 'Nations have *no* permanent *friends* or allies, they only have permanent interests' Managers are like nations so **do not rely on friendships alone**, but rely on mutual interests.

Altitude sickness

This is a common management disease, and it is fatal to your career. Altitude sickness often happens in the low foothills of management, when a team member is first promoted to become a team leader. The person does not realize that the rules of survival and success change at every level. This is obvious when you look at a sports team. As a team player, you may be expected to run hard, make all the tackles, score the occasional goal. If the manager suddenly jumped onto the pitch and tackled a player, there would be uproar. **The job of the manager is not to run hard, make all the tackles and score all the goals.** The job of the manager is to pick the right people for the team, train them in the right skills, coach them on the right tactics and analyse and avert the potential competitive pitfalls they face.

In the world of management, too many first-time managers think they are still players: with more responsibility they think they now have to run harder than ever. They simply burn out, underperform and are eventually fired. They have not suddenly become incompetent: they simply failed to realize that the rules of the game have changed.

And the rules keep on changing. The more you advance, the more your agenda reduces down to the IPM rule – ideas, people and politics, money:

- *Idea*. Are we working on the right things – do we have the right strategy?

- *People*. Have we got the right people in place? Do we need to move them around? Do they need support and training?

- *Politics*. Have we got the right support across the organization to achieve our goals? What are the risks and obstacles we must remove?

- *Money*. Is the budget large enough? Can we keep our commitments to the rest of the firm?

When you are at a low level in the organization, these things are fairly clear. You are told what your goals are and you do not have much discretion. As you progress, your power and discretion increases, but so does the ambiguity. If you let other people dictate your agenda, team and budget to you, you will have a very uncomfortable time. The more senior you become, the more adept you have to be at using ambiguity to your favour and working the people and the politics.

Annual evaluations

These are often exercises in equivocation. People do not like hurting other people's feelings, so the euphemisms and code words come flooding out. You need a cryptographer to find out what is really meant. The result is disaster. The reviewees do not understand their position, do not understand what is really required in terms of future development. They are being set up for failure and disappointment, which will be all the worse when it comes because it will be a surprise to them. Meanwhile, promotion and bonus decisions become arcane exercises in trying to decipher what all the different evaluations mean. Different reviewers have different degrees of equivocation.

The truth only comes out when all the reviewers sit in a room together and are asked exactly what they thought of all the reviewees. Here are some translations of the more common review comments:

- Outstanding performance: the reviewee saved the reviewer's backside on several occasions during the period in review.
- Above average performance: average performance.
- Average performance: barely acceptable performance.
- Below average performance: who hired this turkey?
- A challenging year: catastrophic performance, but the reviewer does not want to say so.
- Development challenges: the reviewee has no chance of developing or progressing.
- Needs to develop analytical skills: the reviewee does not have a brain.
- Analytically outstanding: the reviewee is smarter than the reviewer.
- Needs to develop interpersonal skills: the reviewer never wants this person on his or her team again.
- Strong interpersonal skills: political snake oil salesperson.

The list goes on forever. The question is how to avoid it. There are two responses. First, oblige reviewers to live with the consequences of their decisions. As long as staff and managers are constantly being shuffled, the chances are that a reviewer will not have responsibility for a reviewee for long. That means that nasty problems can be shuffled off onto the next manager. In the meantime, the manager can focus on promoting the great performers, which makes everyone feel happy. Or, second, shift evaluations away from the traditional good/bad or below/above average evaluation. The very nature of these evaluations creates conflict and tension: **it is difficult to tell another human being they are no good or below average**. It is a judgement that invites denial and hostility, which does not move anyone forward.

There is an alternative. Map out the typical time it takes for someone to progress to the next stage in his or her career, be it three, five or seven years. Show what sorts of skills, responsibilities and accomplishments need to be achieved as the person progresses. Then assess his or her skills and performance in terms of progression, not an absolute good/bad judgement. No one who has just been promoted minds being told that his or her performance is consistent with someone who is only one year into a five-year career step. The same person, just promoted, would be mortified to hear that his or her performance is below average. In performance terms, both messages say the same thing, but with radically different results. The growth maturity evaluation looks something like this.

TABLE A.1

Performance level Criteria	New	Developing	Maturing	Mature
Interpersonal skills			X	
Leadership skills		X		
Analytical skills				X
Presentation skills	X			
Sales results		X		
Other (give details and performance level)				

If this individual has been around a while, the messages would be clear, positive and constructive about where he or she is strong and where he or she needs to develop. Note that most of the marks are in what would be a 'below average' column if the individual was being judged against everyone at his or her level. The development approach works because:

- It is less confrontational than the good/bad approach.
- It is more constructive: you end up with an agenda about what to do about going forward.
- It gives the reviewer a fighting chance of being honest and the reviewee a fighting chance of being able to listen without too much angst.
- It gives a good picture of who is ready for promotion and when. And if someone is not developing, it gives clear signals about who is at risk and why.

Even if the formal evaluation system is the good/bad one, using the development approach informally with reviewees will help build trust and understanding on both sides.

Association with success

Beware of people who are associated with success. They will have a long list of successful initiatives with which they have been associated. What they really mean is that at some point they offered some advice. It may or may not have been used, helpful or positive but it was enough for them to then claim that they were associated with the initiative if it was a success. If it was a failure, then they can either claim that they were not responsible for it, or that the turkey who was responsible for it did not follow their advice. They have set themselves up with a win/win situation every time.

Of course, they have made zero contribution to the organization. They mainly exist in flat organizations where it is possible for people to jump on and off passing bandwagons at ease. All the risk lies with the person actually leading the bandwagon. If the leader succeeds, all his or her passengers will say it was down to them, if it fails then they will all point the finger of blame at the leader. These are the only solutions:

- Go back to a traditional functional hierarchy where responsibilities are clearer and hiding is more difficult.
- Set very clear management by objectives (MBO) criteria and enforce them.
- **Kneecap anyone who claims to be 'associated' with success.** They either put themselves on the line, or they did not. Find out which is the case.

Attrition is good

Planned headcount attrition is good, at all levels of the business. It keeps the corporate gene pool fresh, it keeps the performance bar high within the business, and it enables the business to manage changes in the shape and volume of demand smoothly.

The question is how to manage attrition effectively. Where it is managed spectacularly badly, the attrition disasters give some idea of how not to do it, and by implication how it could be done. Here's how not do it:

- Set a high, fixed attrition rate and force rank everyone. Automatically lose those in the bottom 20 per cent. It keeps the performance bar high, and it is a great way of encouraging competition, politics and paranoia among those subject to the force ranking. And it encourages arrogance among those who survive.

- Set a low attrition rate that represents no more than natural wastage. If this is the case, the performance bar is not being maintained. The chances are that good people are leaving and average people are arriving.

- Exclude senior managers from the attrition targets. Encourage complacency, create an 'us and them' set of rules, ensure that the gene pool of senior management is not refreshed. Not smart.

- Have a single target for planned and unplanned attrition. Do not track the unplanned losses or the reasons for the losses. This is a good way to ensure that there is no useful information to manage performance or to minimize unplanned attrition.

- Have a weak evaluation system. This causes double chaos. It denies management any rational basis for making decisions, which will increasingly look political and irrational to outsiders. It fails to manage expectations of the individual. With a good evaluation system, the individual will see the way the wind is blowing and will jump, with plenty of goodwill all around, before being pushed involuntarily. The weak system leads to surprises and unenforceable decisions with the lack of data. It is an invitation to legal action.

Averages and the drunkard

Statistics lie. **Managers use statistics the way a drunk uses a lamp post: for support rather than illumination.** Of all statistics, the average is the best liar. It sounds so reasonable that few want to question it. But any statistic that is an average or refers to an average should be questioned and challenged. Normally, a lie will be discovered lurking behind the average. These are the most common average lies:

- *People performance relative to the average*. In every consulting firm, about 95 per cent of the staff are rated as 'above average' performers. The remaining 5 per cent are fired. Statistically, this is impossible, unless the benchmark is the general population, which is useless. Clearly, 'above average' performance ratings make for an easy evaluation for the reviewer, and keeps the reviewee happy. But it simply stores up trouble when it comes to promotions and bonuses. Forced rankings at least create some clarity and help decision making. In a forced ranking, half the reviewees will be below average, and about half will be above. This clarifies where the performance bar is.

- *Investment performance.* Look at the financial pages of any paper. A hundred per cent of the advertisements for established funds will claim above average performance. There is some self-selection in this: successful funds advertise, unsuccessful ones do not. Although for the most part this has the perverse effect of encouraging investors to move into asset types just as they hit their peak after a long run of outperformance: new investors can then look forward to a long period of underperformance. Above average performance is claimed by creative benchmarking of assets (versus bonds, cash, other markets) and over creative periods (6 months to 20 years). Most funds can claim overperformance by fudging the reference.

- *Customer satisfaction.* Customers always try to be nice in customer surveys. Satisfaction is only rated below average if it is truly awful. Even 'average' performance normally reflects fairly deep dissatisfaction. These surveys can lull management into a false sense of security.

Averages are less useful to management than exceptions. **The average consumer is 51 per cent female** (but not in China or India) **and has slightly fewer than two eyes**. This misleads. The exceptions are where both the insight and the money can be found. The customers who leave, or rejoin, or are particularly inactive or particularly active say more about what we are doing right or wrong than the average.

And it is the exceptions that are profitable. Procter & Gamble (P&G) launched a toilet soap (Zest) with a very strong fragrance. On average, it got a poor reception and some people hated it because of the fragrance. Then there were the exceptions: about 15 per cent of the target market thought this soap (including its fragrance) was outstanding. They turned out to be very loyal customers willing to pay a high premium for the product.

Baselines

The fallacy of forecasting

The fallacy of forecasting is based on the stable, historic baseline. **The best predictor of next year's budget and strategy is this year's budget and strategy.** The assumed baseline for next year's performance is last year's performance with some sort of historical trend extrapolated into the future. For a laugh, look at a five-year plan from five years ago. Its projections for today will bear no resemblance to the reality of today, unless you are a monopoly in a static industry.

Part of the problem comes from unpredictable external shocks, from the internet, through takeovers, government intervention and recessions. Inability to forecast these shocks is excusable. The purpose of scenario planning is to give a basis for looking at such shocks.

The greater part of the problem comes from assuming that current performance can be maintained without special management action. This is nonsense. **The true baseline for any business is one of rapidly deteriorating performance.** The reasons for this are obvious:

- Operationally, everything tends to slide towards chaos. Anyone who has worked in a store sees how quickly displays, stock and prices go awry. In professional service firms the constant loss of experienced talent and the introduction of inexperienced talent means that just maintaining the overall skills level is a major challenge.

- Those in competition with you, on average, are likely to be as smart as you. Certainly, basing a plan on the assumption that they are stupid is unwise. And yet, this is the implicit assumption in most plans. They assume that the profit improvement programme, cost savings, new marketing plan will all lead to cost savings and share improvements. Then there is surprise when they don't. Somehow, the competition has a way of cutting costs and prices and creating marketing programmes at the same rate as you do. Any successes tend to be short-lived.

- External pressures are rarely benign. Customers do not volunteer to pay higher prices, suppliers do not offer lower prices, employees do not work for less, and, for every dollar the government gives, it will take away another three.

Given this, any performance baseline must be assumed to be negative. In the extreme, over four years one company achieved cost savings equivalent to four times its profits. Over those four years, its profits declined. Clearly, without the cost savings the business would have been in dire straits, but the pace of change was nothing like what managers had hoped for.

The only time that managers understand the nature of the declining baseline is when it comes to setting budgets. At budget time managers become experts at predicting all the problems and disasters that justify having a very low profit and revenue commitment, supported by an extraordinary increase in resources. Suddenly the stable baseline becomes the famous hockey stick. Normally managers can deliver on the downward element of the hockey stick.

The salvation of management

This is the oldest trick in the book. Whenever you are given a new responsibility, dig out every last bit of dirt and disaster that you have inherited. Paint the bleakest picture possible of all the chaos you have inherited, of a business or project that is about to spin out of control and suffer fatal setbacks and losses. From there on, any performance will look like a relative improvement on the appalling situation you apparently inherited.

Conversely, your predecessor will have tried to stress how the business has been brought to the cusp of a breakthrough and everything is poised for the most sensational success. If this version of history is the accepted one, you are dead meat. You will struggle to fulfil what your predecessor has promised. If you do achieve it, it will be because of the groundwork of your predecessor. If you do not achieve it, it will be because you are a turkey. You cannot win, and the only surprises will be nasty.

This game playing is not just for scheming middle managers. Watch how often a change of CEO is followed shortly by results that include major provisions, write-offs and exceptional items. Done early, the CEO can implicitly blame it all on the previous regime. At the same time, the new CEO builds him- or herself financial wriggle room against unforeseen disasters, like poor leadership from the CEO.

Battles

Corporate battles are a way of life. **The most vicious battles are not between businesses, they are within the business.** One department battling against another for resources. One manager against another, battling for recognition and promotion. The challenge for managers is knowing which battles to fight and when. There are three rules to picking a fight. These rules come from Sun Tsu who wrote the Art of War about 2,600 years ago. They are:

- *Only fight if there is a prize worth fighting for.* Don't fight over whether coffee from the coffee machine should be free of charge or not. Better to make your point and graciously concede. Don't waste personal capital on it.

- *Only fight if you know you can win.* On Wall Street, **if you don't know who the fall guy is, you are**. In corporate battles, if you don't know who the loser will be, you are. In other words, if you don't know if you can win, you will lose. This means that most battles are won and lost before they are fought. You must know before you start whether you have lined up all the political alliances and support, as well as the rational arguments, to win.

- *Only fight if there is no other way of winning.* If possible, give your opponents a way out. Don't back them into a corner where they are forced to fight. There is no point in incurring all the damage that a fight, even a victory, brings if you can avoid it. Remember, once a battle is fought and lost you have probably acquired an enemy for life.

People who fight battles too often and too obviously, eventually lose. And when they do, there will be no shortage of enemies waiting to come out of the woodwork and apply the coup de grâce. At the other extreme, avoiding all battles results in the agreement plague and very weak management.

Benchmarking

Benchmarking is better in theory than in practice. In theory, benchmarking helps identify where you are relative to the competition, and can help guide and focus remedial action. In practice, it suffers severe challenges:

- Benchmarking results are totally deniable. At one large electronics group, benchmarking showed that the company was hopelessly uncompetitive with Asian competition. The reaction was not to sort the problem, but to challenge the data. The essential argument was you had to equalize the data to allow for different accounting treatments, product specifications and product mix, different exchange rates and so on. Ultimately, the argument in the electronics group was 'if the competition was the same as us, it would have the same benchmark data as us'. Logically true but practically useless. Meanwhile the business was hammered in the marketplace.

- Getting good benchmark data is difficult, unless the competitors cooperate in syndicated research. Or you have excellent industrial espionage.

- Any strategy that is focused on catching up with those in competition is doomed to failure. By the time you get to where they were at the time of the benchmarking, they have already moved ahead. You never catch up, you are always in catch-up mode. Equally, if the data shows that you are ahead of the competition, that will not be a call to arms: it will be a call to complacency.

At best, benchmarking can be a call to arms to mobilize an organization into making major change fast. At worst it is a charter for consultants to make money, and for management to plunge into arcane debate about the data while losing focus on the business. Benchmarking should be treated less as an intellectual analytical tool, and more as part of a process of mobilizing and focusing management.

The big bad boss

Having boss trouble? Print and display the checklist below of how to be a bad boss. Let everyone figure out who it refers to. And remember not to inflict this misery on your team.

- *Lead your team.* Anyone who does not do what he or she is told is clearly not a team player. Staff are there to serve you and make sure they realize that. Don't let them forget who's the boss.

- *Delegate effectively.* Delegate the routine rubbish that will otherwise waste your time. And delegate the blame when things go wrong. Don't delegate meaningful work: your team might grow, develop and make you replaceable.

- *Stay in control.* Make sure no one has any budget discretion: keep the photocopier key. Stay on top of the budget and make sure members of the team know you cannot possibly trust them with money, or anything else.

- *Monitor progress.* Insist on daily updates from members of your team on everything they do: keep the pressure up.

- *Manage well.* Manage your bosses, manage your profile and manage your career. Associate yourself with successes, walk away from disasters. Don't waste too much time on your underlings.

- *Be a hero.* Show that you can do it all yourself. Don't trust members of your team to do anything: they will mess up. Make sure your bosses know you have been the hero, except when things go wrong because of your team.

- *Be strong.* When anything goes wrong, shout at people. Dress them down in public so that everyone realizes you do not tolerate fools: show that you are above such folly yourself.

- *Be flexible.* Consistency is the hobgoblin of a tiny mind. Of course things change. You have to surf the waves of business. And if those in your team are not smart enough or psychic enough to work out when you have changed your mind, that simply shows they are not up to the job.

- *Don't waste time.* Ignore all the rubbish about motivation and communication. Members of your team are paid to work, aren't they? If you go on pandering to all their petty demands you will spend your whole day stroking their egos. You are a boss, not a shrink. Tell them to get on with it.

- *Be a role model.* Staff should aspire to your success: have a fancy office and fancy car; work the expense system so that your team has the chance to admire your lifestyle.

Bluffing

Never let someone bluff you. If they try it, call their bluff every time. Bluffing is just a power game. The moment you give in, you have lost. Typical bluffs worth calling include:

- 'You must accept this job offer by Friday, or it will be withdrawn.' Do you want to work for a company that bullies people even before they have joined? If they really want you, they will come back again.

- 'If I don't get a 20 per cent rise, I'll resign.' Do you want the organization to discover that this is how salaries are negotiated? Even if the individual merits 20 per cent, give 19 per cent. Let the person decide what to do.

- 'If you don't change your decision, I'll take it up with the CEO.' Pick up the phone and arrange the meeting with the CEO. If you are right, the person will back down before you have got through. If you are wrong, you should not have made the decision in the first place.

Boundaries

Clear organization boundaries are essential for corporate success:

- Clear boundaries clarify roles and sharpen accountabilities. There is nowhere to hide. Everyone knows what they are meant to do. The ambiguities of flat organizations are eliminated.

- Clear hierarchy clarifies and simplifies the decision-making process: authority levels are well understood.

- Costs and budgets are easily managed if they live in well-defined departmental buckets.

- Time and effort are not wasted in the countless internal meetings needed to coordinate the efforts of flat organizations.

- Functional expertise is encouraged.

Clear organization boundaries are a disaster in 21st-century business:

- Strong boundaries mitigate against cross-functional cooperation. Most business problems and processes flow across functions and need cross-functional cooperation.

- Strong boundaries encourage functions to focus on their functional goals at the expense of broader business goals.

- Hierarchy boundaries send the wrong messages about delegation, trust and empowerment and lead to slow decision making as decisions flow up and down the hierarchy.

- True costs and profitability are obscured by the departmental focus: costs are driven by activities that run across departments (order fulfilment, new account acquisition and set up). And customers, not just products, drive profitability.
- General management expertise is fostered by encouraging people to work with and across functions.

You pay your money, you make your choice.

Branding

Be true to yourself

Every product, business and person is a brand. Some are good, some are not. Strong brands have a good product and good values, which are well communicated. The product and how it is communicated and developed have to fit. Strong brands know their franchise, know themselves and remain true unto themselves.

Product branding in action

Product branding started by manufacturers putting their logo on their products. Procter & Gamble put their moon and stars stamp on blocks of soap, which acted as a quality guarantee to customers. Traditional product branding remains true to this custom. The traditional brand will communicate three things:

- a distinctive performance benefit;
- a reason why consumers should believe they benefit;
- a character for the brand.

Confusing the message with multiple benefits, or changing the message, is disaster. For instance, the detergent Ariel is meant to be exceptionally good at stain removal. Dreft is meant to be good for caring for delicate fabrics and colours. Mixing the messages so that Ariel blasts out all known dirt while caring for delicate fabrics would have low credibility. The products have to stay true to themselves. In a crowded marketplace, consumers will not remember complex messages: they will remember one simple thing about each brand. Lifestyle brands such as Nike or Louis Vuitton lead on the character and values of the brand, allowing people to aspire to a desired identity through their choice of clothes. They both have products that support their lifestyle claims. Neither could credibly try to occupy the other brand's territory. They have to stay true to themselves.

Personal branding

Like the product brand, we should be able to answer three questions:

- What is distinctive about our performance for the business?
- What is our distinctive capability?
- What is the character or style we wish to convey?

In a large organization, you will not be remembered for all the small things you do day to day. You will be remembered for one thing. Make sure it is the right thing. And you cannot be what you are not. You have to stay true to yourself.

Branding and the advertising agency

Unfortunately, everyone thinks that they are expert at advertising. Because we all see so much advertising, we have strong views on what we like and what we dislike. Advertising is not about what we like or dislike. It is about what works. This is a message that both advertising agencies and clients forget. The agency focuses on winning creative awards, and the client uses his or her 'person-in-the-street' expertise to pronounce judgement based on what he or she likes. This is not a recipe for good results.

Discussing advertising is hazardous to your mental health. Agencies will blitz you with nonsense. Having asked what sort of car, celebrity or animal your brand would be (if it were a car, celebrity or animal) they will go on to tell you about their wonderful production values, the meaning of different types of calligraphy and more. They will try to bamboozle you into submission. You can retaliate by telling them that you want certain colours banned because you, or your aunt, or your aunt's parrot, dislikes such colours. It will be an entertaining, but wholly unproductive, discussion.

So how do you have a sensible discussion about some proposed advertising, without resorting to your aunt's parrot? This is your health check to make sure that the agency has not gone completely off the wall:

- Is the advertising in line with the strategy? In other words, do you clearly get the message? For TV advertising try listening to the sound alone, and then watching the pictures alone. Both should be clear in their own right.

- Does it target the right people? Targeting 'everyone' is hopeless. If you are targeting ethnic urban youth, do not ask your middle-aged white CEO to judge the advertising.

- Is the brand the hero of the advertising? One commercial showed Claudia Schiffer, the supermodel, taking her knickers off. I have no idea what the brand was. In this case the hero was the personality, not the brand.

- Is the message distinctive? If you put one of your competitors in place of your brand, would it still be credible? No one will confuse Nike and Benetton advertising: they know how to stay distinctive. Most financial service brands are wholly interchangeable.

- Is the content accurate (and legal)? This is important detail: right logos, right colours, right uniforms, right packaging and right product.

- Does the advertising fit with the rest of the marketing strategy? Everything should coordinate.

Brand values and the value of brands

Two CEOs were indiscreetly bragging to each other in the Executive Lounge at Heathrow. Both were involved in M&A deals. The tall CEO mentioned that he was using Goldman Sachs as his advisers. The shorter CEO shrank even further as he admitted that he was using HSBC as his advisers. Then he perked up 'But we are using McKinsey as our consultants. Who are you using?' Suddenly the tall CEO began to squirm with embarrassment. He finally admitted that he was using PwC as his consultants.

HSBC and PwC are very fine firms and could probably do very good work for the two CEOs. But they were a source of embarrassment, whereas McKinsey and Goldman Sachs were a source of pride to the two CEOs.

The CEOs were acting the same way as the housewives of Aberdeen. I was selling Fairy Liquid, and I noticed that many households kept a bottle of Fairy Liquid on their kitchen shelf, where their neighbours could see it. Anyone who bought a cheaper alternative quietly hid it from view beneath the kitchen sink. They were ashamed to be seen as cheapskates who were not house proud.

Neither the housewives nor the CEOs were just buying a product. They were buying an image, an identity. They all wanted to be seen to be buying the best, (and most expensive), to show that they were successful CEOs and housewives.

Brands were originally a mark of quality assurance. In medieval times the King's head on a coin assured people that the coin was worth what it said it was worth. The stamp of a moon and stars on blocks of soap assured nineteenth century shoppers that the soap was good quality and that it came from P&G. But brands are much more than products. They are a mixture of features, benefits and hopes and dreams. To understand the difference, think about why someone might buy a big off-road car.

TABLE B.1

	Features	Benefits	Hopes and dreams
Drive	Four-wheel drive	Gets you out of mud	Be an adventurer
Engine capacity	6 litres	Acceleration, takes heavy loads	Have power, control
Driving position	High	Good visibility	Look down on everyone else

You can do the same exercise for Fairy Liquid, handbags, sports cars, perfumes, investment banks or consulting firms. In theory, we make a rational decision based on price and benefits. In practice, we are doing much more: we are buying a self-image, we are buying hopes and dreams. Even Coca Cola got this wrong. The company was being hammered by Pepsi and its taste challenge: people preferred Pepsi to Coca-Cola in a blind test. So Coca-Cola revamped its product and ditched the old one. There was uproar, such that the original had to be brought back within weeks. Coca Cola discovered that it was not just selling sweet fizzy pop: it was selling an identity and hopes and dreams: Coca Cola was about the United States, freedom and youth. You do not mess with values like that.

The classic mistake is to fall in love with your own product. We have all heard people boring for Britain about the details of the product they love.

They are obsessed by features that no one else cares about. The car may have a twin overhead camshaft, but do I care?

To be more effective, you have to focus on benefits. These change according to each person. So maybe some people want a high driving position for the sake of visibility; others want it because a high position is safe for the driver and passengers (but not for other road users).

The most effective way to sell is to sell to people's hopes and dreams. But this is hard: you cannot say to a CEO: 'Use us because we are prestigious, exclusive and expensive.' You have to demonstrate it. Off-road vehicles often advertise in a way that hints at adventure, even though over half their UK sales are to people who never take their car outside the M25. They will sponsor adventurers who will use their car. Once the dream has been established, it is left to the salesman to emphasize the more mundane benefits: 'very safe for your children on the school run...'

Everyone has hopes and fears and dreams. Once you tap into those hopes and fears you can sell more or less any idea or product to them.

Budget codes

Budget codes can be deployed effectively to demoralize staff, prevent cooperation between different parts of the business, stifle initiative, encourage power games and escalate costs. The way to do this is to insist that everything has a budget code. Every photocopy, every hour of everyone's day should be accounted for by a budget code. This means that nothing can move without the say-so of the great panjandrum who holds all the budget codes. He or she should only let them out in small amounts to minimize an individual's discretion, and to maximize his or her own power. On no account should secretaries have purchasing cards or discretion to buy office supplies. Make them use budget codes and formal purchasing procedures: make sure they understand who is really the boss.

Budgets

Why waste 11 months a year trying to achieve an ambitious budget? It is much easier to play hardball for one month a year and agree an unambitious budget that can then be beaten with ease. Then watch the bonuses and promotions flow your way.

Ultimately, **all budgets are political**. A budget represents a contract between two parts of management to deliver certain results for certain resources. Depending where you are in the negotiating chain you either want to maximize results and minimize resources or vice versa. All the data that is brought to the budget process is simply ammunition for the different points of view. Like the drunk using the lamp post, the data is used for support, not illumination. An effective budget process achieves the following:

- It represents a stretching, but achievable, goal for the business.

- The budget process itself helps managers understand the priorities, risks and opportunities for the business: it creates a common management view of the business.

- It is a process of generating managers' commitment to a course of action and goals. Without achieving the commitment objective, the budget process will have failed.

Achieving a stretching but achievable budget requires unreasonable management. Reasonable managers will listen to all the arguments about why next year's performance will be tough. The result will be a soft budget and low performance. Unreasonable managers see from top–down the 'must have' performance imperatives and stick to them. If this forces managers to think creatively about how to improve performance, the budget process will have served some purpose.

The most common error with the budget process is to let staff functions dominate it. Staff functions have value in adding up the numbers and providing an umpiring service to the budget process. But when they take over they cause more trouble than they are worth:

- They obstruct the process of developing management commitment.

- They wear the organization down by looking for far greater detail than is reasonably required for making a management judgement.

- They land up justifying a job for themselves with endless rounds of budget revisions and forecasts through the year, which again represent a drain on management time.

Business schools

Business schools do three things for emerging management talent:

- They attract the best young talent and the top employers and act as a dating agency between the two. There is a market for a new school that drops all the grind of two years' tuition, charges half the fees and simply acts as the dating agency. The cost and time saving would delight graduates. Employers would still get the same quality and the business school would make a fortune. Someone will figure this out, make it work and make a fortune.

- They provide a core of business knowledge, not skills. This knowledge probably has a half-life of 18 months. Most of the knowledge is not directly usable to someone who becomes a bond salesperson. Even consultants use only a fraction of the knowledge they glean. This makes the non-studying MBA feasible for both graduate and employer: the knowledge simply is not that critical. It only becomes really important years later as the graduate enters general management. By then the knowledge has been forgotten and relearned three times over.

- They give the graduates confidence. Just as a dating agency gives customers a structure and confidence to enter into a new environment with new people, business schools do the same.

The things that graduates really need to learn, like how to survive the management jungle on a day-to-day basis, **are not taught at business schools**. You will look in vain for courses on:

- How do I succeed?
- How do I deal with stroppy customers, unreasonable bosses and impossible deadlines?
- How do I really get promoted?
- How do I manage the politics of the organization?
- How do I avoid becoming an involuntary member of the cock-up club?

Business schools teach explicit knowledge, which can be codified. In that sense, the MBA is a well-named degree: it is about business administration. But the MBA does not teach the tacit skills of management survival. This is a business opportunity waiting to happen. Be the first corporate MBA: the corporate Marriage Bureau Agency for graduates and employers.

To buy or not to buy

All managers are salespeople: we have to learn how to sell our ideas, our needs and our priorities to colleagues and bosses who may or may not have our best interests at heart. But if we want to sell, we first have to learn why we buy and why we don't buy. One in-store salesperson gave a master class in how not to sell. This is why I did not buy from him:

- He talked instead of listening to my needs.
- He asked no questions about my needs.
- He gave me no space and tried to hustle me.
- He was condescending and ignored my concerns.
- He said 'Trust me.' A golden in rule in life is **never trust anyone who says 'Trust me.'**

He probably thought he was the perfect salesman: he had a patter; he could drown any objections and he had probably mastered the reverse flip-flop bi-active power close. But no one will sell like that inside an organization. Thanks to him, though, we can discover how to sell by doing the opposite of what he did:

- *Listen.* This is the secret weapon that lets opponents talk themselves into submission, colleagues talk themselves into agreement and lovers talk themselves into bed.
- *Ask questions.* Find out what people really want, and then you can align your idea with their needs and wishes.
- *Give people space and create options.* If you hustle, you create a win/lose game. Even if you win the argument, you lose a friend. Avoid single point solutions that lead to the win/lose.
- *Don't talk down to people and don't try to ride over their objections.* Far smarter is to agree with the objection: 'Yes, I was worried about that as well. But when I discussed the problem with Finance, they suggested a couple of very good solutions...' Or even simpler: 'That troubles me too... how would you deal with that challenge?'

Don't be an adversary, be a colleague working with others to find a solution.

- *Never say 'Trust me.'* Instead, show that you can be trusted by the way you act. Let people feel that they are being respected; their concerns are valid and have been listened to; that there is a win in the conversation for them. Then they will trust you instead of fighting you.

In a retail store, you can hustle some people into buying. If that means they will never buy from you again, that will not be your problem as you will have moved on with your sales bonus. Inside an organization, you hustle people once and then no one trusts you again. So the gentle art of persuasion is more time-consuming. But **the quickest way between two points is not a straight line: when the wind is against you, you have to zigzag to get to where you want to be**.

C

Calculators and spreadsheets

Throw them away. Using a calculator is normally a way of ensuring that the maths is right to eight decimal places, even when the logic is 100 per cent wrong. Actuaries and accountants are experts at this problem. When looking at a page with data on it, there are better ways of testing it than using a calculator:

- *Do the simple maths test.* Do the last digits in the column produce a result consistent with the last digit in the total?

- *Do the reasonableness test.* Most managers should have at their fingertips the key data for their business or department. If they see data that shows that share will suddenly double and costs halve, it's time to start asking questions, however robust the maths may be.

- *Test definitions.* I used to work on a product called Flash. It had 40 per cent market share, but was in terminal decline because the market was falling. This was because we defined our market as powdered household cleaners. Meanwhile liquid and cream cleaners were growing like crazy. We did not take the obvious action of introducing a cream or liquid product because it was not our market: if it *was* our market it would make our share look small and declining.

- *Test assumptions.* All forecast data is simply a reflection of assumptions made about the market, share, costs and prices. Normally, the assumptions are made to produce the answer that is required. So the answer is meaningless unless the assumptions are good.

Using spreadsheets simply obscures the need to think about data. It does not help test for reasonableness, or for assumptions or for definitions. It also helps people become innumerate. **Better to use the brain than a spreadsheet.**

Call centres and contempt for the customer

Call centres are wonderful vehicles for showing how deeply you feel contempt for your customers. There are three golden rules for making sure the customer knows how little you value them:

- *Understaff the call centre.* Plan staffing levels for average call rates, not for peak call rates. Most people, by definition, call at peak times so understaffing for peaks ensures that you can keep them all waiting. This conveys a simple message to your customers: 'We value your time as less than the time of our underpaid staff, so we will keep you waiting and make you pay for the privilege of it (phone charges)'. Of course, the person waiting may be a CEO or vital customer: the call centre should not discriminate. It should keep them all waiting. To rub salt into the wound, force the customers to listen to some advertising. Insert some messages about how much you value their call: you value it so much that you cannot be bothered to answer it promptly.
- *Make the customer do all the work.* This has three benefits:
  - It reduces the costs of the call centre.
  - It irritates the customer who will be deterred from using the call centre again, further reducing costs.
  - It allows the business to claim high levels of customer service because it is putting the customer in control.

It also reinforces your contempt for the customer. Make it complicated for the customer, with lots of screens with lots of options, which are intended to cover every eventuality. The message this sends is: 'We do not want to waste money on helping you, we will do our best to stop you talking to anyone and we cannot be bothered to figure out a simple call screening method that would help you: you are on your own, tough luck.'

If the customer should breach the defences of the call centre and speak to a human being, make the customer go through elaborate identification and security features, including full details of serial numbers of registration documents, which were probably lost years ago. This should see the customer off. This can also be creatively applied to outbound sales calls. British Telecom rang its customers to sell them a new service. When the customers answered the phone, they had to identify themselves: this was based on the customer confirming the phone number that BT had just called and the customer had just answered. A sense of the surreal helps.

- *Underpay the call centre staff.* Don't give the staff proper training, just give them scripts that they have to follow so that they are no different from automatic voice response (AVR) systems. This means that it does not matter if you suffer high staff turnover rates, you can always replace your staff with an AVR system if necessary. It also ensures that customers do not get the help or support they need, and leads to a miserable life for the underpaid staff who have to deal with torrents of irate customers.

But the good news in all this, is that the call centre will be able to show that it has achieved its budget and productivity targets.

Capital asset pricing model (CAPM)

CAPM is one of the cornerstones of the MBA. Learned finance professors will lecture at length about CAPM. The one thing they will not tell you about it is that CAPM is garbage in theory and in practice. But like priests in the Counter-Reformation, they still inflict their theological nonsense on students and will burn any deviants at the stake for questioning them.

In theory, CAPM tells you how much a project should earn for it to be a viable investment. This can be estimated as follows:

$$COE = R_f + \beta R_m$$

Where:

COE is the cost of equity (any investment should earn more than this)

R_f is the risk-free rate of return

β is beta, or the specific risk for your project

R_m is the risk premium required for holding stocks (equities) instead of risk free assets.

CAPM looks very neat and tidy, but the world is not neat and tidy. It is messy. Let's see how CAPM performs in theory and in practice.

R_f, the risk-free rate of return, can be represented by US government debt. Immediately, the problems start. Who says US government debt is risk free? Even if the United States does not formally default on its spiralling obligations, it may inflate its way out of trouble. No asset is risk free. Even currency hidden beneath your mattress eventually reverts to zero value: no currency lasts for ever. But let's take a huge leap of faith and assume that US government debt is risk free: do we look at 1-year returns or 10-year returns? Our choice will lead us to picking somewhere between 1 per cent and 3 per cent as our risk-free rate. This is already a huge variation.

β, beta, is a sensible concept. Some ideas are riskier than others. My brilliant idea for gold mining at the bottom of the Pacific may be riskier than your idea of changing suppliers to reduce costs. Beta adjusts for this. In the stock market, beta normally varies between about 0.5 and 1.5 (dull utilities versus adventurous high-tech start-ups). But in practice, an individual project may be more or less risk free (such as your change of supplier) versus downright lunatic (my gold mining idea). So we need to assign a beta of somewhere between 0.2 and 5 to different sorts of projects.

R_m recognizes that you will want a higher return for holding stocks than for holding risk-free assets. Academics estimate that historically stocks have delivered an excess return of between 5 per cent and 9 per cent over government bonds. But those estimates are skewed by survivor bias: they tend to look at US and UK stock markets. Anyone who had invested in Russian, German or Chinese stock markets in 1900 would have experienced 100 per cent wipeout. Anyone who invested in Japan in 1990 would be sitting on a 75 per cent loss over 20 years later. As an alternative, you can estimate a forecast risk premium, which normally comes out at roughly 2 per cent. So the risk premium comes to somewhere between 2 per cent and 9 per cent.

Now put this all together:

R_f varies between 1 per cent and 3 per cent

β varies from 0.2 to 5

R_m varies from 2 per cent to 9 per cent

Choose the most conservative assumptions and you land up deciding that a 1.4 per cent return is very nice, thank you. Choose the most aggressive assumptions and you will want at least a 48 per cent return. You may as well stick a pin a dartboard.

CAPM is useless in theory: it is even more dangerous in practice. **If a firm is happy with a return based on CAPM it will go bust**. In practice, firms need to have a few products or services that are wildly profitable, to make up for all the projects that fall short, all the overhead that makes no money and all the longer-term investments that may or may not eventually pay off. You need some fat to survive the hard times. And of course, CAPM has absolutely nothing to say to non-profit organizations such as the public sector and mission-driven firms such as charities, church and the army.

Fortunately, most businesses are more practical. Every finance department will have its own method for deciding what return is required for any investment. The return may be expressed as a payback period, an internal rate of return or a net present value (NPV) calculation. It really does not matter whether the method is good, bad or ugly. Your job is not to find the perfect method, but to work with the method that exists and to use it to your advantage. **Find out the rules of the game before you start playing.**

Change

The bell curve

People have different levels of enthusiasm for change. The bell curve is a normal distribution. In terms of their enthusiasm for change, 95 per cent of the management population exists within two standard deviations of the mean. They are neither openly hostile, nor are they actively supportive of change. It is this mass of the management population that you need to shift. Passive acceptance or resistance to change needs to be converted into willing support. They will never become change zealots, but their active cooperation is nevertheless required.

The interesting challenges lie with the outliers. There will be 2.5 per cent who are change zealots and an equal number who will man the barricades in defence of the status quo.

The change zealots

These are the shock troops of your change programme. Theirs will be the glory if it succeeds and they are also most exposed if it fails. Clearly, these troops are invaluable to leading the change programme. The challenge is to find the right ones in the right places. Good change leaders are not just in powerful positions, although those are needed. They are people who have influence at all levels of the organization. They will work the grapevine with more credibility and authority than any official newsletter.

The right person may be the 50-year-old called Jack who is in a quiet staff job that apparently has no power. Because he has no power he is no threat, he is not seen as part of the official power structure. Because he has been around for ages, people tend to trust him. He is the person you want as a change leader. The acid test is when someone asks Jack what he thinks of the latest change programme. If the answer is that it is the normal management nonsense that will float by, an opportunity is lost. If he perks up and says that for once managers may be on to something worthwhile, the right message starts spreading to the 95 per cent who are stuck in the middle. They will sit up and take notice.

Spending time gaining the commitment of these key influencers is a strong investment. It pays by giving the change programme credibility, and commitment, with the majority of the business.

The reactionaries

These people will fight change tooth and nail. They may be a tiny minority, but they will spread poison. The temptation is to spend countless hours trying to convert them. You may as well try to convert a Jesuit to Buddhism. If the reactionary is in a leadership position, it could be fatal. The choice for the reactionary leader is simple: get on the train, or try standing in front of it. Either way, the train will leave the station. Elsewhere in the organization, the focus should be on gaining the support of the 95 per cent, not dealing with the resistance of the 2 or 3 per cent. As the minority see the majority board the change train, they will start to feel pretty lonely. They will then break into three camps: some will join the train, some will run away and a couple of diehards will lie down on the tracks in front of the train. Let them come to their own conclusions. The train will move on.

The change equation

Change equation for business

Most **normal human beings hate change**. It takes effort, is risky and you never quite know where things may end. And then there are consultants. They love change. Change equals revenues for consultants. A new IT system, a new strategy, a new organization: the consultants will be there to help. They get the revenues, and they do not have to live with the consequences. They get all the benefit and none of the risk. How do you know if the organization is ready for change? After 25 years' use, the change equation still provides an accurate assessment of whether the organization is ready for change. Here it is, with all its spurious mathematical elegance:

$$(P \times V \times C \times F) > R$$

In English, the business is ready for change if there is pain (P) today, a vision (V) for the future coupled with the capability (C) to get there and some practical first steps (F). All of these together need to be greater than the perceived risks and costs of change (R). If a change programme goes awry, it is normally because some or all of these preconditions have not been fulfilled:

- *P is for pain.* There is no point in having a brilliant solution (re-engineering, TQM, time-based management) if it does not solve a problem where the organization feels real pain. The first question to ask of any idea is: 'What problem does it solve?' Without any pain there will be no interest in or commitment to change. At best, people will go through the motions.

- *V is for vision.* The devil you know is better than the devil you don't. So the pain has to be linked to a vision of the future that is clear and has demonstrable benefits to the business. You must size the prize. The benefits must be big to justify the costs of change that will be incurred. Don't play for small prizes. With no common vision, management change efforts will be like headless chickens running around in all directions. Time, effort and morale will evaporate.

- *C is the organization's capacity to change.* This is partly about priorities: knowing what you will not do in order to free up people, time and money to focus on the required change. It also requires the right skills, strong sponsorship and credible managers who have a track record of delivering. If the organization lacks the capacity to change, launching another change effort is an invitation to cynicism all round as people wait for yet another management initiative to fail.

- *F is for practical first steps.* People want instant gratification. Or, at least, they want to know that they are on the winning side, and to see a sense of momentum. Ensure that the change programme gets some early easy and visible wins. It builds confidence. Without it, enthusiasm wanes and momentum evaporates.

- *R is for the risks and costs of change.* These are high: financial costs are small relative to the opportunity cost of not doing other things while focusing priorities on the change effort. The more the risks and costs can be reduced, the more readily change will be accepted. If the risks are high, the opposition to change will be high, and will be both rational and political.

Change equation for people

Ultimately, businesses cannot change unless people do. And people have strong emotional resistance to change. Fear of the unknown tends to outweigh greed for the opportunity. People are risk and loss averse. The change equation works for individuals as well as for businesses. People will change where:

$(P \times V \times C \times F) > R.$

- *P is for pain*. When people are hurting, they are ready to change. This can be in the form of a risk (threat of takeover, redundancy) or simply unsatisfactory current conditions. If everyone is fat and happy, complacency rules and change will not happen. Occasionally, you need to create the crisis to stimulate change.

- *V is for vision*. People want to know where they are going and what it means to them personally. They may listen to all the good stuff about how the business will be transformed by some change. But they will not be engaged. Tell them what it means to them in terms of their career opportunities and what they can get out of it, and you will have their full attention. Get personal.

- *C is for capacity to change*. People don't know if they can handle change. They don't know what it will mean to them in terms of new skills and performance requirements. You are taking away what they can do and replacing it with something they do not know. They need reassurance that they either have the capability, or that they will get the capability, to succeed in the new world.

- *F is for first steps*. People want to know they have backed the right horse, they want to see some early results and early recognition of their personal contribution. Give it. Otherwise morale and momentum will go.

- *R is for risks*. Change is risky to individuals. They do not know how or if they will succeed in the new world. The more you de-risk a change programme, the more easily it will be accepted. Naturally, this can run counter to the need to stretch the organization to force it into new ways of working. Change needs to do a balancing act between risk and stretch.

Claims to fame

Everyone needs a claim to fame. Simply doing the job as required is not enough. **In large organizations, it is easy to hide, but harder to shine.** Your claim to fame gives you an identity, which managers recognize. With hundreds, or thousands, of the people in the organization it is a success to be known for one thing. To be known, your claim to fame has to be big.

Once you become known as an expert at something, or great for achieving something, then life changes. Instead of drifting between assignments, you will be in demand from staff and managers alike. It will give you choices about where to focus time and effort, and will give you visibility when it comes to bonus and promotion time.

A claim to fame is about doing something that has impact and relevance at least two levels up the hierarchy. This is unlikely to come from doing business as usual. It comes from taking an extra risk, making an extra effort and finding out what really is on the agenda of management. Drifting is possible in some organizations, but it is the slow boat to nowhere.

Claims to fame are critical at promotion time. Promotion decisions should be rational, based on a proper understanding of a candidate's achievements and skills. Perhaps in some businesses, this degree of detailed objectivity is achieved. In many businesses, the decision is cruder and simpler.

Evaluations may be written by your immediate boss, who may put up a promotion recommendation. But the actual decision will be made by people two or three levels up the hierarchy. Their knowledge of each individual is sketchy and simplistic. So they will rely on three pieces of evidence to make up their mind. In each piece of evidence it is the exceptional, not the standard, that grabs attention and determines the outcome:

- *The detailed promotion packages.* They may be looking at 20 or 30 of these in a day. All of them will be persuasive and all will be about good candidates. They tend to cancel each other out, unless there is some outstanding achievement or problem associated with the candidate. Each candidate needs a claim to fame.

- *The credibility and strength of advocacy of the person recommending the promotion.* The strength of advocacy is a reflection of the individual's political skills as well as the strength of the advocate's opinion. The advocacy is always strongest when the person can point to a single, distinctive claim to fame that sets the candidate apart from the crowd.

- *Personal knowledge of the candidate*. This may be trivial, like a meeting that went well or badly. This trivial event can assume disproportionate significance. What will swing the decision comprehensively is if the decision makers have personal awareness of the individual's claim to fame. With 20 or 30 candidates under review, and many more within their area of responsibility, most individuals will struggle to be known for just one claim to fame. The stronger it is, the more it will influence the decision.

The client rule

The client rule is: The client rules. There is one other client rule: **The person who owns the client, rules.** The client rule applies to marketplace competition and to internal organizational competition.

The client rule in the organization

In any firm there are power struggles between staff types, product people, marketing, finance, operations and all the different functions. A matrix simply makes the contest between the functions more equal, more ambiguous and more vicious. Ultimately, the winners are those who unambiguously own the clients.

In private banks, the relationship managers own the clients and bring in the revenues. Ultimately, they have the power. In consulting, partners who own big clients have all the power. Greed (everyone wants to be on the big project) and fear (no one wants to lose the revenue stream) drive behaviour.

Salespeople do not own the client. They come, they sell, they go. They are dispensable. It is the person on whom the client relationship depends that is indispensable. At bonus time, this helps.

The client rule in the market

The business that owns the client is strong. Businesses that do not are weak. This shows up in profitability. Ford owns the customer. Contractors are squeezed: they depend on Ford to deliver the volumes. And subcontractors get squeezed by the contractors. They are at the wrong end of the food chain. The same is true of suppliers to the big retailers: the only way of fighting back is through strong branding. This gives the chance of the brand owning the customer, not the retailer. Client ownership is a struggle of power and profit.

Cock-ups and blame

As long as there are people, there are cock-ups. Every cock-up results in a vicious game called 'pin the blame'. There is a hunt to find a victim, and to ensure that the blame is pinned elsewhere than on your own doorstep. This is natural: no one wants to wear the managerial equivalent of the dunce's cap.

Weak managers happily play the blame game. It is a way of ducking responsibility and simplifying, shuffling off a problem. But a witch hunt hardly helps improve levels of trust and cooperation among managers.

Strong managers do not play the blame game. They recognize that the blame game is destructive to individuals and counterproductive to the business. When something goes wrong, it is normally a symptom of some more systemic problem in the organization. The hunt should focus on what went wrong with the system that enabled this fault to occur. By looking at the system first, not the individual, the hunt is depersonalized and managers have a fighting chance of finding out what actually happened, instead of being met with a wall of political fog and obfuscation. Once managers know what happened, they can then act to stop it happening again.

Strong managers will also stand up when the fault lies in their own backyard. By having them stand up, the rest of the organization breathes a huge sigh of relief, and there is an implicit sense of gratitude for letting other people associated with the cock-up off the hook. If the manager reports to enlightened senior managers, this act of statesmanship will tend to strengthen, not weaken, the manager – provided the cock-up is not fatal and does not occur again.

The message of this is simple: when there is a cock-up, **blame the system not the person**. That way the business can learn and improve.

Commercial confidentiality

This is a useful panic button to press occasionally. It is used in particular by governments whenever they want to cover up some major cock-up. It is also used by managers to avoid defending the indefensible.

A minor variation is the legal version of client privilege. This can be used to great effect by managers. When asked for a reference for a litigious individual who has been fired, simply refer the matter to the lawyers and have them draft the response. This will kill the reference stone dead.

Committees

Committees are the land of the living dead. Put them out of their misery.
Kill them. Committees normally suffer from four problems:

- *Responsibility and accountability.* A committee is a great way of
  diffusing accountability and responsibility. If a committee makes a
  decision, then it is hard to pin responsibility on any one individual.
  Even the chairperson can hide behind the excuse of expressing the
  will of the majority.

- *Bad decisions.* Committees make bad decisions. They tend to
  compromise. If there are two proposals to be judged, a committee
  will find a compromise designed to save face all round. You do not
  beat competition by compromising.

- *Speed.* Committees tend to be slow and bureaucratic: they meet on
  a regular basis and need papers in advance. This means that if the new
  sales opportunity or credit request comes on the wrong day, you will
  be left waiting a week or a month for a reply. By then, the competition
  will have stitched you up.

- *Performance metrics and rewards.* Committees rarely have clear
  performance metrics, clear goals that are then measured and reflected
  in the evaluation and bonuses of the committee members.

There are two good alternatives to committees. First, give management
responsibility to individual managers. If the manager then needs support from
colleagues in executing that responsibility, he or she will find a way of doing it
efficiently. But at least you retain clear accountability, with the flexibility to
meet the demands of the situation.

Second, create a small task force with a time-limited objective that can be
measured, and with a leader who has clear accountability for delivering the
objectives of the task force. And, when the deadline is up, disband the task
force with an appropriate celebration. The leader of the task force should also
be responsible for implementing its suggestions: this encourages clearer,
better and more practical recommendations.

Committees, compromise and the US $12 billion challenge

I was sued once for US $12 billion, in the days when a billion was worth something. My only regret is that they did not sue for more: it would have made no difference as I could not pay anyway.

Both sides were obliged to go to binding arbitration. My opponents wanted a committee to judge the case. We wanted one person to judge the case. The reasoning was simple. A committee is always going to make a compromise, whereas an individual might make a decision. So a committee would 'compromise' on a US $6 billion award and both the business and I would be bust. But an individual might just have the courage to throw the entire case out.

In the end, an individual was agreed as the arbitrator and he did throw the case out. The only thing our opponents were allowed to keep was the brand name. We were forced to change our name (from Andersen Consulting to Accenture) and they kept their glorious brand name: Arthur Andersen. And then they got caught with Enron and went out of business, and Accenture escaped completely because it was now clearly a different firm with a different name. We really did not laugh. Well, not that much.

If you want compromise, use a committee. But if you want a real decision, use an individual.

Competitive advantage for the 21st century

Forget sustainable competitive advantage. That is very 20th century. To survive, you need a source of unfair competitive advantage, which gives you excess and sustainable profits. Excess profits pay for all the setbacks, shocks, test markets, R&D and other investment you have elsewhere. **With no fat, the lean organization quickly becomes emaciated.** All successful organizations have some source of unfair advantage, such as:

- virtual monopoly on desktop operating systems;
- owning the best place to drill for oil or dig for coal, iron or gold;
- owning a top brand, such as Coca-Cola;
- occupying the best site to operate on the high street;
- owning patents or other intellectual property.

In too many organizations, competitive advantage is fleeting. It lasts until your competitor copies your product or your price. In a professional services firm, such as law or accounting, it might be as long as it takes for your competitor to walk through your client's door.

Competitive advantage is becoming harder to find and sustain. Competitive advantage in the 21st century is different from traditional 20th-century competitive advantage in five key areas. These are the areas to focus on and to test your own position against.

From tangible to intangible advantages to customers

Traditional product marketing is based on demonstrable product advantages: for example, Daz washes whiter. Now brands have to offer more than performance and a quality assurance. Coca-Cola loses taste tests against Pepsi, but wins on market share. It is not just selling dark fizzy liquid, it is selling youth and US values to the rest of the world. It is a rich brand. Nike clothing is not necessarily better than other sporting and leisure clothes. People buy not just clothes, but a lifestyle from the brand.

Intangibles are more than brand. The service industry promises and delivers intangible benefits that may or may not be bundled with a physical product. Restaurants offer food and ambience, overnight delivery is a time promise, consulting is an insight promise, aero engines offer both a loss-making product and a profit-making service. The challenge is to demonstrate the value of these intangibles to the customer.

From single point to multiple advantages

In the past, the corporate Olympics included three events: better, faster, cheaper. Now there is just one event: betterfastercheaper. The market wants it all, and wants it now.

This is about layering one advantage on top of another over time. The Japanese auto manufacturers entered the US market with cheap but reliable cars. It was a new price/quality trade-off based on innovative production methods. Over time, they added new layers of advantage. First, they increased the level of features; then they moved upmarket into higher profit segments; then they started introducing new models up to three times faster than the competition. The competition could not keep up with all the different layers of advantage the Japanese were introducing.

From formulaic advantages to creative and customized advantages

The formulaic advantages of the 20th century are not enough. These advantages were typically described as scale versus differentiation, price versus quality. Today the answer is as likely to be price and quality and scale and differentiation. Arguably, dot.com businesses allow for all of the objectives to be achieved at the same time. Amazon.com started with a highly differentiated offering, which allowed for high customization. It is building scale and price, making it hard for the competition to enter. It has thrown the formulaic trade-offs out of the window.

Other competitive advantages are likely to be more creative. Honda entered the US motorbike market thinking it would have to compete head on with the traditional Harley type of bike business. It stumbled upon and developed the family leisure bike business, gained volume and eventually outflanked the traditional players.

Creative thinking allows competitors to thrive in the same market. In the PC market, Apple invented a whole new market for personal computers. It has sustained a position based on design and ease of use, targeting education and publishing sectors. IBM (now Lenovo) entered, trying to use its muscle in the corporate market and the implicit assurance of quality. Dell entered the market with a disintermediated mass-customized approach, which enables it largely to eliminate stocks and the hazards of forecasting. These are three totally different approaches to the same market.

From sustainable to temporary advantage

Traditional thinking regards competitive advantage as sustainable. It is not sustainable any more. Perhaps in the past, you could build a railway and no one could compete with that; or build a huge chemical plant and deter anyone else from following suit.

A good test of the strength of the business is the innovation index. This is the proportion of sales derived from products less than three years old. Traditional industries should be able to achieve 25 per cent. The computer industry, fashion, consulting and investment banking should be achieving nearer 100 per cent, and they should be looking for a shorter time frame over which to measure innovation. The proportion of sales to new customers should also be high, especially for growth businesses.

From external to internal and external drivers of advantage

Advantage is no longer sustainable based on the strategic position of the business. Advantage is temporary. If the business is not moving ahead at least as fast as the competition, it is falling back in a relative way. Competition can reduce costs and raise quality by 25 per cent each in three years. Our 20 per cent improvement means we are falling back.

In this world, competitive advantage may be expressed in marketplace performance, but it is driven by the internal strengths of the business. These strengths are not about a static core competence (for example 'We are good at small motors.'). They are about dynamic strengths that enable the business to innovate and move forward.

This is most notable in the talent-driven businesses. Investment banks and consulting companies find it easy to copy each other's products. There is no competitive advantage there. Advantage comes from having the right talent that can consistently innovate and brings those innovations to market.

Competitive intelligence: use it or lose it

Forget the sleuths and the expensive consulting reports. If you know you will act on it, do it yourself. If you just want it for information, don't bother. There are other more creative ways of wasting the company's money.

Most of what you need to find out about the competition is readily available. It is simply a matter of focus. For consultants, competitor profiles have always been money for old rope. It's a job either for the library or for a junior consultant as a test of their ability. There are no magic sources. Here are the real ones:

- annual reports and stock exchange disclosures;
- brokers' reports, media coverage and even Google;
- trade associations;
- special reports (existing benchmark data, syndicated research);
- ex-employees of the competition on your payroll;
- headhunters, suppliers and customers, who are normally helpful and will tell you where you differ from the competition, what you can do better;
- your own R&D analysis of competitors' product performance and costs;

- sales force intelligence: salespeople find out early about pricing changes, promotions, new products, and price lists often leak.

This is all very basic stuff. Even if you use consultants, they will need you to give them access to headhunters, customers, suppliers, sales, brokers and employees. Once you have gone through the effort of giving them access, you should be able to complete the job yourself. The issue for most businesses is not about collecting the data: it is about using it. It normally lives in some remote staff functionary's office. Competitor intelligence is only worth collecting if it is acted on.

Compounding success

'Compounding is the most powerful force in the universe' is one of the more unlikely remarks attributed to Albert Einstein. But on planet business, it is nearly true.

To make the point, if one of my feckless ancestors had bothered to invest one measly dollar on my behalf at the time of Christ, at a mere 2 per cent interest, then I would now have over one trillion trillion dollars, which is more than the entire wealth of our known galaxy. Sadly, taxes, wars, revolutions, death, outrageous fund management fees and a few million other claimants for the fabled dollar have seriously impaired my prospects of acquiring such wealth.

To bring it closer to the modern day, Procter & Gamble (P&G) had a very modest goal of doubling volumes every 10 years: that is just 7 per cent growth annually. Do that for 160 years and you move from US $1 million turnover to US $33 billion turnover. In fact, P&G managed to grow at 7.3 per cent annually in the last 160 years. Beating target by just 0.3 per cent compound sounds trivial. In practice, it means that P&G is more than twice the size it would have been if it had stayed at just 7 per cent growth.

The same effect works on your pension. Invest US $1,000 today and see what happens to it in 40 years' time. At 5 per cent growth, your US $1,000 will magically transform itself into US $7,000. But then your fund manager rakes off a modest 1.5 per cent annually and suddenly you are left with under US $4,000 and your fund manager is left with a very tidy bonus.

Compounding maths sounds complicated, but there is a secret short cut for all geeks out there. The secret is 69 (or 70 if you find round numbers easier). To work out how fast a compound rate of interest will lead to a doubling of your starting number, use 69 (or 70) as follows:

5 per cent compound growth: 70/5 = 14. So 5 per cent doubles your starting number in 14 years.

7 per cent compound growth: 70/7 = 10. So 7 per cent growth doubles your starting number in 10 years.

15 per cent compound growth: 70/15 = about 4.7. So 15 per cent growth doubles your starting number in just over four and a half years.

This is one of those small mathematical oddities that can make even the numerically challenged appear to be a minor mathematical genius.

Computer abuse

We use computers because we have them. This does not mean we should use them, or that we are wise in how we use them. For every one hour of time the computer saves, it wastes anything between five minutes and five hours. The most common abuses of the computer include:

- *Managers acting as typists or production experts.* I have seen a room full of consultants billing an average of US $2,000 a day, busily producing graphics for a presentation. This is not their job. They are slow, and the results are low quality. For US $400 a day, I could hire a great specialist who would produce far better quality at twice the speed. If you see consultants wasting your money like this, fire them.

- *Reporting by the gigabyte.* Volume of reporting information does not equate to quality. More reporting data simply leads to more questions, more analysis, more data revision and more managers chasing their tails. Reporting requirements should focus on what is needed, not on what is possible.

- *Upgrading to the latest gizmo.* Senior managers are particularly prone to this because personal computers are not simply work tools, they are status symbols. So senior managers must have the latest and best computers, even though functionally they are way beyond their modest office requirements. The people who most need all the latest functionality are those on the front line: they are the last to get the upgrade.

- *The solitaire supremos.* The blame should not be attached to the individuals who have enough spare time to start honing their chess, solitaire or bridge skills on the computer. The real question is why there is so much spare capacity in the office, and why it is not being used more effectively.

- *From face time to Facebook time.* Just because staff are present, it does not mean they are working. **If the bureaucrats behind working time regulations actually had to work 35 hours a week, they would probably have to be present in the office 100 hours a week.** Working and being present are different: Facebook, Google and other sites make up much of the difference.

- *Placing computers between you and the customer.* Every day I can buy a newspaper from my local news-stand or from a high street shop. The news-stand knows me, and we exchange papers, money and pleasantries in a moment. The shop has a computer that tracks stock. There is always a queue because the operator has to swipe each transaction through the till, there are always mistakes that then need to eliminated and re-entered. The customer then has to wait while a receipt is printed out. The computer keeps the accountants happy. It drives the service staff and the customers crazy. Computers can enhance the customer's buying experience, but only if it is designed for the customer and not for the accountants.

Conferences: the survival guide

Corporate conferences at least provide the opportunity to get out of the office, perhaps see somewhere nice and, you hope, earn a few more frequent flyer miles. You might also get a decent meal and a big drinking session. The price to pay is high: sitting in a dark, stuffy conference hall for hours on end listening to some self-important panjandrum making an instantly forgettable speech. Most conferences have three elements, which the management survivalist can use to good advantage:

- *Plenary sessions.* Many of these will be a waste of time. This is where important people get on the stage and, like dogs pissing to mark their territory, make speeches to show that they are big shots. Some you may have to attend. But the agenda should reveal several that have no relevance to you, and you will not be missed. This is a good opportunity to catch up with paperwork, phone calls or your exercise programme if there is a health club. You are doing no more than follow the example of the panjandrums who believe they are too busy and important to attend all the plenary sessions. Make your exits and your entrances discreetly.

- *Break-out sessions*. You know that **any work you put into the break-out session will receive a short, garbled summary in the plenary session and will then be ignored**. But the big shots like to think that you have now been involved, you have therefore bought into whatever they are proposing. Because these groups are small, you will be missed and you should go. Survive them.

- *Informal time, coffee breaks and meals*. These are the most useful parts of conferences. Most people waste them. People only speak to people they already know: London office speaks to London office, IT speaks to IT. But, if you have prepared, you will know there are some people out there with interesting ideas, or with interesting projects and career opportunities. Make a point of searching them out. Have your story ready. Do not try to negotiate your next career move there and then, but use the opportunity to put a marker down and ensure that there is a promise of a follow-up after the conference. Then make sure you follow up. These opportunities are not just with bosses, but with your peer group and others with good ideas.

Consultants

You get the consultants you deserve. If you find that they have set up camp permanently in your building, charge outrageous fees and produce little by way of results, tough. You know what you should do about it.

Essentially, consultants are tarts. They will do anything for anyone, provided the customer can pay up. It is worth knowing what motivates the highly plausible consulting partner sitting opposite you:

- The partner will be rewarded for making a sale, not for giving you best advice.

- Partners prefer to sell what they know, regardless of whether the solution fits your problem. The answer you get lies less in the nature of your problem than in the experience of the consultant you are talking to.

- Once in through your door, the partner is aware that selling an engagement to a new client is roughly seven times more expensive, difficult and risky than selling a second engagement to an existing client.

- Partners will expect to spend roughly one third of their effort in the engagement finding the solution for you, one third convincing you of the solution and one third of the time selling you on the next engagement.

- All partners want to swim upstream to the source of all power: the CEO. CEOs are the softest touch in terms of pricing, terms, conditions and payment. They have the biggest budgets, and give the best overview of where the next engagement might come from. Finally, CEOs give the consultants the most power within the organization.

- No partner will commit the consulting organization to any real liability concerning performance.

All of this is fairly self-evident. It means that consultants, for all their protestations, are not on your side. They are in it for the fees. This has some inevitable consequences:

- They will do more or less whatever you want, even if it is not the right thing.

- They will represent that they have the right skills for your task: whether you ever see the person with the right skills beyond the pitch is doubtful; in all probability he or she is a very scarce resource much in demand elsewhere.

- They will promise results based on the fallacy of the stable baseline: given the baseline is moving you will never be able to quantify their contribution to the business relative to all the other moving variables. Their performance promises are usually worthless.

- They all have great products to sell from time to time: re-engineering, core competence, time-based competition, quality. They will apply this solution, regardless of what your problem is, because that is what they know how to sell and how to do.

- They will try to make themselves indispensable to the organization, which in effect means hollowing out and disempowering middle management.

- Forget confidentiality. No consulting firm will actually take your confidential plans and tout them round the market. But they will take all the experience they have gained from you and wrap it up in an anonymous case and start selling it to all your competitors. They will at least use another partner when selling your experience to your direct competition.

This leaves the challenge of how to use consultants effectively. There are a few principles that work:

- Make it very hard for the organization to take on consultants. It should be an executive committee decision and, more or less on principle, the board should turn down all first requests for consulting support. When the squeals of agony get very loud, then you might start listening.

- Managers must be able to prove that they do not have the technical skills that the consultants claim to bring: if it is simply a question of bodies and resources, then the discussion should be about corporate priorities, not about consultants.

- Managers must be able to show that the consultants are actually working on the right problem.

- Pick not just the right firm of consultants, but the right individuals. The partner you are talking to is probably having a struggle to identify and release the right people to work with you, and is under huge pressure to take new recruits (20 per cent of the workforce annually) and weak performers onto his or her team. Your pressure is essential in getting to the A team, not the B team.

- Once the consultants are in, manage them effectively. This means being able to make rapid decisions. A good way to escalate IT implementation costs is to make decisions slowly and then reverse them.

- Keep the consultants hungry. Make them happy, dangle the carrot of extra work in front of them: then they will put their best resources into the effort. Then kick them out.

If you are in middle management and you find that consultants are suddenly swirling around, don't fight. Be helpful, and quietly try to co-opt them in support of your agenda. They are also a useful source of finding out what the agenda is of senior managers. Remember, consultants often have a direct line into the executive committee. This can be used to your advantage, but make them into enemies and it could be fatal. I am yet to meet a CEO who does not, at some point, pull one of the consultants to one side and ask for an opinion of his management team.

Contracts

Contracts are scary. Lawyers often like to make them even more scary. They point out all the dangers and surround the contract with unintelligible gobbledegook. As the world becomes more legalistic, contracts are becoming more important. Contracts are management reality.

From a management perspective, there are four things a manager should do about contracts. They are all common sense. This means that most managers will at some time have a personal or professional contract disaster because one of the four rules have not been followed:

- *Know when you do and do not have a contract.* Just because there is no written document, this does not mean there is no contract. There may be a duty of care. And, as soon as money is exchanged for services, there is a contract.
- **Never sign a contract until you are ready.** The moment you sign, your negotiating position evaporates and the obligations begin. This is normally discovered by new employees, when it is too late. Always negotiate.
- *Never sign a contract you do not understand.* Good lawyers, who can translate legalese into plain English and can give practical as well as legal advice, are worth their weight in gold. Which is roughly how much they charge. But use them.
- *Standard contracts are never in your favour.* They favour the person offering the standard contract. Because it is standard, people think it is a take it or leave it proposition. I just go through the document striking out clauses I do not like and adding new ones in where I want them. If the contract bearer defends the contract on the basis that 'It's what other people sign', he or she has no defence. The only good contract is one you are happy with.

Control, compliance and commitment

Every business needs to stay in control. If there are new tools for controlling the business, it is reckless not to use them. Except that control and commitment work in opposite directions. And, ultimately commitment is a more productive form of control than mere compliance. **Less formal control is often better than *more*.**

There are five control levers open to managers. Most managers use all five levers, in different proportions. The challenge is to get the balance right.

Rules and hierarchy

This is the traditional command and control model. If the business is one where managers think and workers work, having checked their brains and souls out at the front door, command and control is fine. This is the land of the multi-volume policy manual. The policy manual tells people what they cannot do. It is designed to stop disaster. But it does not tell people what they should do, it does not empower them and it does not create a culture of trust and commitment. It is long on compliance, short on commitment.

Information and reporting

The explosion of communications and information technology has led to an explosion in the frequency, breadth and depth of management reporting. The volume of reporting is inversely proportional to the trust you have in your team. The provincial governors in the Roman Empire had to be empowered and trusted to manage: they could not send a trireme back to Rome with a few hundredweight of stone tablets asking for guidance every time a problem came up in Judaea. The Roman Empire lasted longer and achieved more than most business empires can ever hope to. Just because the technology enables us to have mountains of reporting, it does not mean we should have it. **Excessive reporting is a comfort blanket for insecure senior managers.**

Skills and standards

The medieval guilds were a way of ensuring that all the butchers, bakers and candlestick makers had the skills to produce goods to a standard that was acceptable to the community. It did not require long policy manuals: most candlestick makers were illiterate; nor was there much in the way of reporting. Today, the professions such as doctors, lawyers and accountants maintain the same approach. This creates a curious mix of cultural conformity, control and individual commitment. Making it work across a business encompassing multiple skills, trades and cultures is close to impossible, unless you are a firm of accountants or lawyers.

Control of outcomes

This is the classic conglomerate approach to business. Strong financial measures and rewards are put in place, together with tight financial control. Then managers are left to get on with it, provided they are achieving their goals. This maximizes flexibility, and is a high commitment model, based on the twin human motivations of fear and greed. Within organizations effective delegation is about controlling outcomes, not processes. It is fundamentally a high-trust, high-commitment form of control.

Cultural control

This is a high-commitment, but potentially low-compliance form of management. In the extreme, millions of people have volunteered to die to defend communism, fascism and democracy. They may have been brainwashed by years of propaganda, but from the leader's point of view, that person got the result he or she needed: a highly committed and dedicated following. High-commitment businesses normally have strong cultures. This does not need to be high-energy passion, with 100-hour weeks in a new economy business. The traditional 'job for life' company, still present in some businesses in Japan, proves its commitment to the individual over a career and expects the same in return.

Control your destiny

The best book you never need to buy is called *Control Your Destiny or Someone Else Will*, by Noel Tichy and Stratford Sherman (1995). You don't need to buy the book because once you have read the title, you have got the message.

Plenty of managers and leaders are not in control of their destiny: they are simply turning a treadmill that someone else has designed for them. The mouse on the treadmill may think it is making progress: we can all see it is simply spinning its wheel and going nowhere.

Gaining real control over your team or your business is remarkably elusive, especially if we accept the definition of leadership as 'taking people where they would not have got by themselves'. To be in control, you have to be making a difference. If you are put in charge of a team or business, here are three things you should do to make sure you are in control. This is the IPM agenda – idea, people and politics, money – that we met earlier. To recap:

- *Idea*. So how will this unit be different as a result of your leadership of it? Call your idea a strategy if you want to impress people. If you do not have a clear agenda, you are not in control.

- *People*. Do not assume that the team you inherited is the one you need for the future. Work hard to get the 'A' team. The 'B' team is a recipe for underperformance, stress and sleepless nights.

- *Politics*. You can only get the right agenda, team and money if you work the politics, build alliances, do the right deals and fight the right battles.

- *Money*. Get the right budget. That means enough resources for your commitments: either increase your resources or decrease your commitments. You can be sure that your predecessor painted a picture of a unit on the cusp of success. If you accept that story, you are dead meat: any success will be down to your predecessor and if you fall short of wild expectations, you fail. You have to reset expectations very fast: get all the skeletons out of all the cupboards within your first month.

Some newly appointed managers drift and hope to get lucky. But **hope is not a method and luck is not a strategy**. Take control of your destiny or someone else will.

Corruption, bribery and skulduggery

Some countries and industries are awash in corruption, bribery and skulduggery. Managers and businesses can play this in one of four ways:

- Don't play in those countries and industries.

- Avert your gaze and shade the truth. This is popular. Your local sales agent works on 10 per cent commission. Of course, you have no idea that the 10 per cent mostly goes on kickbacks: that's not your business. Naturally, you should invite the clients to the trade show at Disney World, pay their expenses (first class) for them and assistants (lovers or family) and reimburse them through their travel company (which they own, and they are expensing both their employer and another company for the same trip). But you would never bribe them with a free trip for their family to Disney World, would you? Just don't expect the judge to understand the difference.

- Play to lose: enter countries awash with corruption, bribery and skulduggery, avoid all the unethical and illegal activity and accept you will lose. But in 20 or 30 years' time, if the country cleans its act up, you may still have a reputation to build on.

● Play to the local rules of the game.

From an economic point of view corruption and bribery is irrational: it leads to poor allocation of resources and poor economic performance. This is why most advanced economies act strongly against skulduggery. The kindest thing to say about countries that still suffer corruption is that they are simply at an early stage of economic development. The UK at the start of the industrial revolution was still deeply corrupt in many areas: the running of the naval shipyards being best documented for its corruption.

But from the short-term point of view for individuals with power, corruption is highly profitable. They can sing while the country burns. Corruption will not disappear soon.

Courtesy

Let's make this simple. Do you want to deal with people who keep you waiting, put their feet on the table, take phone calls in the middle of your discussion and are perpetually foul mouthed and abusive? You may have to work with such people, but you probably do not want to.

Courtesy and etiquette is not about learning how to use the fish knives. It is about being treated the way you would like to be treated: do unto others as you would have them do unto you. So if you know how you want to be treated, that is your practical guide to business courtesy.

It is also a way of living in a happier office. Courtesy pays. Being pleasant to support staff helps when you have a sudden crunch and you need a favour from them. They will help you without you having to shout at them. Harassed production staff or technical support staff are more likely to put your work to the top of the pile, or to stay the extra hour if they know you and like you. Headhunters are more likely to be helpful if you are always responsive and helpful to them. It is the simple things that count. Outlined below are some easy things that are common sense but are commonly not done.

Telephone etiquette

Always return telephone calls. Something good may come out of it. Even if it is no good, at least you have dealt with the problem right away, and you look professional.

- When someone returns your call, thank them for returning the call.
- Answer the phone promptly: after three rings at the most.
- Never leave the phone on during meetings, unless you want to show the people you are meeting that they are extremely unimportant to you.

Support staff

- Learn their names, and use their names. Say good morning.
- Say thank you.
- Take time to chat and find out a bit about them.
- Respect their personal lives: if you know that you need extra help, tell them in advance so that they can make arrangements.
- Treat them with respect. They are professionals in their own field, they are busy. Don't condescend: treat them as equals.

Courtesy is not wimpish. **Courtesy is a low-effort method of getting your way.**

Culture, crabs and the death of the tea lady

Cultural change programmes do not work. Announce that you are going to change the culture of the organization, and watch the opposition grow. Telling people that you will change their culture is like telling them that you are going to mess with their heads because what they have being doing and thinking in the past is all wrong. And, by definition, **all cultural change is an attack on the majority**. So, even if there is a minority cheerfully egging you on, there is sullen resistance from the majority.

Cultural change programmes carry overtones of the cultural revolution, Mao, Pol Pot and extreme dictatorship. Not the best start for creating a new, open and empowering culture. Culture is best changed crabwise: attacked sideways on.

Values statements do not help. Values statements have meaning only to those who have spent months carefully crafting and bitterly arguing over the nuances of every word in the statement. To the rest of the world, it is more meaningless management babble. People take their cultural cues not from what is said, but from what is done. There are four key levers.

Reward systems

If call centre staff are rewarded for productivity (number of calls handled) do not expect a service-intensive, customer-friendly culture to emerge. They will be too busy getting through the calls for that.

Promotion criteria

Forget about the written criteria. Most businesses have similar criteria that list various skills, levels of responsibility and achievement. But what people really focus on are the unwritten rules. For instance, in most consulting companies the rules for getting to be a partner are:

- Sell loads of work: own clients that will generate revenues.
- Do something to show at least a notional contribution to recruiting, firm management and intellectual property development.
- Don't trample over the bodies of too many people on the way to the top.

The last rule is relaxed in one consulting company, which formally releases a set percentage of its staff after force ranking them. This positively encourages trampling and politics. In one life insurance company, the unwritten rules looked something like this:

- Become an expert in your chosen technical field.
- Never, never make a mistake: meet budgets, cause no nasty surprises, don't rock the boat, don't argue.
- Serve your time and wait your turn.

These promotion criteria are largely unrelated to the formal criteria, but absolutely drive the behaviour of individuals.

Management behaviour

If the department head is a miserable, Machiavellian miser, it is unusual to find an open, enthusiastic team working within the department. People take their cues from what managers do, not what they say. This can work positively for managers. A new CEO took over in a very traditional, hierarchical company. In his first week, he started wandering around the office and talking to staff at their desks. It was as if the Pope had come from Mars to visit. There was shock and disbelief. At first people found it difficult to talk to him. Then at one desk, there was nowhere for him to sit. Instinctively, he turned a waste basket upside down, sat on it and talked to the clerk at her level. The story went round the building like wildfire. Suddenly, the CEO was not just human, he was approachable.

Symbols matter

In one office, there was the tea lady ritual. Technically, her job was to give tea twice a day to managers. Culturally, her job was to reinforce the hierarchy and humiliate the staff. She did this very well. Twice a day she would stroll around each floor: if you were important she stopped and gave you a cup of tea. If you were not important, you got to watch as she walked by, and then you went to the coffee machine and bought your plastic cup of gunk.

The first step in the popular revolution was to **shoot the tea lady** (revolutions can be cruel) and put in free vending machines. From there the revolution went on to dismantle all the other symbols of hierarchy and status: the three levels of executive dining room, the reserved parking spaces, the separate executive lavatories and lifts, and so on.

Communication

Many companies assume that communication is about broadcasting loud clear messages. This does not work. Management propaganda has all the integrity of Pravda in the Soviet era, and gains as much respect. Good communication is critical. The key principles are:

- Words and actions must agree. Don't pretend to want an entrepreneurial culture unless you can manage and accept risk and failure.

- Communications are two-way: make sure you listen to what the organization says. And act on it: if you listen and nothing happens, cynicism is simply reinforced.

- Communication is personal: people respond better to personal communication than broadcast. They trust the grapevine more than official news. Work the grapevine. Find out which people really move and shake in the world of the grapevine and feed them messages.

- Keep the message the same: repeat it through multiple channels time and again. Advertising is often a war of attrition; internal advertising is the same. The more you repeat the message, the more likely it is to be heard and understood.

Customer loyalty and the moment of truth

Doing things right helps build customer loyalty. Doing things wrong does not necessarily destroy the relationship. It can enhance the customer relationship. When things go wrong, it is the moment of truth for the relationship.

The most successful ways of screwing up a customer relationship, as practised by a leading airline, include:

- Do not empower your employees to sort out the problem on the spot.
- Tell the customer he or she is wrong.
- Put bureaucratic obstacles in the way of the customer.
- Do not answer any letters of complaint that may follow.
- When forced to respond, offer too little too late.

Everyone has their own war stories of service from hell, and enjoys recounting them. Typically, one service disaster will get recounted 10 times. The poorly handled moment of truth has not just lost a customer, but has created someone who is busily unselling your service.

Equally, everyone has their tales of service above and beyond the call of duty. It normally revolves around a service disaster that is turned into triumph. Shortly after the airline service disaster above, I flew with Virgin Atlantic and received an involuntary downgrade on a 14-hour flight. This was a disaster that they turned into triumph:

- Employees were empowered on the spot to sort things out: the seat was not there, but they did everything else they could to make the trip a success.
- They accepted responsibility, they sympathized. At stressful moments, a little sympathy goes a long way. Most customers realize cock-ups happen, and are prepared to be reasonable.
- They did not wait for me to write a letter. Richard Branson, the owner of the airline, called directly. This is extreme, but effective.
- They made amends early and fully. A potentially irate customer was turned into a representative for the airline.

Empowering staff in the front line goes against the grain for old style businesses. It implies a loss of control. It may result in staff spending money when not strictly necessary. But it is also a way of losing customers fast. And that, ultimately, is a far greater cost.

Customer research: lies and statistics

Businesses must know their customers. And customer research is a good way of not finding the truth.

Customers lie: attitudes versus behaviour

Customers do not mean to lie, but they do. Most customer research is based on attitudes, opinions and post-rationalization. We conducted two pieces of research for a retailer. The first research asked customers why they bought their television. They gave post-rationalizations about price, features, performance and quality. This showed the store should focus on price, features, performance and quality.

The second piece of research focused on behaviour, and caught people as they left stores either with or without buying. It showed that they wandered around a few shops and became increasingly confused about all the choices. Just after they had bought, they could not recall the different prices or features of different models. If they did not know this basic information, they could not have been making a completely rational decision.

In practice, the customers wanted to be told a story. They wanted to be reassured that they were making a smart choice and that they would not be embarrassed by finding their neighbours had made a better choice. This led the stores to provide an umbrella of price reassurance, without trying to be price leader all the time. More important were the in-store sales skills to provide customers with the reassurance that they wanted, which might focus on price, or on some special features or a warranty. Understanding behaviour was more powerful than recording attitudes.

Similarly, in the UK savings market customers claim to make rational choices about comparing rates and terms. Looking at behaviour shows that 68 per cent of retail customers considered only one supplier in picking their savings account: this was normally their existing bank. Even small businesses fall into the same trap: over half do not shop around for the best savings or borrowing terms. This has profound implications in terms of pricing: existing customers can be penalized for their loyalty or laziness.

Even where attitudinal research is relevant, customers still lie. It is an exceptionally awful product or service that gets a 'below average' rating. Customers are too nice to the researchers. When something is bad, they rate it average. But equally, they find it difficult to be enthusiastic: 'exceptional' ratings are rare. So the research always tends to come back with ratings that give minor variations around the 'above average' rating. The research department then has a field day analysing the data for statistical significance, while missing the bigger picture completely.

Researching the wrong customer

Business-to-business research normally focuses on the immediate buyer. This carries two problems. Like the retail customers, buyers lie. Brokers in the life insurance industry invariably claim that the size of commission does not affect the choice of insurer that they recommend to customers. They lie through their teeth as any basic comparison of commissions and sales shows.

But often the immediate buyer is the wrong person to talk to. Typically the buyer will beef about price. His or her performance is measured on the costs achieved. But this may not be what the rest of the organization wants. Marketing may want short runs of product for test markets or to meet surges in demand. Paying a higher price for a small component that then allows them to increase sales is well worth it.

Similarly, engineering, production and even stock control may have specific product needs for which they would happily pay more. Talking to the buyer will not flush this out.

Effective customer research

Effective customer research is based on two principles. First, ask the right questions. Focus on behaviours and on the product in use, not on attitudes. Behaviours do not lie. Behaviour is becoming ever easier to research: Amazon (for books and hard goods), supermarket loyalty cards; your smartphone and credit card, TripAdvisor for hotels and restaurants tell more about us and what we buy than we can imagine.

Second, ask the right people: focus on the users of the product, not just the buyers. Look not just at the car buyer, but how the whole family uses the car.

You can pay a research agency a small fortune to find this out. You can also go and find out yourself. Customers are normally intrigued and delighted when a real manager from one of their suppliers sits with them to see how their product is used, and how it could be changed to help them even better. They have a tendency to produce insights that a numbers exercise cannot produce.

Customer service: living with reality

If you want to know how good your customer service is, use it yourself:

- Phone your own receptionist, go through the switchboard. Do not use the direct lines.
- Phone the standard call centre number, not the VIP hotline.
- Be a mystery shopper at your stores or dealers.

If you and your staff have to suffer the same service levels that you inflict on your customers, the business will quickly find out how to improve service. Aircrew pick up their bags before the passengers, and have priority clearance through customs and immigration. The howls of pain that would arise if they had to suffer the delays and queues of their passengers would quickly put an end to airport queues. Car executives who have their new cars delivered never have to go through the pain of being ripped off on buying the new car and selling the old car, or of getting the car serviced and maintained. Intellectually they may see the problem, but they do not understand it.

And if government ministers had to suffer all the indignities of lousy public transport instead of chauffeured cars, health systems that do not work and government agencies that are powerful, arrogant and incompetent in equal proportion, there might be a chance of getting some improvement.

Customers versus accountants

The NPV of a customer is a nightmare from the traditional accounting perspective. None of the data fits into the neat little departmental boxes beloved of accountants. From a managerial point of view, customer profitability helps identify where to invest in customer acquisition, where to cross-sell, how to manage different types of customer. In other words, it is useful. At this point, make the accountants help. Make them serve the business and the customer, not the other way round.

Decision time

At school we are taught to work by ourselves to answer pre-determined questions that have clear and logical answers. Any manager who hopes to succeed by working alone to solve pre-determined questions that have a clear answer is going to have a very long wait. As managers we have to answer uncertain questions where all our colleagues have clear but conflicting answers. So how can we make decisions effectively? Here are the basics of good decision making:

- *Know what the question is.* A good answer to 'What is seven times six?' is '42'. For fans of Douglas Adams' novels, it is also the answer to 'What is the meaning of life?' But it is not a great answer to 'What is the capital of Croatia?' On planet business there are plenty of brilliant solutions out there, all in search of a problem: re-engineering, strategic intent, cloud computing and all the fads come and go. So before trying to answer the question, challenge it. A good starting point is to ask: 'What is the problem we are trying to solve?'

- *Know who owns the problem or question.* Just as all bosses are not equal, so all questions are not equal. Some are worth answering well, others merit the toss of a coin. Once you know who owns the problem and what they really want to achieve, you are probably most of the way to success.

- *Ask someone.* You do not have to answer all the questions yourself: **management is not a quiz show**. Your job is to find the right answer. If an expert knows the answer, find it. If you face a tough call but those in your team want to go one way, back them: it is far better to have them working hard to make a flawed decision of their own succeed, than to have them quietly sabotage the brilliant decision you imposed on them.

- *Make a decision, any decision.* Quite often everyone knows what the decision should be, but they lack the courage or authority to make it. So make the decision: your experience will probably guide you in the right direction. If you are wrong, someone will tell you very fast and you can change course. And in a crisis, when everyone is paralyzed by fear and doubt, any decision is a good decision. The challenge is to build momentum and drive to action, rather than get caught in the traps of analysis and finger pointing.

- *Explore the options and build a coalition.* When there is real ambiguity, explore all the options. Avoid getting trapped into an either/or discussion that can rapidly become antagonistic. As you explore options, encourage people to look at the benefits of an idea before the concerns. Best of all, let them think they came up with the brilliant solution: not many people argue against their own ideas. This process is not just about finding the best solution: it is about building support for a solution. There is no such thing as a good idea that did not happen: an idea is only any good if it happens.

- Finally, notice what is missing from this list: all the formal decision making tools you learned on your MBA course. The main value of Bayesian analysis is to show you are smart and to get a good grade: its practical application for most managers is close to zero. Other tools, such as mind maps, decision trees, fishbone analyses, field force analysis, have their places. Some zealots have a whole philosophy about their favourite technique, which they are more than keen to inflict on you for an immodest fee. These tools can be used to engage colleagues in a structured conversation: remember that the tool should be the servant, not the master, of the conversation.

Delegation, empowerment and deception

For the last 200 years delegation has been getting worse. Empowerment has become more or less non-existent except in the speeches made by the big chiefs. Their speeches are deceptions.

The two great enemies of delegation and empowerment are communications and information. Two hundred years ago, the empire builders delegated and empowered without thinking about it. They had no alternative. Once the boat left Europe for India or the colonies it was gone. The next time the people on board would see the big chiefs who had sent them away, it would be years later. By then, they had either succeeded or failed.

If problems arose, they did not refer it to head office. The boat would take six months to travel from India to England and back again. By then the riot, or whatever the problem was, would have faded into history. Even getting a message from one part of India to another and back again would take weeks. The man on the spot had to take control, had to use initiative.

The same pattern of delegation and empowerment was true of the Navy: Nelson did not have to fear being double guessed or countermanded by politicians in Westminster. And equally, he expected his captains to take the initiative. He had a simple command for his captains: 'Any captain that lays his ship alongside that of the enemy can do no wrong.' In other words, get on with it and attack. Don't ask for advice.

Nowadays, if we want to take a penny off the price of a detergent there will be committees, reviews, presentations, research groups, analysis and the whole panoply of corporate oversight and help will swing into force. And they call this delegation and empowerment. And once we have embarked on our course of action, we are under the microscope. There are weekly and monthly reports, progress updates, exception reporting, budget reviews and revisions.

Management trust, **delegation and empowerment are inversely proportional to the frequency and volume of reporting required**. By this measure we live in deeply mistrustful times, and the mistrust is getting deeper. Managers fall into the trap of 'because there is better communication and more information we should use it'. And we use it because it gives us more control and reduces the risks implicit in real delegation and empowerment.

Demotivation and cynicism are not merely products of the administrative burden that the deadweight of reporting represents. The cynicism also comes from knowing that the reporting is a vote of no confidence in the person having to report, and that it lays that person open to being second guessed and overruled by the bosses. The individual is not being entrusted to get on with the business.

But there are other ways of getting control that can leave managers more motivated and more focused on the marketplace than on internal reporting (see page 51 on control).

Democracy and dictatorship at work

The revolution has already happened. Most of the old dictators have been swept away. The traditional command and control through a formal hierarchy is largely dead. There are still a few dinosaurs out there, but their time is up.

Dictatorship at work is a high-control, low-commitment way of managing people. It invites an 'us and them' attitude in which managers hide behind status, rules and hierarchy while workers organize to protect their rights from the dictators. As long as labour was in greater supply than capital, dictators could dictate. As workers built more skills, became more mobile and more important to the enterprise, their value as individuals, not mere units of production, rose. The question is what to replace the dictatorship with. The new age school of thought takes us down the full democratic, tree-hugging, world-saving route. Business is normally not about tree hugging or saving the world. Democracy is not a viable alternative at work. **Businesses are not democracies**: they need clear and effective decision-making processes, linked to clear and effective responsibilities and accountabilities. Clarity and accountability do not come through groups, they come through individuals. There has to be a decision-making hierarchy. Not everyone can be involved in all the decisions all the time, and not everyone will like all the decisions.

For managers the challenge is how to maintain control, enhance commitment and make effective decisions without resorting to authority based solely on rank. The new non-dictatorial and non-democratic leadership model has to based on:

- Respect. The leader must be seen as capable.
- Mutual trust. There have to be common goals backed up by guidelines that help both the manager and the managed achieve the goals.
- Individual responsibility.
- Collective involvement.

Diversity

Diversity is a dirty word in most organizations. Of course, for legal reasons and reasons of political correctness, organizations will try to get a smattering of different minority groups onto the payroll. Although there is some tolerance of minority groups, real diversity is avoided. Indeed, organizations pride themselves on their 'one-firm' approach, which means that you get the same approach, same skills and same culture right around the world supported by global standards and management systems. So, regardless of your sex, race or religion you either adapt to the one firm way or you leave. **Organizations preach diversity but practice conformity.**

The one-firm approach is linked to the preponderance of middle-aged white males in suits in all the top management positions. They set the culture, the standards and the systems. And the culture and the values just happen to reflect the culture and values of white middle-aged males. This is not some white male conspiracy. Japanese companies are even more zealous in promoting a single, homogenous culture across the globe in their global businesses. The only non-Japanese in leading management positions in Japan are in companies that have been taken over by foreigners, such as Mazda and Nissan, plus the notable exception of Sony.

Intolerance of diversity is natural and unavoidable. Working on a global basis, managers need a common set of assumptions and beliefs if they are to operate effectively, make good decisions on a timely basis and communicate and understand each other properly. The Tower of Babel is not a good starting point for a global business. The only way an employee can manage this is to be aware of it at the recruiting stage. Find out what the rules of the game are, and if you don't fit in, don't join.

Warren Buffett wrote: 'I find that when a manager with a great reputation joins a business with a lousy reputation, it is normally the reputation of the business that stays intact.' It is the same with a culture. If you represent a different culture from the firm you join, rest assured that the culture of the firm will not change. Either you will change, or you will leave.

Dress, schizophrenia and the caste system

Dress shows how we want to be seen in the world: who we are, which groups we belong to and, just as importantly, which groups we do not belong to. In the age of conformity, this made life pretty simple for both the individual and the institution. Everyone got to wear the corporate uniform, and no one had to think about identity very much. The only crisis came in deciding just how boring today's tie should be.

Dress codes now cause chaos. Institutions realize they want to be seen differently by different groups. The large-scale systems firm wants to be seen as big, trusty and infinitely reliable by their risk-averse customers. Conservative suits and ties send the right message. But to employment recruits, the firm wants to be seen as hip, high-tech and fun. Suits and ties are not quite the way to do this. The firm's schizophrenia has been revealed by dress codes. It cannot be all things to all people at all times without large-scale deceit. The dress crisis goes into the heart of the institution itself. In place of one uniform, there are hundreds of uniforms that define a person's position in the business with the precision of the caste system:

- Each function has its own style: finance and accounting want to look conservative and trustworthy, creative types try to look creative, IT types try to look hip.

- Each level of management has its own style: bespoke for top managers, designer labels for aspiring middle managers, off the peg for junior managers and dead casual for support staff.

- Each country has its own style, from the overwhelming conformity of the Japanese, to the tyranny of the buff chinos for the US employees; each nationality dresses its culture.

Connoisseurs of dress can tell exactly which country people are from, their department and level just from the dress worn. This matters because it says that people feel a sense of community not with the organization, but with their function or peer group or country. Years of corporate disloyalty to staff through downsizing, restructuring and re-engineering is being repaid by a comprehensive expression of non-loyalty to the organization in the business. If people feel that their identity is primarily as an IT professional, not as an employee of MegaBucks, it is no surprise that they feel relaxed about hawking their skills to the employer with the best package.

Trying to turn the tide back and go to 1960s or Japanese standards of dress conformity is pushing against history. The battle has been fought and comprehensively lost. The greater battle for trying to rebuild a sense of community and loyalty, a psychological contract based on mutual commitment has hardly begun.

Due diligence

This is a process in which the following happens:

- A lot of very highly paid advisers sit in a room amidst the increasing chaos of half-eaten pizzas, smelly socks, fuzzy milk and fuzzy thinking.

- The advisers charge outrageous fees, regardless of whether the outcome of the bid is successful or not.

- The advisers seek to justify in every way possible that the client's gut instinct to launch a takeover bid was correct, in spite of overwhelming evidence to the contrary.

- The thrill of the chase overwhelms managers and advisers alike, throwing objectivity out of the window. Winning is all, even if the cost is out of hand.

Generally, the only antidote is a used envelope. On the back of it write out clearly why you believe the takeover is right, and what the top price is that you should pay. Do this before you talk to the advisers. Keep the envelope with you at all times. Then you know when you should walk away.

E

Easy does it

Make it easy. For your customers, for your staff, for yourself. Put idleness to your advantage.

Make it easy for your customers

Customers are busy. They have lives to lead. It may be climbing mountains, or sitting in front of the TV watching the football. But it is almost certainly more enjoyable and important to them than worrying about your product and service. And they do not want to spend their lives figuring out how to use your service. Equally, they do not have the time, inclination or expertise to do a full assessment of your offering versus all of those in the marketplace. This is true of retail products. Even businesses do only limited beauty parades and comparison shopping.

This is wonderful news for business. It means that price is not always the most important thing. Make it easy for the customer to pick you and use you, and the customer will stay. Make it easy to pick you: branding (retail markets) and reputation (business-to-business markets) count. Make the decision an easy one.

Make it easy for customers to use your service. Look at e-business websites to see how not to do it. Some websites have been hijacked by the techies. They are so keen to show off their technical prowess that the site is fit only for rocket scientists or those with the patience of a saint. Or the product people have hijacked it. They are so keen to show all the bells and whistles of their great service that it is unusable to all bar the initiated. The simple sites are intuitive, invite people to use them and make it easy. The simple sites win. The sophisticated sites lose. If you make the complex easy, people will reward you with loyalty and pay higher prices.

Make it easy for your staff

This is not about idleness, it is about effectiveness. There are three ways to make it easy for staff:

- *Focus*. Keep it simple. Know the priorities, know what you will not do. This makes life easier for staff, and makes for better results.

- *Delegation*. Don't put the staff in a position where they are always second guessing you, checking with you and reiterating work. Delegate. Put the pressure on them to get it right first time. Avoid rework.

- *Expectations*. Be clear about what is and is not expected. It is not enough to have focus, the staff need to understand the focus and what it means to them personally.

Make it easy for yourself

If you have made it easy for your staff, you have probably made it easy for yourself. You should have staff doing what they should be doing, leaving you to focus on what you need to focus on. The wrinkle is that the focus and expectations setting also needs upwards management: the boss needs to have the same expectations as you and your team. The easy life is the good life.

Enthusiasm

'All creatures of the universe: rejoice! On pain of death', Emperor Ming to the creatures of the universe in *Flash Gordon*. Being told to be enthusiastic is the best way to destroy enthusiasm. But unless people have some sense of enthusiasm and enjoyment, they are not going to have that extra commitment that will make the business succeed. People are not good at what they do not enjoy. **You only excel at what you enjoy.**

There is one thing that will not help you create a sense of enthusiasm: taking staff away to corporate events, team-building exercises and forced fun parties are a waste of time. Some of the staff will like the event, but the moment they return to a miserable office, the misery and old habits kick straight back in. The rest of the staff probably don't want to go abseiling or building rafts, and hate every moment of it but know that they are not allowed to say so. Practically, there are three things a manager can do to build a sense of enthusiasm:

- *Be enthusiastic yourself*. You either have it, or you don't. But staff take their cues from managers. If you are a miserable, political bastard, do not be surprised if the staff seem like miserable, political bastards. Cultures are self-reinforcing. Bad ones get worse, good ones get better. If you have no enthusiasm for what you do, you are probably doing the wrong thing. And **if you are not enthusiastic, no one else will be enthusiastic for you**.

- *Show that you know your staff and care for them.* A survey of how staff rated managers showed that if staff believed that a manager cared for them personally, then all the other attributes of the manager (intelligence, insight, effectiveness, results, etc) were seen positively. Managers who did not care for staff were rated badly on all other management criteria as well. If you ever want a good 360-degree feedback, showing you care is the way to get it. This does not mean being false-nice: it means being honest and taking the time and trouble to listen to and talk with each staff member.

- *Give staff a sense of direction and purpose.* Human nature hates ambiguity and risk. You can take that away by painting a clear picture of where you are trying to go, and of what it means to them in terms of opportunities. You may need them to climb Everest, but that is better than leaving them meandering, lost in the foothills.

Enthusiasm is not a certifiable mental disorder, although some organizations seem to think so. It is often a great way of breaking through the dull grey shadows in which many managers live.

Entrepreneurs, business and the pact with the devil

Businesses like to think they are entrepreneurial. They lie, and fool only themselves. **The entrepreneurial approach is as palatable to business as salt to a slug.** Try a simple test. **When your boss asks for more entrepreneurial zeal, ask if he or she wants more risk, ambiguity, cost and failure.** Bosses like the successful outcomes of enterprise, but hate the process and will not tolerate the failures. So all crazy innovations are fine, as long as they have been tried, tested and are guaranteed to succeed.

Ambiguity, risk and speed

Corporations tolerate risk but hate ambiguity. Planned risk is part of any investment or new market initiative. But there are no mechanisms for dealing with ambiguity.

The entrepreneur will seek to minimize risk: his or her house is probably on the line. But ambiguity is tolerable: it creates opportunities to do things differently and create some new competitive space. So where there are two or three different ways of attacking a market, the entrepreneur will probably try a couple of ways, see which works and then scale up fast. The corporation will want to research everything in detail, document and prove the best case before teams of functionaries and then proceed. By which time, the entrepreneurs have already moved.

Hustle

In the corporate world everyone takes holidays. When employees take holidays, fall sick, retire, resign or die, the business moves on. Entrepreneurs quickly discover that unless they hustle, nothing happens. And the hustle has to be hustle on all fronts: finding customers, recruiting talent, managing people, sorting out the finances. There are no large company departments to take all of these problems away.

Corporate life support systems and the pact with the devil

Anyone who has escaped from the corporate to the entrepreneurial world is shocked:

- Flunkies do not come round with fresh flowers for the office.
- You have to do your own photocopying at a local print shop.
- The air-conditioning system means opening the window.
- Getting more money is not a matter of politics and a new budget system: it means crawling on your knees to hard-nosed banks and venture capitalists.
- Managing cash flow is not a budget item: it means either paying the rent or not.
- Travelling in economy class is possible without dying.
- There are no committees to block you, but none to support you and share the blame. You are responsible for your own decisions.

This is the pact with the devil that employees sign up to with their employer. **Employees are enabled and imprisoned by corporate life support**

systems. As long as you go along with the corporate systems, life is fine. Buck the system, and it will strike back. This does not make big company employees into natural entrepreneurs. It does not make it easy for big companies to accommodate the true entrepreneur. They are different beasts.

The solution for corporates is not to pretend to be entrepreneurial. It quickly leads to corporate confusion and schizophrenia. Entrepreneurialism has to exist outside the safe confines of the corporate world. Fostering entrepreneurialism means creating a unit outside all the normal controls of the business, preferably far away geographically, with a powerful political sponsor who shoots any corporate functionary that tries to help.

Executive excess

It is easy to explode with anger, tinged with just a little hint of envy, when we hear of the latest excess of corporate greed. In 2011, the FTSE 100 CEOs each paid themselves an average of £3.7 million. An average worker would have to work non-stop for 145 years to earn what the CEO earns in 12 months. And it is not as if these CEOs have delivered for their shareholders: in the last 10 years, their pay has gone up four fold, while share prices have gone down. Nice work if you can get it.

But if you are angry now, be prepared to become apoplectic later on: it is only going to get worse. CEOs are not being paid for performance, or for risk. They are being paid because they control the company. The shareholder only gets a look in when there is a takeover, which leads to the CEO either getting a bonus for succeeding or getting a massive golden parachute for being taken over. **Heads you lose, tails they win.**

The basic problem was recognized by Adam Smith in *The Wealth of Nations* (1776). The problem is the separation of control and ownership. We look after things we own better than we look after things that are not ours. Someone who owns a company they started cares about every penny: this is not an accusation that can be levelled at CEOs of top FTSE companies. They do not own the company, but they have the power and the control to milk it for as much as they can. In theory, shareholders control the company. In practice, they do not. Indeed, when shareholders object to the latest CEO pay rise, it is called a shareholder revolt. Marx would be spinning in his grave: the workers were meant to revolt against the evil owners and shareholders. Instead, shareholders are now reduced to revolting against the overmighty workers in the executive suite.

CEO pay will continue to spiral, regardless of performance. The board, which will probably consist of senior executives from other companies, will review CEO pay. For this, they will refer to compensation experts who will tell them that the average CEO pay for a FTSE 100 CEO is £3.7 million per annum. Well, we cannot hire a sub-standard CEO, can we? So of course we need to pay above average. So every board decides to pay above average and the average remorselessly rises. The only ultimate check is objection by the shareholders, but they are largely irrelevant.

As Adam Smith wrote: 'Negligence and profusion, therefore, must always prevail, more or less, in the management of the affairs of such a company (with owners who are not managers).' Expect much more negligence and profusion. You have only two reasonable responses: indulge your moral indignation, or become a CEO.

Excess capacity

Excess capacity is not a sin. It may well represent a smart investment. Think of all the times you have been stuck in checkout queues, or waiting at the airport or waiting on the line for the call centre to answer. You, as the customer, are being forced to pay for the service provider's lack of capacity. You may get slightly lower prices, in return for service that sucks.

Think of all the initiatives you would like to start, the research that needs to be done, the markets that need to be tested and opened, but cannot because of lack of capacity. The organization may be extremely lean and efficient, but at the cost of underinvesting in its future.

Any system that operates with no excess capacity, that strives for 100 per cent efficiency **is inherently unstable**. It cannot cope with any unexpected demand, or to any unexpected problems. An office where all the staff are already working 50–60 hours a week just to maintain the status quo is not a happy place, and probably does not have a good future.

Excess capacity in the office is rarely measured in individuals who are doing nothing at all. It is more likely that 6 or 10 or 12 people each have a quarter or half their time that could be redeployed effectively.

The art is to know where that slack exists and then focus it. Keep a list of all the initiatives you would like to start, and then you can marry the excess supply to the demand. As and when a business shock comes along, you can then redeploy that excess capacity away from the discretionary efforts and on to the full-time work. You have a business that can deal with peaks and troughs, and can pursue the discretionary efforts that are the investment in the future.

Excuses

Never use or accept excuses. If there is a problem, explain clearly why the problem occurred. If you know why it happened, you should also have the solution. Bring both the problem and the solution to the table. Then you look positive, proactive and in control.

Weak and defensive managers simply turn up with their excuse. Worse, they try to hide or shift responsibility. When found out they appear untrustworthy, defensive, reactive and not in control.

Equally, do not accept excuses. Prevention is far better than cure. Set your team up to succeed, and help them win, then no excuses are necessary. If excuses start appearing, then it is as much your fault as the fault of the people making excuses. First, get the team to come back with solutions, not excuses. Then work out what you need to do to stop the problem and the excuse reaction recurring.

Expatriates

Expatriates are rarely worth the trouble for either the corporation or the individual. I should know: I was one. From the corporate point of view, the expatriate in theory does a lot. He or she helps transfer skills, helps build the one-firm organization globally, helps maintain global standards, and provides insight to global management about regional opportunities and performance. An expatriate posting is also a way of stretching and developing individuals. There is, however, an alternative reality:

- Expatriates are extremely expensive compared to local hires.
- Expatriates take time to get up to speed: they underperform relative to their capabilities while they learn the local language and local business.
- They do not represent a vote of confidence in local managers: morale can be damaged and it becomes harder to recruit good locals if they see the path to the top obstructed by foreigners.
- Expatriates are likely to leave once they have finished their tour of duty: the skills so expensively nurtured will be lost.

From the expatriate's point of view, things do not look much better:

- Culture shock is real: about 40 per cent of the people we sent to Japan washed out inside two months. This was a typical experience.

- Reintegration into the home business is difficult. No position can be held open for three years. And no one will be overly keen to give up their chance of promotion to someone who has not been around.

- Culture shock on the return is real. Having got used to running a business and being a big shot far away, it is difficult to readjust to being stuck in the matrix of middle management back in the home office. Many expatriates leave the company at this point.

There is always going to be the need for some expatriates. From the corporate point of view, they should be minimized. From the individual point of view, be very wary of accepting an expatriate position. And never believe any of the promises of what will happen when you return. The boss who made the promises has probably been reorganized twice into a completely different role. And your new boss will have no interest in keeping promises he or she didn't make.

Eyes of management

Managers can look at the same thing and see completely different things. This is a source of huge strength when all the different angles are brought together to create a common picture. It is also a source of endless conflict when the different points of view are in competition with each other.

Try walking into a grocery store and doing the 'eyes of management' test. See how different people will see exactly the same thing. A good grocery store is a beautifully choreographed show, which the consumer is scarcely aware of. Looking through the eyes of the different players illustrates how radically different perspectives have to come together. For example:

- The manufacturer's salesperson sees just his or her own products and how they are displayed relative to the competition, whether the promotional messages and the prices are correct and whether each brand has the correct number of facings for its market share. This then leads to a discussion with the buyer about how to position the products better.

- Shelf-fillers see the gaps in the shelves and the sell-by dates on the products that need to be rotated.

- The store manager sees detail, detail, detail: looking for stock-outs, display errors, checkout queues, staff deployment and behaviour, pilferage, maintenance issues, compliance with head office guidelines on displays and promotions, as well as the general administration of the store.

- Security staff are looking at customers and staff and for the typical patterns of pilferage.

- Maintenance staff see broken light bulbs, dirt, faulty electrics and fittings that are, they hope, invisible to others.

- The area manager is seeing the detail of the store manager, but is also looking at how the store manager is interacting with the staff, what is going wrong, where the store manager needs support or coaching.

- The marketing manager starts looking in the car park: how many people there are, what sorts of people they are (singles, families, age, affluence) and what the local environment is (competition, transport, other complementary stores). Implicitly he or she is looking at the potential of the store, which can then be checked against the reality of what is happening in the store: how customers are moving around the store, where they are stopping and buying and where they just pass through.

Through this, the customer wanders barely aware of the extraordinary performance being choreographed around the shopping trolley. It is not possible for the customer to see everything that all the managers and staff see. **The strength of the organization is in the choreography of the show.** Managerially, the challenge is to move from the cacophony of management to the choreography of management: to see and coordinate all the different perspectives of all the different players.

Fear or friendship?

Gordon Gekko, the banking villain of the 1987 film *Wall Street*, famously announced, 'If you want a friend, buy a dog.' He joins a long line of bankers who are hated and thinkers who doubt the value of friendship. Machiavelli in *The Prince* (published formally in 1532) advises rulers that it is better to be feared than loved, because love is fickle. Nothing much has changed in the last 500 years or so.

For weak managers, **friendship is the low road to an easy life and poor performance**. Managers who seek friendship curry favour, avoid hard decisions, duck conflict and ask for modest performance. The reward for chasing popularity is weakness.

There are some managers who follow the Machiavelli rule and like to be feared. Machiavelli recommends a few executions to keep the public in line; some managers like to fire a few people to make their mark. These are the sort of managers we may have to work for, but we do not want to work for.

So if neither fear nor friendship is the solution, what is the way forward? The most **effective managers need to be respected and trusted**. We may not want to go out for a beer with them every evening, but we will feel comfortable working for them. Here is how to earn trust and respect:

- *Be consistent.* Avoid flip-flops; set expectations and stick to them. Inconsistency is the hallmark of a weak leader.

- *Stay positive, especially when times are tough.* Avoid blame: focus on the future and drive to action, not to analysis.

- *Face up to problems.* If a team member is not performing, don't hide the fact and keep it as a nasty surprise for the annual review. Have the awkward conversation early and positively: help the individual correct course while he or she still has time.

- *Deliver on your promises.* So take care about what you say and set expectations very carefully: people hear what they want to hear, not what you say. When you say 'I will do my best for your promotion/

bonus (etc)' they will hear 'I promise to get you your promotion/bonus (etc).' If later you have to tell them you 'did your best' as promised, but it was not enough, you will have lost all credibility.

- *Be loyal.* Loyalty is a two-way street: you should expect the members of your team to be loyal to you and you should be loyal to them, especially when it comes to bonus and promotion time. Loyalty also means shielding them from unfair criticism and taking flak for them when required.

- *Show you care.* Take an interest in who they are, what they do and in their hopes, fears and dreams. You do not have to indulge their whims, but you should show you understand and respect them.

If you can do all this, you will be way ahead of most managers in most organizations. Doing simple things well and consistently is very hard.

Financial accounting: the road to irrelevance

Financial accounting was never perfect. A system that was born hundreds of years ago is looking as relevant to today's business as the quill pens that were used in the first ledgers. There were always some basic problems:

- Financial accounting looks backward, not forward. This is fine for keeping score, but not for scoring goals.

- Accounting conventions leave enough room for interpretation that there is huge potential to mislead. Profit figures massaged year on year by exceptional items, write-offs, depreciation of goodwill, different treatment of stocks, inventory and even different ways of recognizing sales give plenty of room for manoeuvre. No wonder analysts and fund managers trash companies that miss earnings targets by a penny. If they miss even after all the setting of expectations and massaging of numbers, then something fairly profound must be wrong.

- Financial accounting is only a starting point for understanding corporate performance. Market share, sales, growth, productivity and new products are probably better forward indicators of performance than backward-looking financial data.

The 21st century is making the problems worse. **The financial accounting profession is still fighting the battles of the last century.** The profession is trying to harmonize irrelevant standards. The challenge for the profession is not standardization, it is relevance.

At the heart of the problem are intangible assets. When Pacciole invented double entry bookkeeping, it was based on the presumption that the book entries represented real, tangible assets that had a clear market, cash value. This 500-year-old assumption is still at the heart of accounting. But a look at the shape of 21st-century business shows that this assumption is wrong. The assets of today's businesses are not physical or tradable assets:

- *Nike:* the value of the business is in the brand. Production is outsourced. There is not that much in the way of physical assets beyond a lot of old posters. Heroic, but unconvincing, efforts are being made to value brands. From the accounting point of view, there is no reliable way of putting the brand on the balance sheet: is advertising an expense or a capital investment building the value of the brand?

- *Investment banks:* the assets are walking out of the door each evening. The assets are the skills of the staff. A hundred years ago, accounting did not have to worry about skills: capitalists provided the capital, managers managed and workers worked. Workers were not skilled, and were easily replaced.

- *Dot.coms:* the value of the business is not physical assets. It is based on the value of the intellectual property, the business idea of the dot.com.

- *Pharmaceutical companies:* the value of the business is in patents supported by a strong distribution network. The physical assets are largely irrelevant, except for their cash mountains. Financial accounting does not reflect the value of those assets, nor how investment in those assets should be treated.

The shift from physical to intangible assets is also linked to a parallel shift from costs being largely variable to largely fixed. When Adam Smith observed the pin makers in Gloucester, the cost of each pin was related to two main variable costs: raw materials and labour. There were virtually no overheads. The pin makers did not have advertisers, training departments, strategy or HR functions, computer systems, telephone networks, corporate headquarters, accounting staff, or any of the other overheads that represent today's corporate life support system. This explosion of overhead and semi-fixed costs is a nightmare for traditional financial accounting systems:

- Costs and profits are becomingly increasingly dependent on potentially arbitrary decisions about overhead allocation. Financial accounting, based on departmental budgets, does not give management a rational basis on which to make allocation decisions.
- The balance sheet is becoming increasingly disconnected from the value of the business and the true, intangible, assets that underpin it.
- The profit figure is open to distortion: a good starting point for looking at an annual report is not the profit and loss but the notes to see how the figures will have been massaged.

About the only figure that has much integrity left is the cash flow statement, but even that can be distorted on an annual basis by timing sales and expenses smartly. Over a three- to five-year period, it is hard to have a cash flow statement that lies. But five years is history, not an actionable time frame for managers or investors. Management accounting is starting to get to grips with the challenges of the 21st century. Financial accounting is stuck in the wrong century.

Flat organizations, flat results

The flat organization can be a very high performing organization. At its best it is a high commitment, high energy, flexible business in which people work closely together. Seeing this, some traditional organizations have tried to flatten themselves. In the process they have flattened their results. They lack the culture, legacy or capability to perform as a flat organization. They should be true to what they are, and not pretend to be what they cannot be. Despite claims to the contrary, **elephants do not learn to dance** except as a comic routine in old-fashioned circuses. Here's how one very successful but traditional organization tried to flatten the organization and succeeded in flattening its performance:

- There was massive centralization and bureaucracy. The new organization still needed to integrate and coordinate its efforts. This used to be achieved through the hierarchy. In place of the formal hierarchical control, lots of staff jobs appeared to coordinate training policies, recruiting policies, standards, quality, communications, financial controls and firm-wide initiatives. Once in, the staffers are impossible to shift.

- There was exponential growth of internal communications and focus. Decisions that used to require two or three people would suddenly require 10 or 20 people. The number of points of contact and communication grew exponentially with the introduction of each new dimension of the matrix. The flat organization had a five-dimensional matrix. Normal human beings cannot think in more than three dimensions (or four, if time is a dimension). This meant decisions would now involve industry groups, geographical groups, functional groups, product or service groups and skills-based groups. Each had competing agendas, overlapping responsibilities.

- Politics rose and accountability declined. The matrix allowed people and performance to hide. It enabled individuals to associate themselves with initiatives if they looked like being successful, and to disassociate themselves if it looked like being unsuccessful.

- Managers stopped talking to each other. The complexity of communication became so great that at first a few managers found it easiest to call large meetings of all the interested parties together, rather than talk to other managers one to one. It was the easiest way of squaring up all the different agendas. Where previously one manager would call another directly and discuss the issue or arrange to meet, the secretaries took over to coordinate multiple diaries.

- Internal meetings and conferences proliferated. Everyone belonged to all five sides of the matrix. To assert their authority and influence, managers of each dimension would summon their underlings to meetings, training events and increasingly lavish offsite jollies designed to woo the underlings.

Naturally, the business was so busy coordinating itself that it lost sight of the customer.

A flat organization is as much a cultural statement as an organizational statement. Put a flat organization chart onto a hierarchical organization and the nightmare starts. The traditional hierarchical managers take the flat organization chart too seriously, and spend the whole time looking at what it means in terms of accountability, responsibility, power and authority. They make the mistake of believing the chart. The result is not a lean, flexible and market-focused business but a bureaucratic, political muddle.

Flattery

Research shows that **there is no point at which flattery becomes counter-productive**. The more outrageously you flatter people, the more they will think that you are a wonderful person. Forget the academic research, test this idea yourself.

For a start, how many of your colleagues think that they are under promoted, underpaid and under recognized? And how many people you know think that they are below average in terms of honesty, hard work, intelligence, driving cars or loving? In fact **95 per cent of people think they are above average: this is statistically impossible but emotionally inevitable**. And you can use this to your advantage.

We live in a cruel and uncaring world that does not always recognize our innate brilliance and humanity. And then someone comes along who suddenly seems to realize that we are as great as we always thought we were. So will we think that person is an idiot, or will we conclude that he or she has very fine judgement? Even better, when we flatter someone the person will feel the need to reciprocate the favour: so we will find ourselves on the receiving end of much deserved praise.

If you are going to flatter, make sure it works. Here's how:

- *Make it substantive.* Avoid one-minute managing with non-praise: 'Wow, you photocopied that sheet of paper really well.' And avoid generics such as 'You are a wonderful human being.' Find some specific idea, action or trait you can praise.

- *Praise in public.* Private praise is good, public praise is great. Public recognition, especially in front of bosses, is like a Class A drug: a totally addictive high.

- *Flatter everyone:* avoid having a few favourites, because then you become divisive.

- *Use the contradiction principle:* 'I really did not think that could possibly work, but what a great result!' This works particularly well with bosses: they often need confirmation that they have superior insight and business acumen.

- *Enquire:* 'How on earth did you manage to do that?' Then look rapt as people explain their own genius. This will give you plenty of chances to 'ooh' and 'aah' and confirm to them that they are truly wonderful. If in doubt, ask people to talk about their favourite subject: themselves. Then coo over their trivial triumphs and travails. They will appreciate someone who recognizes them for what they are: wonderful human beings.

- *Ask for advice.* This strokes anyone's ego: it shows that the person is regarded as a source of wisdom and expertise. And of course, be sure to lavish praise on people for their brilliant insights about how to work out 2 plus 2.

- *Go for it. If you are going to flatter, go the whole hog.* Try using words such as: brilliant, fantastic, outstanding, great, top class, unbelievable. Remember, there is no point at which your praise becomes counter-productive, so don't hold back.

- *Be overly generous:* even if someone only contributed part of an idea or an action, show how without that person's act of genius the sky would have fallen down. Don't worry that you are giving away the credit to someone else: by offering praise you are showing that you were really at the centre of things anyway.

- *Praise at least 10 times as much as you criticize.* Try counting your flattery–criticism ratio. Eventually you will find that criticism is completely unnecessary: instead of criticizing the past, you focus on the future and on action.

Flattery is a very small investment of time that pays large and repeated dividends.

Forecasting and experts

Everyone gets their forecasts wrong. Experts are wrong with greater eloquence and authority than the rest of us. Here's the expert view on:

- *telephones:* 'An amazing invention, but who would want to use one?', US president Rutherford Hayes, 1876;

- *electric lighting:* 'Good enough for our transatlantic friends... but unworthy of practical or scientific men', British Parliamentary Select Committee, 1878;

- *record players:* 'The phonograph is of no commercial value', Thomas Alva Edison;

- *computers:* 'There is no reason for any individual to have a computer in their home', Ken Olson, President of DEC, 1977;

- *computers (again):* 'I think there is a world market for about five computers', IBM founder Thomas J Watson, 1947;

- *radio:* 'I have anticipated its complete disappearance – confident that the unfortunate people who must now subdue themselves to "listening in" will soon find a better pastime for their leisure', HG Wells, 1928;

- *atomic power:* 'Anyone who expects a source of power from the transformation of these atoms is talking moonshine', Nobel prize-winning physicist Lord Rutherford after he had split the atom in 1911;

- *the stock market:* 'Stock prices have reached what looks like a permanently high plateau', Irving Fisher, Professor of Economics at Yale University, September 1929, just before the Wall Street crash.

Of course, corporate forecasts are never so foolish. Are they?

Frequent flying

Frequent flying is a disaster for business. Just because frequent flying is possible, it does not mean managers should fly frequently. Flying may be tedious, uncomfortable, tiring, cause jet lag and destroy productivity, but it is a powerful status symbol. The more you fly, the more important you must be. And if you travel business or first class, then you must be even more important to the business. Complaining about jet lag, poor service and delayed flights is simply a way of articulating your status to people who do not see you travel and do not realize the status it brings with it.

Because flying is still a status symbol, the rot starts at the top. Some of the most frequent, and certainly most expensive travellers, are senior managers. Flying reinforces their status: while they turn left at the aircraft door to go business or first, the underlings enjoy the humiliation of turning right into the cramped seats at the back. The apartheid of status is rigorously laid out by corporate travel policies and enforced by the airlines as you step on the aircraft.

Senior managers are articulate about why they need to spend up to US $10,000 to rent a bed for six hours while they cross the Atlantic. It's all about their productivity. Which is another way of saying that the productivity of their staff travelling economy does not matter so much to them. The airlines reinforce the frequent flyer abuse through their loyalty programmes. The loyalty programmes mean:

- People make more business trips than necessary.
- They pay full fare when they could find a discount with a cheaper airline.
- They fly at awkward times to gain loyalty points with their chosen airline.

Travel policies and procedures do not stop this abuse. Travel policies may dictate class of travel, but do nothing to stop the extent of travel or choice of airline. Stopping this abuse by trying to claim ownership of the air miles earned on corporate expense invites a long emotional battle with staff that is not worth fighting. One solution would be to name and shame the worst culprits. Publish a league table with the number of miles flown per manager, the cost per mile and the total cost. If senior managers set a good example, junior managers would be reluctant to be seen to be outspending and outflying their bosses.

Unfortunately, this is a league table that most senior managers would quietly like to lead, with the junior managers trying to emulate them. Consultancies have an effective, if dishonest answer. They implicitly treat travel as a perk of the job, and simply charge their clients for the expense. It is a cost-free perk to the consultants, and an expensive one for their clients.

G

Global teams

Listen a little and you will hear a tumultuous roar about globalization. Listen a little harder and you will hear much about how global organizations should organize globally (or locally or multi-locally).

Only when you listen very hard will you hear the sound of silence echoing around a subject that is both essential and ignored: how global teams should work. Global teams are not like the team in your office: they speak different languages, work different hours, have different assumptions, and you cannot see or hear them most of the time. But if you are working on designing an aircraft, or on a global supply chain, or advising a global client, you will have to work in a global team. Not all of your global and virtual team will necessarily be in the same organization as yours.

Within the global team, not all team members are equal. Inevitably, the boss lives in one country, which means that the other countries will start to be suspicious. If I work in Wales on the aircraft, but my team boss is in France, will all the decisions be made in France? Will all the promotions favour the French? Will we get a fair hearing for our needs? At least Wales and France are nearly on the same time zone. The opportunities for misunderstanding are huge; the opportunities for resolving the misunderstandings are very limited.

All teams run on trust. If you work closely with the same people day to day, that trust can build naturally. You start to understand each other better: you understand what your colleagues are good or bad at; what they like and dislike; how to help or hinder them. This is how the original global teams worked: empires were administered by people who all came from the same background. But that is not a luxury the modern global team has. Instead, best practice involves apparently wasting time and money on global conferences in exotic locations. The value of this is not in the big speeches. The value lies in people getting to know each other: putting faces to names. But you need more than feasting to make a global team work. Here are some of the basics:

- *Clear team rubrics.* You need clear goals, processes, reporting and decision-making rubrics. Write these down to minimize the chances of confusion, and allow the team to question and challenge them, so that the rubrics are accepted.

- *Clear global rubrics*. Be clear about when you will meet virtually. Middle of the day is great for Europe, early for the United States and very late for Japan. Spread the pain around a little.

- *Clear communication*. If in doubt, over-communicate. Where you can, see people face to face, even if you do rack up the air miles. **Telecoms are great for transactions, lousy for trust.** If you need to build or use trust, do it in person. Once you have the trust, then e-mail and phone is fine for the routine transactions of any team.

- *Smart staffing*. Move key people around. This is expensive, but opens up communications, transfers skills, standardizes global norms and brings cultural misunderstandings out into the open.

- *Global meetings*. Have global meetings where you can talk through issues, clear up misunderstandings, reinforce the rubrics, agree common plans and approaches and build trust.

Glory and lies: the annual report

The company annual report has one main objective: to glorify top managers. The glorification starts with lots of pictures and comments by the great panjandrums. This is where the lies start. To show that the panjandrums are worthy of their glory, the annual report has to show how well the business has done, regardless of the actual results.

Below is the patent lie detector test for annual reports. Any annual report scoring over 75 per cent gets a gold-level award. You will then be entitled to send a scored copy of this test to the chairperson of the company with a raspberry or whatever reward you think is most appropriate for the gold-standard lies you have detected. There are three categories of lie:

- *Category one lies*. We are a happy, politically correct company. Evidence is mainly in the pictures:
  - pictures of the only senior women or minority executives or non-executives to disguise the glass ceiling that operates in the company;
  - pictures of smiling employees with disabilities, women and minority frontline workers who are on low/minimum wages and struggling to survive while doing dirty, dull or dangerous jobs;

- pictures of charities that have benefited from the company's need to appear politically correct;
- statements showing that the firm cares for the environment (the most polluting companies claim this the most vigorously);
- pictures of happy, local employees in exotic destinations: also on low wages – avoiding pictures from exotic but politically incorrect countries (dictatorships, kleptocracies).

● *Category two lies.* Managers are doing a great job. Annual reports will either provide excuses in bad years or will claim management excellence in good years. Any companies that admit management failings in bad years or luck in good years are probably worth investing in: they have a strong grip on reality, if not on deceit. Evidence is found mainly in the chairperson's and CEO's statements:

- In bad years, score points for each excuse: market downturn, government action or inaction, supplier and input costs, currency effects, weather and calamities, and other more creative excuses. In other words, all the bad stuff is down to external factors, not managers.

- In good years, score a point for each claim to fame: new product successes, new strategic direction, cost-cutting programmes, quality programmes, new systems implementation, new advertising, new alliances, and any other actions, which on further examination are common to this company and all its competitors. All the good stuff is down to managers, not to external factors.

- Give double points to any company that gives both excuses and a list of claims to fame, which are no different from those of its competition.

● *Category three lies.* The numbers are not so bad. This is where the financial director earns his or her money. The goal is to make sure that the numbers are in line with analysts' expectations, regardless of the underlying performance of the business. The evidence is in the profit and loss account, the balance sheet and the cash flow statement. The notes are where the forensic evidence can be found to nail the lies. These lies could fill several books. The highlights are:

- smoothing the profit and loss downwards using higher than normal write-offs and exceptional items, special pension contributions, provisions for restructuring, bad debts;

- smoothing the profit and loss upwards using lower than normal write-offs and exceptional items, pension holidays, write-backs, gains on sale of assets, capitalization of expense items (IT investments);
- massaging the balance sheet to make the ratios look good using off balance sheet financing and obligations, stocks valuations and write-offs, property revaluations;
- massaging the cash flow statement by fixing the timing of major payments or income streams to fall just outside the accounting period.

If the financial director cannot make the numbers come in line with expectations then either he or she is incompetent or the results are truly awful. Either way, the overreaction of the investment analysts and the share price plunge will be well justified.

Grass is greener on the other side of the hill

The risks and opportunities of moving on

Everyone likes to believe the grass is greener on the other side of the hill, even successful people. Business people may dream of the power of politicians, who may dream of the glamour of actors, who may dream of the glory of sportsmen, who may dream of the artistry of poets, who may crave the genius of scientists. There is always someone else who seems to be better off. A good starting point is to recognize that no one has it all, even those who appear to have it all still crave something that is beyond the reach of money or power.

Moving jobs is fun. You learn new skills. But it is inherently risky. In the thrill of the chase, both the headhunter and the hunted tend to over promise. The hunter will tend to overplay the strengths of the company and the importance of the role on offer. The hunted will tend to overplay his or her achievements and track record. So, the first thing that happens is disappointment versus the expectations that have been raised. Then reality strikes for the new hire:

- *There is no support network.* In large organizations, this is built up over years, helps people to navigate their way around and is essential for making things happen. Because it happens over years, it seems natural. Without it in the new organization, the new hire is desperately exposed until he or she can build a new network, at speed.

- *The rules of the game are unclear.* Every organization has unwritten rules about how to make things happen, what is good and bad behaviour, what to wear and how to work. Unconsciously, the new hire is stepping on landmines left, right and centre. The politics are totally obscure.

- *People are sceptical.* People will want to see you prove yourself, fast – especially if there were internal candidates for your job. But proving yourself fast in a new environment where you do not know the politics, rules of the game and have no network, is harder than proving yourself in the old organization.

- *Disillusionment results.* The grass is not greener on the other side of the hill. Many companies in the same industry land up with similar sorts of skills, people and styles. They may be new, but not necessarily better. And, even if the culture is different, this leads to the discovery that the strengths and weaknesses are simply different from before. At least this makes the source of frustration different.

Given the credulity of recruiters and their tendency to overvalue outside experience relative to internal experience, it should be possible to promote yourself out of your current firm. Two years later you can always get another promotion and salary rise by rejoining the old firm with your new experience.

Next time a headhunter promises you greener pastures elsewhere, remember that it is greenest where it rains the most.

Guarantees: promises and lies

Businesses like the idea of offering guarantees. It shows that the business has faith in its product and can attract customers. But many businesses wimp out when it comes to offering or fulfilling the guarantee. This is when the caution of the bean counters and the lawyers overwhelms the logic of the marketplace. Wimping out of guarantees is typically driven by three concerns:

- *Some customers will cheat.* At university an old scam was to buy a suit from Marks & Spencer, wear it to an interview and then return it to the store and get a cash refund. The students who did this effectively cashed a cheque and rented a smart suit for free. In return, Marks & Spencer acquired many faithful future customers. And the cheats, students aside, are a small and affordable minority.

- *Acts of God happen.* We cannot guarantee overnight delivery if disaster strikes. This is true. Part of the solution is to stop disaster striking. If delivery people on the ground have their van break down, empower them to do whatever it takes to make the delivery. The guarantee works not just on the customer, it works on the business by forcing staff to find solutions that will improve performance and ensure that customers do not have to call upon the guarantee.

- *A guarantee carries costs.* These are driven by poor performance and some customer cheating. The challenge for the business is that the costs of the guarantee are immediately apparent, the benefits flow only later through improved performance, customer loyalty and word of mouth referrals. This is where managers show their loyalties: to the bean counters or to the market.

The wimp's response to the problems of the service guarantee is to offer a meaningless guarantee. The typical ways of making a guarantee worthless are:

- *Make it highly conditional.* Put onerous maintenance requirements on customers in order for them to keep the guarantee alive.

- *Make it difficult to claim.* Oblige customers to send in a registration form within seven days of purchase, and then require full proof of purchase and the original packaging to be sent at their expense when submitting a claim. This should eliminate 99 per cent of claims.

- *Make the value of the guarantee low.* Consultants often offer a one-month discontinuation clause as a guarantee. This is worthless.

The effect of these non-guarantees is that customers are not encouraged to claim. The business does not hear what is going wrong, it does not receive signals showing how and where it needs to raise performance, it destroys customer loyalty and leads to disaffected customers unselling its reputation in the marketplace. A low claims cost is achieved at a terrible price to the business. In contrast, the effective service guarantee has several key elements:

- *It is relevant.* Delivery by noon next day, guaranteed, is relevant for people shifting important packages. The power of this guarantee meant that one firm in New York had managers using FedEx to send packages from one floor of its office block to another. All the packages went from New York to Memphis and back to New York again at great cost, simply because the guarantee was reassurance the package would arrive there, versus the uncertainties of the internal mail system.

- *It is unconditional.* Domino's Pizza promised to deliver the pizza in 30 minutes, or the pizza was free. The guarantee was unconditional: no excuses for bad weather, traffic, breakdowns. And, importantly, customers did not have to do anything to claim. They simply could take the pizza and not pay. The sting in the tail of this is that the guarantee was withdrawn when a delivery driver rushed too fast, knocked a pedestrian over and Domino's Pizza was sued for US $78 million.

- It is easy to understand and easy to claim, as in the Domino's Pizza case.

- *It is credible.* 'Lose 40 pounds in weight next week or your money back'; 'Speak a foreign language like a native in two weeks or your money back.' These guarantees sound too good to be true. And they are.

Head office: the beauty and the beast

Part of head office should be beautiful. This is the bit reserved for clients and important visitors. The rest of it should be beastly, small and remote. No overflow offices are allowed.

Keeping head office small will make it physically difficult for the corporate functionaries to grow large empires. With small empires, they will be forced to do only the things that are most important and helpful to the business. Corporate functionaries are excellent at justifying their existence, and will grow over time, unless space stops them. Every time functionaries ask for more space, let them have it, on condition they find it within the existing space – either they have to displace another functionary or crowd up like the sardines in a tin.

Keep head office remote from the businesses. Discourage line managers from wanting to go to head office. There is a tendency to treat head office either as the devil in disguise, or as corporate Valhalla for those who graduate from the line. Neither is true. Head office serves some necessary roles.

Finally, make head office beastly: at least do not make it so palatial that senior managers want to spend all their time there talking to each other. Head office is removed from reality, and reporting numbers is not a good way of knowing what's really going on. Encourage managers to get on the road and be with the business and with customers. **Innovation grows the further away you move from head office.**

Hedonic adaptation and slavery

Can you imagine how you would survive without a mobile phone, the internet, a personal computer, satellite TV and fish pedicures? Cast your mind back 20 years, or to your parents' era, and that is how people survived. They not only survived, they were apparently happy despite their appalling taste in big hair, power shoulder pads and an inexplicable liking for Oasis and other dodgy music.

Once we adapt our lifestyle to an improvement, we find it very hard to go back to the previous state. Economists call this hedonic adaptation. As employees, hedonic adaptation is what keeps our feet on the treadmill. **Once we get used to the champagne and caviar lifestyle, we don't want to go back to the beer and chips way of living.** And even if we are prepared to trade off less work for a simpler lifestyle, our families may be less understanding. So we become slaves to work. We may not like it, but we cannot escape it.

The only escape route is to avoid the problem in the first place. Just as the best way to lose weight is to avoid putting it on in the first place, so the best way to deal with hedonic adaptation is to avoid getting strapped onto the treadmill in the first place. This requires real discipline: know what you truly want and what makes you happy. If the only thing that will make you happy is the world's largest collection of shoes and handbags, or cars and gizmos, then get onto the treadmill and start running hard. Otherwise, find the lifestyle you want and stick with it: you will not have to run so hard and you will be at severe risk of enjoying your life.

Herd instincts

Managers are herd animals. **Sticking with the pack is the low risk route to survival.** Just as managers are herd animals, so businesses display herd instincts. They all tend to follow the same fads at the same time. But what may be safe management behaviour can be suicidal business behaviour.

Corporate herd instincts: the Gadarene swine and industry extinction

Corporations, like managers, are herd creatures. But this leads to disaster. Where all the firms in an industry adopt the same strategy, they have a zero sum game. Banking is particularly prone to this problem:

- *1980s.* All banks discovered the beautiful truth that countries cannot go bust, so they went on a lending spree to emerging countries. And then came the Latin American debt crisis, and now even Uncle Sam is no longer gilt edged.

- *1990s.* Financial markets discover a money machine called the internet which means that everything will be different this time – until the dot.com bomb at the turn of the millennium: stock prices have still not recovered.

- *2000s*. Banks discover the brilliance of financial engineering: diversify your holdings of enough toxic rubbish and sub-prime mortgages miraculously become investment grade. Welcome to the crash of 2008 and its hangover that we are still enjoying.

It is easy to bash bankers, but most firms easily fall into 'group think'. This means that there are big wins to be made by firms that do not follow the grain and challenge existing business models. Most innovation in most industries does not come from insiders. They are all playing the percentage game to protect what they have. Innovation comes from outsiders. We all hear the success stories, which look obvious and easy in retrospect, we never hear of the thousand failures which prove that **leaving the herd may be very successful, but it is more often fatal**.

The management herds: insight versus loyalty

Managers show a consistent preference for loyalty over competence. Slightly below average performers will stay on a team far longer than a disloyal team member. So managers may say that they like constant challenge, real insight and people who will 'think outside the box'. They fool only themselves. Managers do not want to be constantly challenged. They want people who will get on with the work with as little fuss as possible. The more you challenge, the more disruptive you will be seen; you will not be seen to be a team player and you may be committing the cardinal sin of disloyalty. If the whole firm goes in the wrong direction, you will not be blamed for driving down the wrong road. But if you are the wise one who says loudly 'I told you so...' you will earn gratitude from no one. **Often it is better to be wrong collectively than right individually.**

Hiring and firing

Our first finance director was incompetent. The second one tried to defraud us. The third turned out to be an armed bank robber in her spare time. Our suspicions should have been raised when staff reported that she had shoe boxes stuffed full of currency at her home. She said she did not trust banks. Not surprising really, when she was robbing them.

I started to realize that there was more to this business of hiring and firing people. Then a CEO gave the game away. **'I hire most people for their technical skills and fire most for their (lack of) personal and political skills.'**

The challenge for most managers is that we spend our early years learning technical skills, while what we need to progress are people and political skills. Many people fail to make the transition from one set of skills to the next, and their careers duly crash and burn.

But our bank robber gave one more clue to hiring success. Look beyond their technical, people and political skills to their values. Most people are not fired because they are incompetent: they are fired because they do not fit. This is clearest in the early stages of a career: starters may go through two or three employers before they finally discover the career that suits them. This is huge waste for employer and employee.

As an alternative, it is possible to hire explicitly to values. Teach First, which is one of the top five graduate recruiters in the UK, explicitly recruits to values. The reasoning is simple: you can train people in new technical skills, like teaching, but you cannot train them to have a new set of values. The result is that Teach First has high retention rates in schools where normally staff turnover is very high.

If you are hiring, hire to values as well as skills. If you are looking for a new employer, look beyond the salary and the job description to the values of the people you will work with.

The history of management

Here is the past, present and future of management in 416 words.

Part 1

Modern management really started with the Industrial Revolution. It was easy. The bosses had the brains and the workers had the hands. Bosses did the thinking and workers did the working, and you never mixed the two up. Motivation was easy: workers got paid if they worked and were out on the street if they did not. In the era of the one company town with no social security, that meant workers would lose everything if they lost their job. Great for bosses, not quite so good for workers.

Part 2

And then it all started to go wrong for managers. Being a brain on sticks was no longer enough. The workers did not revolt: they got educated. That really messed things up. Although they could do more, they also demanded more.

And they started to have choices about where they worked; for the idle or unlucky social security gave a back stop. So workers could no longer be treated as unreliable units of production (and occasionally consumption). Suddenly they had to be treated like... human beings. No longer was high IQ (intelligence quotient) enough to be a boss. You also need to have high EQ: emotional quotient.

Part 3

And now the bar has been raised again. Look around your own organization. You will find plenty of people with high IQ and high EQ who are rapidly going nowhere, while people who are not so smart and not so nice magically gravitate upwards. Something is missing: that something is political quotient (PQ).

Management is now the art of making things happen through people you may not control: colleagues, customers, suppliers, partners. In a flat organization you can no longer command and control. You have to do deals; align agendas; pick your battles; build your network of trust, allies and influence. All of this is the art of organizational politics, or PQ. **Naive managers deny that politics exist; cynical managers complain about it; smart managers use PQ to make things happen** and to help the organization and themselves.

What it means for you

So management has finally become three dimensional. You still need to be smart (IQ); you also need to be effective with people (EQ) and you must know how to make the organization work (PQ). The bad news is that management is getting harder, which means more challenging and more interesting. And at least we are unlikely to be replaced by computers... yet.

Honest feedback

This is up there with military intelligence and the paperless office as one of the great oxymorons of our time. Everyone has been there, asking for or being asked for honest feedback. CEOs are particularly prone to this, because they will never get honest feedback from anyone in their organization. **No one likes giving honest feedback**, least of all to people who have displayed enough trust in us to ask for it. We do not want to hurt their feelings.

But there is a way of giving honest feedback that works. There are three linked principles:

- depersonalize the feedback;
- abstract the feedback;
- tell a story.

Example 1

A slightly underperforming staff member asks about his or her prospects. Telling employees they are slightly, but not seriously, underperforming is devastating to morale, and unnecessary. Depersonalize and abstract the discussion by talking about the challenges faced, and the skills that need to be developed by people at that stage of a career. Highlight the ones that are most important to the person's situation. Relate this to some real life examples of similar people in his or her situation and talk through what they did to tackle the challenges. Ensure that you have specific examples of actions and behaviours that you can identify in the staff member so that the story is relevant and credible. Discuss it. This then creates a positive programme of action for the individual to take forward, rather than a demotivating message that the person is slightly behind.

If, some months later, the challenges are starting to look insurmountable, that is the time to start asking the person how confident he or she feels in taking on the challenges. You can then mutually decide if this is the right business for the person.

Example 2

A CEO asks you to give feedback on how he or she is doing. There are plenty of ways of canvassing for anonymous points of view from his or her team, but the chances are that you already know what they think. And the CEO probably does not want to be embarrassed by the canvassing process. So you need to respond honestly, but positively. This is a risky exercise in which trust is either rapidly built or destroyed.

Again, abstract the problem by telling a story about the challenges that other CEOs in his or her position have typically faced, and what they did about it. Depersonalizing the feedback makes it a lot less threatening. And it makes it easy to discuss: if there is disagreement about some of the feedback, it can easily be dropped from the story. Clearly, doing this needs experience. It is no use trying to invent some stories on the spot. They have to be real and relevant.

All of this is separate from the official bureaucracy of staff assessments. These are important to keep HR happy, for legal reasons if it comes to dismissal and to support decision making around promotions and compensation. But in terms of honest feedback and career counselling, the standard box-ticking exercise that ranks everyone on a good/bad scale is hardly useful.

Humour and the sense of humour test

Passing the sense of humour test should be mandatory for managers. This test occurs on days when one unbelievable disaster follows another. At one moment the world looks like it is about to cave in. This is called the sense of humour test. If you can still step back and see the whole bizarre nightmare in perspective, you have passed the test. If you start losing your rag, you have failed. Failing the test leads to behaviour that upsets everyone else, makes things worse and sends the day into a death spiral. Enough perspective and a fine sense of the bizarre can help defuse the tension. There is a fighting chance of stepping back from the brink.

Next time the outrageous happens remember to tell yourself, 'I think this is a sense of humour test.' Just saying it increases your chances of regaining perspective and passing. Of course, once you have said it, you can also decide to fail the test and to go down with all guns blazing.

Despite plenty of evidence to the contrary, managers believe that management is Not Funny. Senior managers think it is Not Funny At All. Trainees may get away with going out in the evening, drinking beer, getting drunk at the pub and slagging off the managers. Senior managers are meant to go out in the evening, drink wine at the restaurant, pretend not to be drunk and have weighty conversations about the state of the nation.

Lack of humour is not to do with reality, but with culture. Senior managers like to be seen to be serious, and to be dealing with weighty issues with appropriate gravitas. Slapstick is out, although the occasional dry witticism that reflects conventional wisdom is safe. It can show you are intellectually smart if the witticism is clever enough.

Lack of humour is a shame. The bizarre world of management deserves respect, perspective and humour if it is to be valued properly.

Influencing decisions

As managers, we lack the control we might like to make all the decisions ourselves. Instead, we have to influence decisions effectively. If making decisions is harder, influencing other managers' decisions is even more difficult. Surprisingly, some academic work has proven to be very useful showing how we can succeed in influencing decisions, thanks to Daniel Kahnemann who won the Nobel Prize for economics. It is not clear if he used his techniques to influence the Nobel Committee's decision. They are listed here:

- *Strike early.* Anchor the discussion on your terms, not theirs. Do African nations represent more or less than 30 per cent of the member states of the United Nations? The discussion has just been anchored around 30 per cent, which may or may not be anywhere close to the answer. Do the same in budget discussions: set expectations very early and you set them on your terms.

- *Constantly repeat the message.* Advertisers and politicians understand this: the more you repeat a message, the more people will remember it and believe it.

- *Gain social proof.* Celebrity endorsements by film stars and sports stars work. You do not need celebrities to back your proposal: if the top celebrity in your firm, the CEO, backs your idea then everyone will fall into line. Get backing, if not from the CEO then at least from the Finance department and the other groups people listen to.

- *Play on emotional relevance.* If crime statistics rise, so what? If my neighbour is burgled, crime is becoming a problem. If I get mugged, then clearly crime is out of control. So forget the thousand pages of dense data that makes your case. Find the few killer factoids and illustrations that people will remember: let their drama make the case for you.

- *Keep loss aversion in mind.* No one likes to look like a fool. So make your proposal risk free: if there is risk, then people will find a thousand logical reasons why your idea should die.

- *Restrict choice.* Ask people to choose between 3,217 options and they will give up: they will constantly worry that they did not make the best choice. Give people a choice from three (the cheap but useless option, the brilliant but absurdly expensive option and the option you want them to pick) and they will confidently make the right choice for you.

Naive managers think that if they build a brilliant business case, then the decision will be theirs. **Influencing decisions is not about data, it is about people.** Manage the people and the process, and the decision will be the one you want. You can always backfill with the logic later.

Information inflation: back to the future

In the medieval period, each word was precious. It might be painstakingly illuminated by a monk using quill on parchment. There were few books, and those that were around were treasured. Information was valued and nurtured. For many, words were beyond them: pictures on church walls were used to unravel the mysteries of the faith.

With the printing press, and then the photocopier and finally e-mail and the computer, we have gone from information deficit to information overload. And the pace of overload is increasing all the time. Looking back at 1960s advertising for detergents, each advertisement seemed like a soap opera in its own right. It would last 60 or even 90 seconds, while the virtues of the detergent were explored in excruciating detail. By the 1980s, advertisements were down to 30-, perhaps 40-second slots. Now 30 seconds seems like a luxury, 20 seconds is normal and 10 seconds is becoming more common.

Information overload has serious consequences. The value of information deflates as rapidly as the volume inflates. Finding good information is harder, like finding a needle in a haystack. Attention spans are reducing: we listen to a message only briefly before moving onto the next message. Information is trusted to the extent that we trust the information provider.

We are heading back to the medieval period in the way we use words and pictures. Now we want fewer words. Ideally, we do not want words, we want a picture that will sum up the message. Visual literacy is taking over from verbal literacy. All this matters to managers. This is what it means:

- Write short, not long. Use visuals.
- Build credibility into the message through the messenger. As an individual, that's you. As a business, it is your brand. The message supports the brand and vice versa.

- Be consistent in the message: in the world of information an overloaded message takes a long time to get through, and receiving two messages simply confuses everyone. So pick your message with care. This is true of brands, internal corporate communications or how you present yourself to the business. Senior managers will not know everything about you other than perhaps one claim to fame or infamy. Make sure you know what it is you want to be remembered for.

Innovate and die

Large, bureaucratic organizations occasionally lust after innovation and entrepreneurialism. They are like the fat kid at school, who secretly wants to be the sports superhero that everyone looks up to. They are equally unlikely to succeed.

If your boss asks you to be entrepreneurial, ask your boss if he or she likes risk, uncertainty, failure and expense. In practice, bosses like the results of successful innovation, but do not want to accept the downside of innovation. They want innovative and wholly original ideas that have been tried, tested and are bound to succeed.

Fortunately, there is a way out of this mess. You can innovate without going into funky creative sessions where a creative guru asks you what sort of animal, car or musician your unit would be if it were an animal, car or musician. Here are a few simple ways of finding creative and innovative ideas:

- *Copy an idea.* Ryanair simply copied the success of US low-cost airlines such as SouthWest Airlines. Within your functional area, there will be plenty of other companies being very innovative: any good consultants should know who is doing what and which ideas are working. But they may also sell you moonshine, so do your homework.

- *Ask your customers.* They will have ideas about what they want, like and dislike. Do not do general market research that gives you average responses: look for the outliers. People who hate or love your product will give you the greatest insight.

- *Find a problem.* The more specific the problem is, the more likely you are to find a creative solution that works. Asking 'How do we make more money?' leads straight to cost cutting. Asking 'How can we reduce the time to bring a new product to market?' will get focused and practical solutions.

- *Stop doing something.* The essence of capitalism is that bad ideas die and good ideas flourish. Find out what you can kill, and then reinvest the savings in the things that are working the best.

Perhaps the best way to approach the challenge is to ask your boss why there is the sudden lust for innovation. Innovation is a solution in search of a problem. Find out what the problem is, and solve that, rather than going on a wild goose chase in search of the pixie dust of innovation. If gaining more customers is the challenge, focus on that. If reducing costs or lead times is the challenge, then focus on that. It always pays to know the question you are meant to answer.

IT consultants: the builder's brick

IT consultants and builders are the same. You can never find a good one when you want one; the work always costs more and lasts longer than you expected and the people involved cause huge disruption when they are in. Of course, one lot have bellies over their jeans, and others have partners in bespoke suits. Next time the IT consultants come selling, imagine them with their beer barrel bellies and site clothing. It makes it easier to tolerate the builder's speech that they will then give you.

Score them on the speech. When they pass 5 out of 10, quietly get up and give each of them a brick. Do not explain why. One week later, send them a photocopy of this page, complete with your scoring. Here are the builders' comments to look for:

- *They rubbish the previous work.* 'Whoever did that plastering should be shot' versus 'COBOL? Hardly anyone has that nowadays.'
- *The work will be bigger than you thought.* 'That's not a bit of damp mate, you'll need to put in a whole new damp course' versus 'Of course you'll have to replace all those systems as well.'
- *The work is not just big, it's tricky.* 'Flat roofs are always dodgy' versus 'You can't buy a package for that: we have to build something specially.'
- *So, of course, it will be expensive.* 'It's going to cost you' versus 'This will be a big investment.'
- *And it will take a long time.* 'It'll take a long time' versus 'It'll take a long time.'

- *But they can't say how long.* 'Until we've seen what's under the floorboards' versus 'Until we've done a full specification.'

- And they cannot guarantee the price.

- *They will promise a worthless guarantee.* 'We can always fix it up later if you need' versus 'You can give us just one month's notice (once you are totally dependent on us).'

- *They will try to broaden the job.* 'We could do your front drive at the same time' versus 'This needs to be linked to a proper change programme/strategy.'

- *But this is your lucky day: they have just the people for the job.* 'Mick's a great plasterer, he's coming free on Tuesday' versus 'Of course you know how difficult it is to assemble a team with the right skills, but we should be able to do it for next month, if you give the go-ahead now.'

There are other uses for the brick. Do not be tempted.

IT: intermediate technology

For the last 30 years, information technology has been intermediate technology. It has always been promising to do more tomorrow than it can today, and it always does. Moore's Law has held true: processing capacity has doubled and costs have halved roughly every 18 months. This has been a disaster for management, and a gold mine for the IT industry.

The pace of change is what makes IT crippling for business. At least in the last industrial revolution the technology was relatively stable. Railway lines have not had to suffer changes in designs, routes and specifications every three years. And the changes that had to be made could be done fast. When the Great Western line was converted from broad to standard gauge, 213 miles of track were replaced in one weekend by 4,000 workers. Most businesses would happily hire 4,000 workers for a weekend if that were all it took to change their technology infrastructure.

Rapid obsolescence of technology has given managers three broad options:

- Ignore the technology upgrades, stick with current systems and watch the competition sail by as they find ways of serving customers better at lower cost through technology.

- Become upgrade junkies; add little bits of new systems everywhere to keep up to date. The result is a back office that looks like a technology museum: systems and languages from all eras and all parts of the world. Most banks do not even know what systems they have, and do not have the manuals or expertise to know how to fix faults. One bank had 1,290 systems, few of which talked to each other properly. **The bank's systems were like the Tower of Babel hidden in of a bowl of spaghetti.** Total mess.

- Scrap all the existing systems at vast expense and effort to get a clean sheet again. Incur all the data migration and run off difficulties, and then realize that by the time the three-year programme is complete, the technology is already out of date.

Managers are doomed with technology. Whatever they do, it will be expensive and once they have completed the job, they just have to start again. The obvious solution is to get into the IT industry, which has been a licence to print money. Barely competent managers have been able to make fortunes by riding this wave.

The alternative is to hand the technology infrastructure over to one of the technology firms. They are better placed to keep on upgrading all the required skills, know the right technology solutions and deliver the results better than an in-house operation.

Innovation: winning without fighting

The best battles are won without fighting. The bloody battles for a couple of market share points have to be fought. But even better is to occupy territory that no one else has thought about. It is about outflanking the competition. There are two sorts of innovation.

The better mousetrap

This is the world of the inventor. It belongs to James Dyson (bagless vacuum cleaners), Trevor Bayliss (wind-up radios), and 3M (Post-it notes). All these products and people created new markets and built businesses on the back of them. The challenge is to institutionalize this sort of innovation. The evidence is that this sort of innovation is not naturally institutionalized. Corporates have to look to another form of innovation.

Creating new markets

In each of these cases below, an incumbent could have occupied the new market space. In each case, the companies left it to an outsider, which then became a formidable competitor in its own right.

Canon is a good example. The photocopier used to be a central function based on a leased machine with high performance and high maintenance. Canon made the photocopier a cheaper, purchased machine with acceptable performance that could be used across the business in each department locally. It was a totally new way of attacking the market. Xerox was slow to follow because of fear of cannibalizing its own market.

CNN created the first dedicated news channel. Because of the scale of costs of creating a similar network, and the brand image advantage CNN has, competition has found it tough to follow. The BBC and the traditional US networks would have been better placed to be first to build a 24-hour news channel.

FedEx created the overnight parcel delivery service. UPS could have owned it; but followed up a late and poor second.

Apple created the personal computer market – and then created and dominated the markets for iPods and iPads; Microsoft dominated the operating systems market; Dell reinvented the PC market with a direct-to-the-buyer model. All the might of IBM, DEC and Fujitsu was spent fighting the wrong battles, battles for market share among themselves.

Naturally, no one in any of the losing organizations was fired for missing the big opportunity. **No one gets fired for failing to take a risk, even if the risk could save the firm.**

The job of senior managers is to make sure that the business fights the right battles. This requires taking the blinkers off and 'thinking outside the box'. People who think outside the box are likely to be new, younger employees; rebels in the organization; customers; advertising agencies. Go away for a weekend with them and senior managers and brainstorm. It does not matter that 99 per cent of what you get will be rubbish. The real battle is the battle for ideas. Win that battle, and the competitive war is transformed.

Investing to lose

Resource allocation, the investment of money, time and people, is central to the management task. Roosevelt remarked that he was really just a traffic cop: directing people to go in, he hoped, the right direction.

As managers we are also taught to be prudent. This means that we want to make sure every investment dollar is spent wisely. We should not overspend. So we look at investment proposals and see how we can minimize the investment cost. Lower investment has the wonderful ability to raise the return on investment (ROI).

A US $100 investment yielding a marginal 10 per cent can be transformed into a yield of 12.5 per cent if we hold the investment at US $80. We have saved the business US $20, and raised the ROI. We may also have ensured that we have invested just enough to lose the whole lot: US $80 lost for no return. But, by then, everyone will have forgotten how the decision was made and by whom.

The alternative approach is to give the team members everything they ask for. Suddenly, there are no excuses. They have all the resources they need to do the job and to win. And they have the motivation of knowing that they have been backed to the hilt, rather than being nickled and dimed. They will be totally committed to success. And if the proposal is so marginal that the investment needs to be cut back to achieve the desired ROI, it probably should not be approved at all. Invest to win. Prudent investing is investing to lose.

'-ists'

The '-ists' are still out there. The **ageists, racists and sexists are great news** from a competitive perspective. The -ists will help your competitors fail. It's not just the risk of litigation that will hurt. They are losing out in the war for talent. And they are failing to freshen up the gene pool of their business. They are creating a uniform, inward-looking group think.

Today the test is not about hiring across genders, ages, races and faiths. The person doing the hiring still feels in a position of power and is not threatened by the diversity: if it does not work, he or she can always move or fire the person. The challenge is about promoting and then working for people of a different age, race, gender or faith. This is where most businesses fail. The gene pool can be diverse at the bottom of the business, but conformity strikes at the top.

In the UK, about half the workforce are women. A grand total of 1.8 per cent of executive directors of the top 100 companies are women. About 8 per cent of non-executive directors are women. This shows that tokenism is alive and kicking in the boardrooms of Britain. Hiring a woman non-executive director makes for a worthy picture in the annual report and absolves managers from taking real diversity seriously. The challenge is not hiring for diversity, or having diversity in the annual report. The challenge is to promote for diversity.

Working for people younger than yourself or from a different race or sex can be great. Some of them may be brilliant, others may be turkeys. But they are human, and they do offer a different view of the world. It's a great way to learn, and gives the confidence to promote across the gene pool when your turn comes at the top.

Japan: learning to eat sushi and conquer the world

During the 1980s and early 1990s, forests were destroyed to print books on the secrets of Japanese success. Everyone was keen to follow the Japanese example and learn how to conquer the world. There were three problems with these books:

- Most of the authors had not actually worked in Japan. They relied on second-hand material and recycled cases from the same companies. It looked great to outsiders and would generate book sales and speaking engagements. People who had worked in Japan could see most of it was rubbish. Western business was not going to succeed by implementing second-hand recycled rubbish.

- The Japanese miracle was a mirage. Like any economy, Japan has significant areas of relative advantage and significant areas of relative disadvantage. Japan had not discovered the philosopher's stone, the universal recipe for business success. A walk into any Japanese retail store would be enough to dispel notions of universal excellence and world-conquering power. Again, Western business was not going to succeed by copying a mirage.

- Whatever else the Japanese are good or bad at, they are world class at being Japanese. No one else is going to be more Japanese than the Japanese. The West will never appreciate sushi or sumo as much as they do, or learn to bow quite the way they do. And yet the premise of most books was that we had to copy the Japanese.

Copying the competition is the most certain way of losing. It is a game of catch-up in which the others will always be ahead. The only way to compete is by finding ways in which we can be different and better. Ultimately, this is what happened: the United States discovered it had more flexible working patterns, better methods of capital allocation and better use of new technology. US businesses are winning by being different, not by copying the Japanese.

But the same mistake is being made again. Now everyone is learning how to be like a US business, and how to be a dot.com. Now the bubble has burst and the search will be on for new heroes to copy. In the meantime, we should dare to be different.

Job descriptions versus the psychological contract

Job descriptions are primarily job justifiers for underemployed HR staff. If an organization has boxes full of job descriptions, it is probably suffering severe bureaucratic tendencies.

Job descriptions answer questions such as 'What is my role?' and 'What is my status?' Roles and status do not build a business and do not represent achievement. And they are not a basis for judging performance.

The job description is not useful to the business or the employee. What is more useful to both is the psychological contract that the individual has with managers. This psychological contract may not be written down, but the expectations are real. The expectations tend to revolve around five questions:

- What am I expected to achieve?
- What resources will I have?
- What skills do I need to develop?
- How will I be measured and rewarded?
- What will you do to support me?

The psychological contract is more demanding on both sides than the job description. Acrimony arises not so much when the job description is broken, but more when the psychological contract is broken. Because this is a two-way contract it is different from traditional management by objectives (MBO), which is a one-sided commitment. Managing the expectations on both sides of this psychological contract is essential to a successful relationship and business.

Killing ideas

Some managers are brilliant at killing ideas. These same people will complain about the lack of innovation and new thinking in the business. It is human nature to react with hostility to new ideas. New ideas represent a threat to the status quo:

- They involve risk, they may not work.
- They are a challenge to the way we have done things before, implying criticism of us.
- Even if the idea succeeds, it will take extra work and puts extra performance expectations on us.
- We did not come up with the idea, so we are not in control.

Naturally, the hostility is not normally overt. It normally comes in the form of helpful questions. We have all been in meetings where an idea surfaces. First one person shoots a heat-seeking missile, normally characterized by a 'Yes, but...' or 'I think it's a good idea but...' Remember, **everything before the 'but' is baloney**. The real message comes afterwards:

- 'It's great, *but* has it ever been done before?' If yes, then it's old hat and not worth doing; if no, then it is too risky to do. Fight your way out of that one.
- 'I like that, *but* of course funding it would require cancelling this year's advertising.'
- 'Yes, *but* would the unions/regulators/trade accept it?'

Once one person comes up with a killer missile, everyone else in the meeting joins in. The more deadly the missile, the more it shows the commentator is smart. It is easy pickings for everyone, except the person who suggested the idea. By the end of the meeting, the meeting has achieved three things:

- It has killed a potentially good idea.
- It has thoroughly demoralized the person with the idea.
- It has taught everyone in the meeting that **having good ideas is a career-limiting move**.

These are not healthy outcomes. Three things can be done to save ideas:

1 Pre-sell ideas before the meeting, so that by the time of the meeting there is a core of support for the idea and the major concerns have been identified and pre-empted.

2 As chairperson, force people to evaluate the benefits of the idea before they comment on any concerns. Forcing people to think positively is unnatural for them, and is harder work than coming up with criticisms. This makes putting benefits first a good discipline in its own right. Recognizing the benefits of an idea first also puts the criticisms into perspective. If the benefits of the idea are huge, it may be worthwhile overcoming some huge concerns. If the focus is only on the concerns, then the idea will be stillborn.

3 As chairperson, make people express their criticisms positively and in an action-oriented way. The easiest way to do this is to insist that concerns are prefaced with two words: 'How to...' These two words at the start of a sentence are at first unnatural. But they put the concern into an action framework, which invites other people to think up possible solutions to the concern.

Knowledge management

Knowledge management should be important. But it has become a fad trying to hit the wrong target the wrong way.

The knowledge management fad

It is always possible to spot a management fad. When someone appears on the executive committee with an unfamiliar title, the title is normally the clue to the fad. It started with the appointment of chief quality officers, and has moved through to heads of re-engineering, innovation and then knowledge. The appointment of a chief fad officer achieves several goals:

- It demonstrates to investors that the business is up to date with the latest management thinking and practice.

- It provides a useful and harmless role for a displaced executive, who can later be gently eased out of the business when the next fad comes along.

- It gives the impression of doing something while not actually interfering with the organization: we must be a knowledge-based company because we have a knowledge officer on the executive committee. This puts the fad into a nice safe box, away from the business.

Knowledge management is hitting the wrong target

Knowledge management in Western countries assumes that knowledge is explicit. It assumes that any knowledge worth having can be documented, and then reapplied based on the documentation. This has the potential to lead to vast swathes of bureaucracy, which achieves little.

In Japan and other Asian countries, they recognize that much of the most useful knowledge is tacit. It is about how people do things more than what they do. It is much harder to document, and cannot be replicated remotely by simply reading the manual. It assumes learning comes more from the apprenticeship model than from formal academic learning.

Intuitively, most Western managers understand the value of tacit knowledge. When we want to use a new computer, or learn how another salesperson is so successful, we do not reach for the textbooks. We ask someone.

The wrong target is being hit the wrong way

Because there is excess focus on explicit knowledge, there is excessive documentation. Knowledge teams produce self-directed learning discs and manuals. There is often a motivational problem with self-directed learning: people either don't do it or they skimp and cheat. And they are right to skimp and cheat, because it is not teaching what they want, which is the tacit knowledge.

The nadir of knowledge management is when it is reduced to contracting in consultants to build some big knowledge management software at great expense, both in financial cost and the cost of managers' time.

The alternative is to build and strengthen the internal networks of people talking to each other. Staff and managers most value learning from successful peers: it is demonstrably practical and tailored to the needs of the business. And, normally, successful peers have enough vanity to want to share their expertise and to be recognized as experts in the business. Everyone wins, the effort is relatively low and the results are direct.

L

Language and the dirty dozen: the most dangerous words in business

Don't worry about the jargon: at least we all recognize it when we hear it. The really nasty language in business are normal words with abnormal meanings. Here are the dirty dozen worst offenders, and doubtless you can add many more:

- *Just.* This is used to make a huge request or error seem trivial as in: 'Could you just do this (500 page) document by Monday?' – a request usually made late on a Friday afternoon.

- *But.* Remember, whatever is said before 'but' is baloney, as in 'That was a great presentation, but...', or 'I would like to help, but...'

- *From.* This is much loved by advertisers, as in 'Fly to Rome from £10' excluding £100 of taxes and other 'optional' extras for a flight leaving at 4.00 am, going to an airport about 100 kilometres away from Rome and the ticket has to be booked one year in advance.

- *Might (and any other conditional verb).* 'Might' is used to achieve two things: first it sets up a negotiating position as in 'I might be able to do that if...'. Second, it lays the groundwork for excusing failure later on: 'I would have done it, if only...'

- *Only (closely related to 'just').* It is an attempt to make a big request or problem seem small. 'It was only a small error... we only dropped one nuclear bomb over London...'

- *Important (and 'urgent').* This is used to puff up any presentation: 'This important new product/initiative...' Important to whom? And why? Maybe it is important to the speaker, but why is it to me?

- *Strategic.* This is 'important', with bells on. See Strategic Human Capital Division, formerly known as the Personnel department. The term is also used to justify spending that has no financial payback.

- *Rightsize, downsize, best shore, offshore, outsource, optimize, redeploy, downshift, re-engineer.* How many ways are there of avoiding saying straight up: we are going to lay off staff/make staff redundant?

- *Thank you.* Normally 'Thank you' is good, except when used by automated voices at call centres saying 'Thank you for calling, we value your call... (and we have so much contempt for our customers that we cannot be bothered to answer your call promptly so we will put you on hold until you give up and try to use our impenetrable and useless online help instead).'

- *Interesting.* Fear this word. When your lawyer uses it, you are doomed. When your doctor uses it, check that your will is up to date. The recession is certainly interesting. A slightly less interesting time would be preferable.

- *Investment.* When used by financial advisers, this is an invitation to lose all your money, especially if it is a time limited, special, unique offer just for you. When used by politicians this is a polite way to refer to uncontrolled spending on social programmes (investing in the NHS, schools, regeneration, etc).

- *Opportunity.* Because the word 'problem' has been banned in business speak, all problems have become opportunities. This means many opportunities are problems. There is a limit to how many opportunities I can solve. An important, interesting and strategic opportunity is called the death star assignment. Avoid at all costs.

Lawyers and the revolution

When the revolution comes, it will not be all bad news for managers. Of course, we can expect to join our colleagues in being put up against the wall and shot. At least we should have the pleasure of seeing the lawyers shot before us. In the meantime, we have to deal with them.

The world is getting ever more litigious and rights aware. Trust is a good way to do business when things are going well. But it provides no cover when things go wrong. And by then, it is too late to bring in the lawyers.

Bring them in early: prevention is better than cure. But pick your lawyers with care. Lawyers who are business focused are worth their weight in gold. **Good lawyers focus on what you can do, not on what you cannot do.** Avoid the ones who insist on swamping the entire business with legalese. They may minimize all the legal risk, but at the cost of freezing the business in a legal swamp where no one dares to move without taking three lawyers in tow.

The simple test of lawyers is the language they speak. If they start mumbling on about obscure cases and subsections of 200-year-old acts, drop them. If they start talking about your business and how it can be supported, they are at least in the right game.

Leaders and the led

Everyone grumbles about management, if its leaders are understood to be anyone more senior than yourself. To listen to the grumbles, you might believe people hate being led. People love being led. Being led is essentially lazy and low risk. To the extent that people dislike excess work or risk, leaders perform a great function for them. Followers let the leader take all the strain and risk of deciding where to go and what to do. Then the leader can be blamed when things go wrong.

If flat organizations are to have meaning, it requires that partnerships are formed both vertically and horizontally across the organization. The days of the all-knowing and omnipotent leader are long gone, even if they ever existed except in people's minds. But this partnership requires that followers do not passively follow: they push back, advocate new directions and take responsibility themselves. In other words, everyone in a flat organization should be a leader. Being led is lazy, passive and unproductive. But it is also an attractive recipe for an easy life.

Leadership

Most people think of the CEO as the leader. All the academic writing about leadership focuses on the role of the leader. This is totally misleading. Every manager should act as a leader.

Kissinger defined **leadership as the art of 'taking people where they would not have gone by themselves'**. In other words, it is about stretching the organization and enabling it to achieve those stretchy targets. This form of leadership can be achieved at all levels of the organization. It can be as simple as getting a trainee to make his or her first successful sales call.

Most managers land up being somewhere between administrators and leaders. Here is a simple test to see what sort of manager you have got:

TABLE L.1

Criterion	Administrators	Leaders
Basis of authority	Organization chart	Credibility, trust
Key resource	Budget	People
Basis of promotion	No mistakes	Beats stretchy goals
Focus of attention	Inputs, costs	Output, results
Communication	Top–down	360 degrees
Style	Compliance, control	Empowerment
Attitude to change	Risk	Opportunity
Outlook	Details	Big picture

Ideally, managers have both administrative competence and leadership capability. This is rare. Generally, it is easier for a leader to find an administratively competent manager to backfill on his or her deficiencies than it is to find a genuine leader to support an administrator.

Leadership heaven and hell

Leaders from hell can be just as successful as leaders from heaven. This is bad news for employees who have a leader from hell. And it is bad news for all the academics and consultants who try to prescribe what a good leader should and should not do.

For the management survivalist, the point is not to judge the leader, let alone try to change the leader. The point is to learn from the leaders what it is that they do: why they succeed and what behaviours they value and display. This will tell you all about the rules of the game that you need to succeed. Then you can either play by the rules of the game, or get out.

We all have memories of leaders from hell and leaders from heaven. Judging them reflects partly on the leader, and greatly on the person doing the judging. With this is mind, here are personal profiles of two real leaders: one from hell and one from heaven:

TABLE L.2

Leadership criterion	Leader from hell	Leader from heaven
Style	Command and control: 'Do as I tell you'	Inspirational: 'Let's go for it'
Basis of authority	Rank	Trust, respect
Performance	Don't make a mistake	Over perform
Expectations	Risk intolerant	Risk tolerant
Focus of control	Process: meetings and papers on time, neat presentation	Outcomes and results
Attention to detail	High	Low
Insight/big picture focus	Low	High
Communications	Boss: 'I/you' Secretive	Peer: 'We' Open
Political skills	High	High
Technical skills	Fair	High
Social skills	Low	High

From the business point of view, the leader from hell is as successful as the leader from heaven. In a large, traditional hierarchy that is risk averse and process-focused, the leader from hell represents a perfect fit with the culture and needs of the organization. The leader from heaven would be an unmitigated disaster in such a business.

From the personal point of view, some people will prefer the leader from hell to the leader from heaven. In practice, the leader from heaven has much higher expectations and is a much more demanding taskmaster than the leader from hell. The leader from hell simply expects compliance and no mistakes: you can leave your brain at the front door and still succeed. The leader from heaven expects outperformance. Outperformance is tougher than compliance.

The leadership riddle

You will never succeed as a leader by trying to be someone else. Trying to be an implausible mix of Genghis Khan, Mother Theresa, Nelson Mandela and Lord Nelson is a recipe for many hours of therapeutic counselling: it is not a recipe for leadership.

But you will never succeed just by being yourself. If you hang around like a teenager in full hormonal angst, waiting for the world to recognize your innate genius and humanity, you will have a very long wait.

So **we cannot succeed by being someone else, and we cannot succeed just by being ourselves**. We may as well give up.

The solution is that we have to be the best of who we are. We all have some strengths, and we also have weaknesses which our bosses and colleagues never hesitate to tell us about. So the recipe for leadership success has three ingredients:

- *Focus on your strengths.* Corporate evaluation systems focus on weaknesses, which is nonsense. **Don't ask Olympic weightlifters to focus on their synchronized swimming skills**, which are a bit weak. You only succeed by building on your strengths.

- *Work around your weaknesses.* The good news is that leadership is a team sport. You do not have to do it all yourself. So if there are some things you do not enjoy, you will find plenty of people who can fill in for you on accounting, project management, strategy development or whatever fills you with dread.

- *Find your context.* Find roles and organizations that play to your strengths. If you hate risk, don't become an entrepreneur or a trader in an investment bank. If you dislike foreign food, don't join a global company.

Lies

Forget the morality problem. The effectiveness problem is the killer. Most corporate lies get nailed, eventually. It took 30 years to rumble the tobacco companies, but normally it is faster. Most individuals' lies get nailed, because most of us are no good at lying. The occasional bit of inflation on your CV is sustainable. Other lies have a tendency of becoming increasingly complicated, and eventually unravel. Unless you are an expert liar, it's not worth it. The reputation risk is too great, and lasts forever.

About 5 per cent of managers appear to be pathological liars. And the good ones are very good at it. They get a lot of practice. They succeed because most of us are too trusting. Moral outrage is not a defence. Vigilance is.

Luck

Napoleon preferred lucky generals until he met Wellington. He was right. Lucky people have a habit of consistently being lucky. Which means that it is not really luck. Look behind luck, and there are normally three characteristics: practice, persistence and preparation. **You can learn to be lucky.**

Practice

Arnold Palmer said: 'The harder I practice, the luckier I get.' This is true: the 50/50 chance of putting a hole becomes a 60/40, and the 60/40 chance becomes a likely 70/30 chance. Management is the same. There are always close calls. The more practice and the more experience managers have, the more likely they are to make the right call.

Persistence

Many successes come after serial failure. The chilling words of the IRA after they failed to blow up Prime Minister Thatcher in Brighton summed it up: 'This time we were unlucky. Remember, we only need to get lucky once.' The difference between failure and success is often as simple as giving up. Richard Wiseman, author of *The Luck Factor* (2004), describes one sensationally lucky woman. She is always winning prizes: free holidays, free cars and free money. But her luck becomes more understandable when you find she enters over 80 competitions per week. And the more she enters, the better she gets at knowing how to win. Practice and persistence walk hand in hand.

Preparation

Lucky people prepare. When the opportunity comes along, it is there for everyone to see. But only some of the people are looking. In retrospect, most opportunities are so obvious we end up saying: 'We could have done that.' Except that we could not, because we were not looking in the right direction. Often it needs an industry insider who can look at the business with fresh eyes. Examples include instant offices (Regus); selling books over the internet (Amazon) and portable personal music (Sony Walkman). The slings and arrows of outrageous fortune do sometimes make a difference. But for the most part, lucky managers are as consistently lucky as Napoleon's generals.

Management accounting: death and reincarnation

Management accounting as we knew it and hated it, is dying. It is being reincarnated as something that could be useful. It is worth making sure you have the 21st-century version of management accounting, not the 20th-century version. The 21st-century version of management accounting should differ in six critical areas from the 20th-century version.

From functional costs to cross-functional costs

Cost control used to reflect the traditional hierarchy. Each silo had its own budget. This had the huge virtue of simplicity. It was good for budget control purposes, but was lousy at cost management. Most costs are driven by business activities that cut across functions. The process of acquiring and setting up a new banking customer drives costs in marketing, sales or relationship management, credit analysis, documentation and products. Account acquisition drives the volume of activity, and hence the costs, in each of these departments. Controlling budget costs while not controlling the activity is a case of looking in the wrong direction.

From allocated costs to cost drivers

Departmental costs were relevant in an age when most costs were direct and variable costs. The more they become indirect and fixed or semi-variable, the more there is the problem of cost allocation. At worst, this becomes a political dog fight. At minimum, it makes it harder to understand true customer and product profitability. Understanding the drivers of costs across the business improves the chances of not just allocating costs fairly, but enabling managers to focus on actions to manage the costs.

From historic costs to forecast costs

The 20th-century version of management accounting kept a financial scorecard of how well you were doing against forecast, and could produce endless variation analyses and year-on-year analyses to help keep score. But it was essentially after-the-event accounting. By looking at activity costs that cut across functions, it is possible to forecast costs based on forecast demand. It is easier to control costs by looking ahead than looking backward.

From counting beans to making decisions

Traditional cost accounting was backward-looking, so that remedial action was nearly always reactive. With forecasts of costs and volumes managers can look ahead and manage costs proactively. Critically, they can do it with the cooperation of other departments who will drive or influence their own costs.

From cost control to profit management

Cost management is not necessarily good profit management. The most vulnerable items in a cost-cutting drive are the discretionary items. Advertising, promotion and research are soft targets for the cost cutter. These may also be the things that will most help drive up profitability.

A proper understanding of what drives costs also allows managers to see which products and which customers are making profit. Traditional cost accounting methods tend to underestimate the costs of acquiring and serving small-value customers, small deliveries and customized products. Activity-based costing identifies these costs, and allows managers to make informed decisions about segment and product pricing and service strategies to optimize profits, not just costs.

From centralized to decentralized cost management

The traditional cost accounting function was a specialized staff function. Staff did all the analysis and produced the scorecards for managers to look at. The new cost accounting is much more managerially focused: it is about proactively managing for profit across the business. This means that all managers need to be able to speak the language of management accounting, understand it and act on it. It is not simply a question of knowing whether the brackets in the right-hand column are a good thing or a bad thing.

Naturally, new management accounting is not a free lunch. It has several preconditions if it is to succeed:

- There must be accounting literacy across the business.
- There needs to be an understanding of how costs are driven in the business. This is not a static, one-off exercise. The nature of the cost

drivers changes in response to managers' actions. This makes cost management a dynamic, not a static process.

- Systems that allow the information to be gathered in the right way must be present.
- There must be managers who want to make it happen and to use it.

This is still a revolution in progress. It is still more art than science, and feels cumbersome to implement. Switching off the traditional systems is premature. But it is time to start testing the new approach, adapting it to local conditions and creating the capability to exploit it in the future.

Management by walking away

The grandfather of modern management books, *In Search of Excellence* by Tom Peters and Robert Waterman (1982), advocated MBWA: Management By Walking About. The idea is that this would keep you in touch with how things are going on. An equally valid version of MBWA is Management By Walking Away.

Part of the art of management is knowing where you genuinely add value, and where others can do the job as well as you. The key principle is that all jobs should be done by the most junior person possible. This maximizes the leverage for senior managers and maximizes the development of the junior managers. It is also more motivational to be fully entrusted with work, than to have to check every five minutes with the boss.

If you think people are 60 per cent, or even 50 per cent up to the job, give it to them. Stretch them. They may have to work all day and all night because they are slow and making mistakes. But they will learn and grow as a result. And if they make a commitment to deliver a certain result by a certain time, trust them. This can get hairy, but if you try to take away all the risk then you probably land up doing the job yourself. High trust is consistent with a high performance culture where you expect people to deliver on their commitments.

Management by walking away is different from abandoning the team. You may walk away, but you make sure that you are always available to help and counsel whenever members of the team want it. The difference is that instead of intruding on their work, you let them ask for help when they want it. Your intervention will be valued more highly if they ask for it than if you inflict it unilaterally.

Management information systems (MIS)

The years BC (Before desktop Computers) were the golden age of MIS. At least you could see the rubbish. At one insurance company the weekly MIS was printed out onto a mainframe, put onto a low loader and carted up to the executive floor. The MIS weighed in at 20 kilograms. No one read it or understood it. In the years AD (After Desktops) MIS has got worse. We have evolved from reams of rubbish to gigabytes of garbage. This is worse because the technology allows the amount of data to explode. Because no one can see how much garbage there is, there is no incentive to clean it up.

Getting the MIS you need

We all know that MIS is meant to be timely, relevant and accurate. Just as firms are meant to grow profitably. We know what is meant to happen, but not how to make it happen. Here are the key principles of getting the MIS you need:

- You won't get there by starting from here. You probably need to start again with your MIS: create a zero base.
- The MIS you gather should represent a balanced view of performance including financial, market, organizational and innovation data.
- Drive the process top–down.
- Throw away the old system. This forces the pace of change.

CASE STUDY   Taming the MIS beast: a case study

The insurance company eventually got tired of chopping down trees and printing rubbish on them before taking them past executives on the way to the incinerator. This was not productive work. And management needed information to run the business.

Step 1 was for the CEO to sit down and write on one piece of paper the information he needed on a weekly basis to run the business. He reviewed it with his executive committee and then finalized it. It caused shock. The information concerned all sorts of stuff that did not even exist on the computer. Broadly, it fell into four categories:

- *Financial data*. This was the relatively easy bit for the MIS people. It is by its nature backward-looking, a scorecard of how we have done in the past. But it is useful.

Inevitably, the structure of the information required was different from what the system could produce.

- *Market data*. This looks at how the business is performing in real time. But this data was not only about traditional sales measures, but also about service quality, complaints and terminations. These represented warning lights over future performance, and had not been seen at CEO level before.

- *Organization data*. Partly this was about traditional departmental cost and performance data, and partly HR data on headcount and turnover.

- *Innovation*. This blew the mind of the MIS. This information was crucial to understand the future potential performance of the business. It included information on progress of key projects and an innovation index: the proportion of sales coming from new products, channels and customers.

Step 2 was to invite each executive committee member to create his or her own one-page summary, that covered the person's areas of responsibility. The only constraint was that the information the committee members requested had to be consistent with the information that the CEO requested.

Step 3 was to roll the process down through the organization. At each level, there were vast gaps between what people needed and what they had. What they needed was much less in volume but much more in value than what they were used to.

Step 4 was for the executive to start using the new MIS. This involved throwing away the old MIS. Immediately, there was a crisis. Large parts of the MIS simply did not exist. The rest had to be collected or collated manually. This crisis forced the pace of change in producing the new MIS. And as soon as other managers saw senior managers using the new MIS they were keen to use the same system.

Management: who is managing?

In one large bank I found one consistent answer to this question: management is my boss and above. So in the call centre the first line supervisor was management. But equally, very senior managers referred to the level above them as management. Only the executive committee recognized that they were management. Sadly, the belief that management refers only to the people above is widespread. Even partners at one large consulting firm fell into this trap.

'Management is above me' is a symptom of a sick organization. On one hand, it shows a denial of responsibility by the people claiming that management is above them. On the other hand, it is a reflection of disempowerment throughout the ranks of management. It reduces middle managers to their traditional role of mere ciphers communicating orders from the top of a hierarchy to the bottom. Anyone who has responsibility for any people or resources should think of themselves as managers and should act accordingly.

Managing or leading?

Question 1: what is the difference between management and leadership?
Question 2: how many angels can dance on the head of a pin?

Many fancy arguments have been put forward about management versus leadership. I asked my publisher what he thought the difference was. 'Easy' he said, 'leadership sells more books.'

Leadership sells more books because it is sexy: who wants to be a manager when you can be a leader? Now imagine an organization full of leaders transforming their paradigms while no one actually manages anything or does anything. Total chaos.

So let's try and answer the first, if not the second, question. Henry Kissinger came up with an excellent definition of a leader: 'a leader is someone who takes people where they would not have gone by themselves'. That is simple and devastating. It means that there are plenty of people in leadership positions, such as CEOs, who are not leading. They are not taking people where they would not have gone by themselves. They are simply managing a legacy they inherited, and are paying themselves very well for their troubles. John Major, the British Prime Minister, was attacked for being in office, but not in power: he held the title of leader but was not leading. In contrast, William Rodriguez was a great leader: he was the last person out of the World Trade Centre on 9/11 and led many people to safety. His title: janitor. Leadership is not about your title, it is about what you do.

So where does that leave managers? Perhaps the best definition of a manager is someone who 'makes things happen through other people he or she may not control'. Again, simplicity is deceptive. Many new managers do not understand that their job is no longer to do all the work themselves. They are like the player who has been promoted to team manager. They are not meant to make all the tackles and passes and score all the goals themselves. As managers, they have to select the right people for a team, train them, decide the tactics, coach as needed. The difference between doing and managing is night and day: the manager who tries to do it all alone quickly gets frustrated, angry and blows up.

In practice, the manager's job has become much harder. In the old days of command and control life was easy: bosses bossed and workers worked. The bosses had the brains and the workers had the hands. Now things are harder. Workers got educated: they could do more, but they expected more. They wanted more pay, more interesting work and better bosses who might try to motivate them, not just coerce them. And to make it worse, firms became flatter. Command and control went. And now managers have to manage the fine art of persuading colleagues, building coalitions, negotiating, doing deals and making things happen through colleagues, customers and suppliers over whom they have no formal control.

In many ways, managing is harder than leading. As a manager, your responsibilities exceed your authority; expectations exceed your resources; your goals are ambiguous and likely to change; you lack the control you need to succeed. As a leader, life is easier. You are in control of your destiny; you set the expectations and allocate the resources. And you get paid much more. Very nice.

Leaders may lead the revolution, but before and after the revolution the world will be run by managers who create order out of the chaos. Managing may be less glamorous, but it is at least as important and probably much harder than leading.

As for the angels dancing on the head of a pin: have you heard of the pinhead the size of a football field?

Meetings: the good, the bad and the ugly

Meetings are a great way of wasting time while giving the appearance of great activity. We have all spent more hours than we can count in useless meetings. No one is taught what makes a good meeting, or how to run a good meeting. If they were, office productivity would soar, and the office bill for coffee and pastries would plummet. Inevitably, the rules of effective meetings represent little more than common sense, which is routinely ignored whenever a meeting is called.

The model below applies to the typical, run-of-the-mill internal company meeting. It does not apply to brainstorming sessions or to large group meetings or to formal board meetings, where there are other constraints and special requirements.

The purpose of the meeting

A test of a good meeting is to ask the following three questions:

- What will be different as a result of this meeting? This is normally the result of making some decisions. Referring an issue to a committee or asking for more information is not a decision and does not make the business different.
- What did I learn from the meeting? The learning should be significant, relevant and useful.
- What do I do next? There have to be clear next steps coming out of the meeting.

If there are no good answers to these questions, then either it was a lousy meeting, or you should not have been there. In planning a meeting, it is worth thinking about how each of the participants will be able to answer these questions at the end of the meeting. If they will not have good answers, they probably should not be there. Ultimately be clear about what you will get out of the meeting, whether you are chairing it or attending it.

Attendance at meetings

Everyone wants to go to meetings. Junior staff want to go to get exposure to senior staff. Senior staff want the junior staff there, because they have probably done the donkey work and the senior staff feel exposed without their help. Every department wants to send someone so that they are represented. Jamborees do not make for good meetings.

Generally, once attendance rises above six to eight people, it becomes difficult to sustain a significant discussion among the whole group. Either a core group comes to dominate the meeting, or the meeting degenerates into a sequence of bilateral discussions between the chairperson and individual attendees. Either way, many people have become spectators and are not contributing. **Meetings are not meant to be a spectator sport**. Here are a few simple rules on attendance at meetings:

- Avoid meetings with more than six to eight people, unless the purpose is to broadcast a message.
- Only people with a role to play by bringing expertise, resources or authority should be there.

- No duplication of roles should occur: two people are not required to represent one point of view, unless they are representing quite different perspectives on it.

Preparation for a meeting

This is easily skipped, with unfortunate consequences. The key preparation is about setting expectations with other attendees. Setting expectations includes the following:

- The role each person is expected to play must be understood.
- Homework required should be made clear.
- Preview of critical issues is useful. It is better to talk to a potential adversary before the meeting, understand and manage the concerns in private, than to invite a punch-up in public. Build the consensus beforehand, a process institutionalized in Japan as 'nemawashi'.

Clearly, logistical preparation is required. Beyond the obvious points of location, facilities and potentially catering, there are the less obvious decisions about room layout. The traditional long table with a chairperson at its head is about the least effective format for a discussion, and makes looking at a presentation at one end of the table nearly impossible. Room layout is constrained only by your needs and your imagination. Hollow squares are common. One attractive option is to get rid of chairs and tables completely. A standing meeting is guaranteed to be faster and more focused than a meeting with deep comfortable chairs and lots of coffee and cookies. Standing meetings are not outlandish: the Queen uses them when meeting the Privy Council. A good way of keeping long-winded politicians from using too much gas.

Logic of meetings

Agenda items that get the most discussion are those that come close to the start of the meeting, when everyone is still fresh and energetic; where everyone is an expert; where no one will be offended by the outcome or by the discussion. In other words the debate is risk-free for the participants.

This creates great opportunities for manipulation. One of my favourite executive committee meetings met at 11.00 am. The first item was a discussion about giving the staff a glass of champagne at lunchtime to celebrate the recent merger and the official launch of the new brand and the new business. This hit the jackpot in terms of generating discussion. Everyone was fresh and wanted to be seen by the CEO to be contributing.

Everyone was an expert. Some argued that giving champagne would set the wrong example, and make disciplinary action over drinking at work impossible. Others argued that it would be atrocious to celebrate with a glass of water, management would look mean and morale would plummet. For 90 minutes there was moral combat over the glass of champagne. No one present could be offended by the discussion or the outcome: a glass of champagne did not represent the risk of pissing on anyone's turf. Opinions could fly, risk-free.

At about 12.30 pm, coming up to the 1.00 pm lunch break and still with three agenda items to go, a request from the IT director was put to the committee to extend a systems integration programme across the two businesses. This was vital to the business: millions of pounds of investment were at stake, it effectively doomed one set of platforms and one set of employees, and had significant impact on the product development and servicing capability of the business. Inevitably, it went through on the nod, because everyone was exhausted from the champagne battle, and had their eyes on more agenda items before lunch. Only the IT director really understood what was at stake: finance, marketing and personnel were completely out of their depth. And the IT director had the sense to square the CEO beforehand. Any challenge would have been risky: it would have been pissing directly on the IT director's turf. Set the agenda to get the level of discussion and the results you need.

Mergers and acquisitions (M&A)

Theory and practice

All the academic literature shows that most acquisitions fail. M&A activity gets larger every year. Either business people are stupid, or the academics are missing something.

The academics can show that the main benefits of an acquisition flow to the shareholders of the acquired company. Countless studies show that typically an acquirer will have to pay a premium of about 40 per cent above the open market price to secure control of a target company. The target company shareholders lock in a quick 40 per cent gain. The acquirer's stock typically underperforms relative to the market following the acquisition. The result is that less than half of acquisitions succeed from the acquiring shareholders' perspective. This may be rational and logical, but the logic is incomplete.

Acquisitions are about managers not just shareholders. From the management perspective about 50 per cent of managers win. The successful acquirer wins the power and the glory, and the acquired lose. **The dead don't laugh**. Managers' and shareholders' perceptions of victory are not the same.

This is more than vanity. By acquiring another company, the acquirer earns the right to stay in the contest. Acquiring CEOs get to play with a bigger toy. They can drive some short-term financial benefits and cost savings; they give themselves more room to manoeuvre strategically; they give themselves the chance of winning long term. The acquired company has lost, cannot play, cannot win. Game over. Naturally, not all acquirers go on to win: that is the nature of competition. But from the management perspective, it makes more sense to be predator than prey.

Mergers versus acquisitions: the FUD factor

Managers hate the FUD factor: fear, uncertainty, doubt. When the FUD factor rises, morale and performance plummet. Resistance, politicking and internal rivalry rise.

Acquisitions bring the FUD factor to boiling point. And rightly too: the target company's managers and staff have good reason to fear for their jobs. Even if the acquisition is about growth, not scale economies, there is the uncertainty of what the new managers will look like, what they will expect, and how they will manage.

However, a well-managed acquisition will drive through the FUD factor fast. The decisions on who survives, and in what role, will be made quickly. Those who have to go, will go soon. There will be pain. Well managed, the pain will be short if sharp. The FUD factor will be blown away, and managers can get on with managing the business, instead of jockeying for position and survival.

This means that the post-merger integration should be thought out in advance so that the acquirer can strike fast. Normally acquirers are so wrapped up in the thrill of the chase that when they win there is a hiatus that leads to the crisis: they do not know how to integrate the acquired business.

Mergers bring the pain to boiling point, and keep it there for a long time until the entire management team and the business is well stewed. The more equal the merger, the worse it is. In the desperate struggle to be fair to both sides, managers duck all the difficult decisions. This is one case I lived through, where managers were desperate to be fair, rational and even handed. Here's how they approached the key decisions:

- Who will be in charge? We will both share responsibilities.
- Where shall we cut back? We will set up some task forces to look at the question objectively and they will report back in six months.
- Which systems shall we use? We'll think about it.
- Which offices shall we close down? Let's keep both running until the other decisions have been sorted out.
- How will decisions be made? To be fair, we will make sure that all key decisions involve managers from both sides so that we can reach the best solution for the business as a whole.

Naturally, this was a mandate for politics and internal rivalry on a grand scale. The business turned in on itself. Everyone realized the real competition was not in the marketplace: it was the other management team. And this was going to be a fight to the death. There were never going to be two CEOs, two marketing directors, two finance directors. The more managers tried to fudge the issues, the worse became the FUD factor.

The business was put back two years in the marketplace and never really recovered. Instead of a clear direction there was fudge, which confused everyone and sub-optimized the business.

Having been acquired and having lived through a merger, the acquisition is less painful and more effective than the merger. Clear decision making is good management. Compromise is not.

The Midas touch

King Midas wished that everything he touched would turn to gold. The gods granted his wish. He was delighted. He embraced his wife. She turned to gold. Shocked, he turned to pick up a drink. The wooden goblet turned to gold, and then the wine inside turned to gold. He could eat and drink nothing. This is the origin of the old Greek curse: 'May all your wishes come true.'

Corporate wishes are expressed not in prayers to the gods, but in reward and measurement systems for the staff. And some reward and measurement systems have the true Midas touch:

- Call centre staff measured on the number of calls handled. Result: unsatisfactory customer service and large call waiting queues as throughput is maximized.

- Bank relationship managers sold on the size of the loan book generated. Result: low-quality loan books and expensive write-offs. **Lending money is easy, getting it back is hard.** That is banking lesson 101, which many banks seem to have forgotten.

- Insurance salespeople rewarded on commission. Result: mis-selling of inappropriate policies to the wrong people; legal and government action costing the industry nearly $20 billion in the UK.

- Hospitals measured on the length of time between a patient seeing a specialist and having an operation. Result: patients kept off the waiting list by delaying their appointment with the specialist.

- Capital markets dealers who are measured on profits. Result: they take huge risks with the firm's capital, even resorting to deceit to bypass risk control measures. The bigger the risk the bigger the potential gain or loss. Since the first edition of this book was published, we have had the 2008 global financial collapse. The collapse was predictable and nothing has changed: we await the second instalment of disaster fuelled by greed.

Multinationals and multi-locals

It is fashionable for multinationals to present themselves as multi-local. They want to be seen as good citizens of the community and responsive to local needs. They do not want to be seen as fast food or fizzy drink imperialists squashing out the local culture.

The logic of the multinational says that any localization has to be window dressing to pacify the local constituencies. It helps to appear local to the national government when it comes to bargaining time over regulations, or investment incentives for building new factories, or for tax reviews.

Otherwise, the logic of the multinational forces is to be global. The management presumption has to be in favour of the global approach over the local approach, despite the complaints of local managers. Operationally, the multinational succeeds by working globally, not locally:

- Production costs can be minimized by global sourcing.
- Marketing costs are minimized with one global campaign.

- Stock costs are minimized by having a single pack design globally, so that stock can be used internationally. This also drives longer production runs and means fewer changeovers.

- Overhead costs are minimized: ultimately brand groups can go global, and administration can be consolidated, only one set of R&D is required. This can go to extremes. I have seen rice cookers being developed and tested in Groningen, the Netherlands. They don't cook much rice there compared to Asia. The idea of globalization was right, the execution was not.

- Learning is optimized: by having one call centre in Dublin for all its European corporate customers, a bank not only smoothes capacity utilization, but also learns more about the patterns of corporate needs across Europe. A fragmented approach would not drive the learning out so easily.

- Where customers are global, either structurally (business to business) or in taste (consumer) the business has to drive to a global response.

Managerially, multinationals have to take a global perspective. Decisions on resource allocation, production, products and branding have to be global if the global economies of scale are to be achieved. Decision making is easier when there is a cohesive group of managers who understand and trust each other.

At minimum, that requires a common management language. This is driving even some French multinationals to adopt English as the corporate language. It also drives top managers to be homogenous. Members of the executive committees of US multinationals tend to be US born, and the Japanese multinationals have Japanese executives. Multinationalism does not reach the executive suite.

Of course, there are pressures to adapt to local needs. But if the local needs are truly unique, a local company will probably best exploit them. A multinational will never be as local and as responsive as a good local company. A McDonald's will never produce a soufflé quite the way a fine French chef does: it does not need to compete on such local fare. The pressure within the multinational has to be to drive management, operations and ultimately the market and its customers to a standard global model. As with auto manufacturers that use global chassis, engines and parts, the end result may be tailored to local needs, but the economics, management and standards are global.

Myths of management

There are three myths at the heart of management. For those that recognize them and can deal with them, they are useful.

We know where we are

This is a big myth. Of course, it is a mortal sin for any managers to admit that they do not know where they are. And in the course of trying to find out exactly where we are, we gather more and more detailed information ever more frequently on every aspect of our business. But no one is ever satisfied: we can never know enough. Knowing where we are is about being in control. But we can never gain the level of control or information we want. We will never know exactly what is going on in other functions, other parts of the business. We certainly do not understand what the political and emotional agendas are of all our colleagues. We usually do not know until too late what our competition is up to. We are always surprised by random events in the outside world: storms, strikes, new technologies like the internet blow up out of nowhere.

As managers we should recognize that **the search for perfect knowledge is self-defeating**: it consumes so much time we will never do anything except find and file information.

The solution is not to worry. Focus on the few things that are important, that we can control and make a difference in. The tighter the focus, the more chance we have of being in control and making a difference. This is true for individuals and for institutions.

We know where we are going

There is a simple test for this one: dig out the five-year plan from five years ago and see how accurate it is. The world is awash with examples of how forecasts go wrong. In any takeover, there is at least one party for whom the takeover was not part of the five-year plan. Look at economic and financial forecasts and compare them with reality. *Fortune* magazine highlighted 10 attractive technology stocks (18 September 2000). Within a month, five of them had fallen by more than 50 per cent, two had fallen by 80 per cent. The unexpected happens. In the 27 years since the FTSE 100 was formed out of the top 100 public companies in the UK, 71 of them have fallen out of the top 100 ranking: none of them knew that they were going to be taken over or overtaken within one generation.

Since we are not in control of the whole world, we are not entirely in control of our own destiny. Again, the solution is not to try to control everything.

It is impossible. The solution is to fix on a few goals and to focus on the key actions that are likely to get there. Be fixated about the goals, but flexible on the means.

Even if the reality is that the future will not turn out as we intended, it is worth sustaining the myth that we know where we are going. People need a sense of leadership, direction and focus. Giving them focus is not just about motivation: it is about getting results in the areas we believe are important. If we are wrong, we can always start again.

We know how to get there

If we don't really know where we are or where we are going, we are not in a strong position to claim we know how to get there. But the myth that managers are fully in control demands that we are clear about how we are going to get there.

Again, this myth is worth sustaining to the extent that it gives the organization a sense of direction and momentum. Where the myth becomes dangerous is when managers leap onto the latest management fad as a way of demonstrating that they have a plan to get to wherever they think they are going. The eagerness of managers to jump onto fads is indicative of their uncertainty about how they should go forward. Fads are solutions to problems that may not be relevant.

So what do we do about it?

For the health of the business, these three myths should be sustained. It would be a career-limiting move to tell the stockholders at the general meeting: we don't know where we are, we don't know where we are going and we don't know how to get there. People like the sense of security that a direction gives them, even if it is a false sense of security.

The real danger is when managers start believing the myths themselves. Then they try controlling too much, build inflexibility into their plans for the future and are easy prey for the quack doctors selling the latest fad. A healthy scepticism about these myths encourages managers to focus only on what they control and change, to be flexible about adapting for the future, and it will wean them off dependency on fads.

Negotiate to win

The best way to win in any negotiation is to negotiate for a win/win. Make sure the people on the other side can walk away with a win and give it to them.

The traditional win/lose negotiation causes conflict. In a sales pitch it normally ends up focusing on price and ignores other things that may be of value to both sides.

The win/win negotiation requires an understanding of what the people on the other side value. It may be something you can give at low cost. Let them have it. In return, you will probably be able to get what you need.

These negotiations happen all the time in the office. A technology person asks some advice on a business plan: no sweat. I need some technology help, I get it back. This sort of negotiation is as natural as breathing air.

We know how to negotiate informally, but in formal negotiations our instincts often desert us. Here are the most important rules for successful negotiation:

- Make it a win/win, not a win/lose: don't compete, collaborate.

- See it through the eyes of the other people: understand what's in it for them. Let them have a win, let them have a story they can tell themselves and their colleagues to show that they were smart.

- Create options: avoid a single point solution because that becomes win/lose. For instance, a price negotiation is win/lose. But create options by introducing other ideas: service, guarantees, extra features, financing plans, trade-ins and suddenly you can find a win/win. And you can give away something cheap to you (an extra service) but valuable to those on the other side: they now have a story to tell their friends about how they negotiated a great deal.

- Be sociable: if the people on the other side like you, they will find it harder to screw you. So you do not need to enter the negotiation right away. Let them talk about themselves and their needs: you will learn more and they will feel more comfortable dealing with you if they feel they trust you.

Offices

Form follows function

You can tell a business from its building. Learn to read the signals. The interior of the office is a statement of what the business is like. The exterior of the building is a strong statement about how the business wants to be seen. Many are functional, simple offices in business parks. But a clearer statement is possible:

- Traditional banks may be built like marble palaces to give customers a sense of the bank's strength and stability.
- Local government offices with cheap flooring and decoration reassure taxpayers that their money is not being frittered away.
- Central government often occupies magnificent buildings to project the power of the state.
- Modern architectural landmark buildings may house IT consulting firms that want to be seen at the leading edge.
- Anonymous, discreet but rich offices may house strategy consulting firms.

The principle of form follows function applies to the inside as well as the outside of the building. There are two competing forces at work. The first is the simple functional requirements of the building. An investment bank will require a huge, high-tech open area with good air-conditioning and room for cabling to support a trading floor. A media design company requires more intimate space.

Consulting companies increasingly arrange the interior space so that consultants have no permanent desks. They want to keep the consultants out of the office and at the client site, where they can earn fees. So the interior has plenty of hot desk space, personal filing areas and informal meeting spaces.

Internal space is not just about function in the utilitarian sense. The other key function it serves is about status. You can tell how hierarchical a firm is from the amount of private offices it keeps, and whether there are separate lifts, floors and dining rooms for different levels of executive. In contrast, a firm that needs to promote internal communication will have plenty of open space. In between is the compromise of cubicle land. Cubicles are meant to create the best of open-plan communication with personal space. They tend to achieve the worst combination: poor communication and little privacy. Use of space is not just a design issue; it is a management issue that helps to drive costs, behaviour, attitudes, communication and morale.

Status and executive apartheid

Burn the private offices and the executive floor. If the executives are desperate to cling to their offices, burn them anyway. Let the executives fry or flee.

For most offices, form follows function. For executives, function is about status not utility. The executives are the ones who most need to stay in touch with everything that is going on, and they are the ones who put up the greatest barriers to a free flow of information. The separate executive floor is a good way of creating and enforcing the corporate apartheid system: executives only, riff-raff stay away. In one business, the executive floor was known as death row. You only went there to be hired or fired. This was not a business with easy communication, high trust or openness.

Individual private offices ensure that communication is minimized and formality is maximized. The quick chat is made more difficult. The riff-raff are not allowed onto the executive floor without an appointment, so there is no chance of seeing if the boss is available for a quick chat. Even among the executive team, the separate offices mean that each executive is not aware of what the others are doing, unless they meet. There is no point in having an open door policy if no one is allowed to see the door or to get onto the same floor as the door without an appointment booked through a secretary who tenaciously guards the diary.

There is an alternative. It is called 'back to the future'. I have worked as a partner in two firms. The difference illustrates the impact of different executive arrangements.

The very old-fashioned future perfect partnership

This partnership had a Victorian approach to the partners' office: all the partners shared one room. Their status and net worth could have justified magnificent personal suites. But sharing an office worked:

- Formal meetings were not required: we all knew what was happening with the business. If anyone needed help, or there were decisions to make about a client, all it took was a shout across the room.

- We knew how all the staff were performing. You got to know after a while that every time X came into the room, a good conversation would seem to happen. Every time Y came into the room, it would be tense and difficult. You would not listen to the conversation, but the impact was obvious.

- There were no secrets. This helps build trust among the partners.

- Open plan for the partners made for open communication throughout the firm: there would be a steady trickle of people coming in and out of the room. It was not a big deal to see the partners. The partners were literally on top of the business.

- There was no place to hide. If you were being idle or had nothing to do, it was obvious. If you were not contributing, it was obvious. Peer group pressure is a powerful motivator.

- There was a constant buzz. This was energizing. Some people claim only to be able to think in a private space. You get used to the open space fast.

The traditional hierarchy

The second partnership was a traditional command and control hierarchy, with the troops kept at arm's length. The loyalty and commitment of the troops was correspondingly an arm's length affair.

All the partners clung tenaciously to their private offices. They had poor communication among themselves. Nearly all decisions had to be arranged through formal meetings, which would flow up and down the hierarchy of partners. Cooperation was formal and poor.

Most people at all levels had much greater affection for the first firm than for the second; there was a sense of family in the first versus a desire to build a career and make money in the second. And this showed in the quality of people and service.

One-way options

Options serve neither managers nor shareholders. When the tide rises, both the cream and the sewage rise to the top. A rising stock market rewards good and poor management alike. Clearly, some managers do better than others.

Those in fundamental growth industries like software, telecommunications, financial services and pharmaceuticals have done very well. Managers in steel, food manufacturing and old economy industries will have struggled to keep up, however good they are. Managers are not being rewarded for performance. They are being rewarded for working in a growth industry during an economic boom.

Equally, managers should not be punished when the economy hits a recession. The recession, when it comes, will not have been caused by the option holder.

The response of boards in these situations is the wrong response. They reprice the options; so, the options essentially become a one-way bet for management. If the share price rises, they win. If it drops, they get the options repriced and they get to play again until the stock market lifts them out of trouble. This is not an incentive to outperform.

If directors and managers are serious about rewarding performance, they have to focus on outperformance. There are two ways. First, use economic performance measures: incentivize managers to achieve profitability in excess of the required rate of return on the capital employed in the business. This can lead to game playing. Reducing the apparent capital employed through write-offs is an easier way of improving profitability than actually improving performance.

Second, use share price performance measures: reward managers based on outperformance of the share price relative not just to the stock market but to its immediate competitors and peer group in the market. This would enable managers to be rewarded even in a falling market, provided the stock price did not fall as fast as the peer group. Either way, managers would have to earn their results, rather than get lucky.

Organization charts

Boxes are for the dead

Draw them up and throw them away. Big organizations need to draw organization charts. Drawing up the chart is a way of forcing managers to make basic decisions about what roles people will have, where accountabilities will lie, and how decision-making processes will work. Some organizations pride themselves on never having drawn up an organization chart. They are the ones that have the least internal clarity about how things get done. The result is confusion and politics on a grand scale.

Once the discipline of drawing up and communicating the organization chart is complete, throw it away – unless you have a traditional command and control hierarchy, in which case publish it widely so everyone can see which box they lie in. Otherwise, don't let people hide in their little boxes. **Don't put people in boxes until they are dead.**

Organization charts ossify the organization vertically and horizontally. The horizontal divisions of the chart convert the organization into layers, like pancakes layered on a plate. The pancake at the top is the most important. Don't let managers hide in their pancake. It simply reinforces the traditional control versus commitment hierarchy.

The vertical divisions of the chart split the organization up into deep silos. Again, this is consistent with a command and control hierarchy. But if lateral communication and cooperation is important, don't let formal structures get in its way. Silo mentality is a great way of avoiding responsibility and shifting blame.

Silo mentality allows for passing the buck. When sales dropped at an electrical goods manufacturer, the sales force immediately blamed the marketing department for putting together the wrong promotions. The marketing team blamed the product development team for not bringing the right products to market. The product development people inevitably blamed the R&D team who in turn blamed the finance department for cutting their budgets. The finance people pointed back to the sales organization for underselling, which meant the budgets had to be cut.

The silos spent months making sure that the blame did not fall into their silo, when they should have cooperated across the silos to reach a solution. The only winners were the competition.

Upside-down thinking

Upside-down organization charts are very trendy. A 50-year-old manager showing an upside-down organization chart looks as trendy as a 50-year old going out clubbing.

The upside-down organization chart preaches wisdom that the front-line workers are the most important. The chart means to show that the boss at the bottom of the pyramid is simply supporting the people above him or her.

What is said by the boss and what is understood by the listeners is quite different. The people in the audience do not see the upside-down pyramid. They see a spinning top out of control, where the boss likes to believe that everything depends on and revolves around him or her alone. No one is taken in by the claim that the front-line troops are the most important and the boss simply supports them. The decisions all still flow from the boss, while all the salary and status flow to the boss.

The upside-down organization chart is misleading, dishonest, patronizing and not credible. And it is not even original any more. But it makes for a speech the boss feels good about, and convinces the boss that he or she is trendy. So, expect to see a lot more upside-down organization charts.

Overpay people

If people really are your most important asset, then it makes sense to overpay them relative to the market. Paying over the odds has several positive consequences:

- You stand a chance of recruiting the best people. In sales, top-quartile performers are often four to five times as productive as those in the bottom quartile. Overpayment is a good investment.

- You stand a reasonable chance of keeping attrition down. The cost of attrition is not just the recruiting cost, but the far greater cost of bringing new people up to speed, together with the risk that they may not work out.

- Overpayment sets high expectations of performance. People tend to achieve what is expected: low expectations get low performance, high expectations create the potential for high performance.

Low pay may ensure lower costs, but it also ensures lower performance and lower morale. Employing more low-paid staff is not a substitute for quality.

There are bad and good ways of overpaying. Overpaying should be linked to performance. And it should be linked to a culture of high performance and putting people first. Overpayment is not just for the management big shots. At least as important are the receptionists, call centre staff and front-line service people who represent the business to the customer. They should be excellent.

Pareto principle

Originally, this was an assertion by the Italian economist Vilfredo Pareto that about 80 per cent of the wealth in any country was held by 20 per cent of the population. This has found its way into management thinking in the theory that 20 per cent of the effort produces 80 per cent of the result. This is inaccurate. For management, the 20/80 principle is often much more like 5/95. Everyone knows this, but does not apply it. These examples are worth testing in your own business to see how well the 20/80 stacks up. The real challenge is for managers to then act on the results:

- Look at customer profitability. Typically, 20 per cent of the customers produce over 100 per cent of the profit contribution. This is fairly consistently true when activity-based costing is used to measure the true cost to serve different customers. Most businesses do not differentiate customer service and pricing in line with profitability and the cost to serve.

- Consider product profitability. Perhaps 20–30 per cent of the products produce over 100 per cent of the profits. This is a powerful message that is being applied by Unilever and P&G as they refocus their businesses on the most successful global brands.

- Examine effort and results. For example, 95 per cent of managers' effort is used to maintain the business or to justify work that will move the business forward; **95 per cent of work is spinning wheels, 5 per cent results in moving forward.**

- Ten per cent of the managers produce 90 per cent of the value. Names, please.

- Ten per cent of the people cause 90 per cent of the problems. Names, please.

- Ten per cent of salespeople's time is spent selling to customers, 90 per cent is spent on administration, souped-up service and some sales call preparation. This is tried and tested as a ratio. In business-to-business selling the ratio can be nearer 5/95. It represents a great opportunity for performance improvement.

- Before a project starts, 95 per cent of the probability of its success is determined, and after it starts 95 per cent of the effort happens. Projects, like battles, tend to be won and lost before they start: the right problem with the right team and the right resources is set up to win against a project on the wrong problem with the wrong sponsor and the wrong team.

- Ten per cent of the specifications drive 90 per cent of the cost of the new IT programme.

- Managers spend 90 per cent of budget reviews testing 10 per cent of the budget: they test not the most important parts, but the bits that are easiest for everyone to understand; are most discretionary; and are least volatile politically.

- Five per cent of this book will give you 95 per cent of the value. But for each person, it will be a different 5 per cent. Good luck!

Parkinson's Law

Few management insights stand the test of time. *Parkinson's Law*, by C N Parkinson (1958), is one of them. It will be as true during the 21st century as it was during the 20th:

1 'Work expands so as to fill the time available.'
2 'Officials make work for each other.'
3 'An official wants to multiply subordinates.'

Rules one and three are self-evident in the daily work of managers. Rule two is the killer for the 21st century. As organizations become flatter, so the number of officials tends to grow.

Previously, a factory manager could probably decide if the washrooms needed to be refurbished and would get the work done. Now the corporate life support systems swing into action to help the factory manager. The health and safety people offer all advice on the standards that need to be applied; the purchasing people produce a list of preferred suppliers; the lawyers check the contracts; the accountants check the estimates and control the payments; the HR people make sure that the staff understand what is happening and get the newsletter to communicate the refurbishment; and of course the whole management chain gets involved in the procurement process, giving approvals, with staff checking the submissions and other staff checking progress with yet more checkers checking that the checkers are doing the checking the right way. Then the designers, consultants, architects, surveyors, cleaning contractors and builders get involved. The result is a jamboree for all. The refurbishment should have cost US $1,500, but just managing it will have cost US $15,000.

The flat organization does not make it worthwhile challenging this management feeding frenzy. From the factory manager's point of view it takes longer to fight the system than it does to go along with it. And none of the zoo of managers needs to challenge their own existence. Finally, each one of them can demonstrate that they, individually, are adding value to the process.

There is no one in the system who has an incentive to stop it spinning out of control. Even top managers have other battles to fight, rather than grappling with the internecine warfare of the internal bureaucracy. The beast is out of control until it causes a crisis. Then it is chopped back ruthlessly. Like pruning, this simply allows it to flower yet more vigorously the next time around.

Perfect predators

Some consultants were on safari, and they decided to design the perfect predator. Each took responsibility for one limb. The result combined the best of all the animals. The perfect predator had the legs of a cheetah, the neck of a giraffe, the head of an elephant, the hide of a rhino, the teeth of an alligator and the wings of an eagle. The animal collapsed under the weight of its own improbability.

When they returned to work, the consultants decided to create the perfect company. Each contributed his or her greatest strength. This was the business that came out:

- It would be a high commitment workplace, for as long as managers wanted the staff.

- It would have detailed, world-class reporting and control systems and highly empowered managers.

- It would have great strategic intent to beat the world and be ruthlessly re-engineered to minimize costs.

- It would be a flat organization with a clear decision-making hierarchy.
- It would have the lowest prices and highest service in the marketplace.
- It would be global and local.
- It would serve its shareholders, customers, staff and the community outstandingly.

This business did not turn to be a world-beater. It was just the same as all the other businesses in the marketplace. And it too, eventually collapsed under the weight of its own improbability.

The perfect predator is not a mix of all the best bits of best practices from elsewhere. It is not a mix of every fad to have wafted through academia and boardrooms in the last 10 years. The perfect predator, like the lion or the crocodile or the eagle, is perfectly adapted to its own environment and has made the trade-offs required to become perfect. Luckily for business, as the environment changes there are endless opportunities to achieve perfection by not being the same as everyone else. **Perfection does not exist.** Do not chase it. If you fit your environment, that is as close to perfect as you will ever achieve.

Perspectives and the jigsaw puzzle

We decided to walk up the mountain. In England we think of it as a mountain, anywhere else it would be a hill.

In the morning we walked through the village. A cat jumped out of our way and waited to be let into a house. We could see the sheep and pigs in the farmyard. The bottles of milk on the doorstep had just been delivered and the local shop had put some fruit and veg outside for sale. We bought our supplies and set off.

A couple of hours later we stopped and took in the view, which had changed completely. We could no longer see the cats, pigs and sheep. We could see the pattern of fields laid out below us; we could see a stream disappearing into the woods and small lanes winding their way through the countryside.

Eventually, we got to the summit and our view changed again. We could see forever: across distant ridges into the blue-green horizon where land, sea and sky merged into one.

So which view was the right view: the view from the bottom, middle or top of the mountain?

Clearly, they were all different and none was right or wrong. And it is the same in business. The senior executives at the top may see the big picture, but the front-line worker dealing with the customer has an equally valid view. At every level and in every department, people have a different view. It is not right and it is not wrong.

Most organization conflict arises because people see things differently, as they should do: we do not expect marketing, finance and operations all to be looking at the same thing. The real problems arise when each unit insists that it has the only true version of reality. In practice, we all hold one small part of a giant jigsaw puzzle. The challenge for senior managers is to make sure that all the pieces come together to make a coherent picture. That is hard work, made even harder by the fact that each piece of the jigsaw has a mind of its own and argues with other pieces; the pieces tend to change shape and colour over time, and the big picture is constantly changing anyway.

Who said management was easy?

Planning heaven and hell

Good planning can move a business forward quickly. Bad planning is a bureaucratic hell that sucks up management time and achieves nothing. Every business has its own unique planning system, normally guarded by functionaries for whom the planning cycle is their meal ticket for life. Attack the process at your peril: the functionaries will defend their system with eloquence.

Planning should not be a dry technical process. It should be about mobilizing, aligning and committing managers to a course of action. That will not happen with plans dictated by staff.

You probably know intuitively if your planning process comes from heaven or from hell. Here's how you can substantiate your instinct.

Planning hell

- Planning is driven by staff, not managers. Once staff start leading with their numbers and judgements of the business, it wastes an inordinate amount of time and effort to change what they are writing.
- A historic trend-line mindset exists: the past is extrapolated into the future. This is a surefire way to guarantee incrementalist thinking.

It does not encourage ambition, and it ignores the changing obstacles and opportunities for each business.

- There is single point planning. This normally dissolves into the debate about what the target for next year should be. Some testing for sensitivities under different scenarios is more useful, as well as differentiating between base and stretch objectives.

- There is 'bottom right-hand box' bias. Everyone knows what the answer in the bottom right-hand box of the spreadsheet should be, so they fix and fudge all the assumptions to get there. If the box is meant to show US $10 million profit or 15 per cent return on equity, it will always manage to come in just above the number. Do not test the number. Test the assumptions behind it.

- Planning is politically driven. Power and selective facts are used to drive targets up or down.

- It is complicated: people search for endless detail and spurious accuracy. This is normally linked to control by the staff. Arguing over secretaries' salary assumptions is not going to make for a plan that builds the enterprise successfully.

- It is long-winded. Managers have other things to do than go through endless iterations of a plan.

Planning heaven

- Planning is driven by business managers. The planning process simply articulates the commitments that managers make to each other. Intermediation by functionaries does not help the process of commitment.

- Market-based assumptions are made about what will happen. This is better than plans that are based on looking backward (at historical trends) and inward (extrapolating costs and results forward).

- There is sensitivity testing against different scenarios, which is a natural consequence of being outward- and future-focused.

- Balanced goals are in place. Get away from the tyranny of simply trying to fix on the profit target. The plan should reflect progress for the business in four areas:
  - financial progress: profit, capital effectiveness, revenues;
  - market progress: share, service, quality, satisfaction;

   – organization: new skills, capabilities, focus;

   – innovation: this is about working smarter rather than just trying to work harder to get more results. Long term, this is the only way progress will be sustained.

Ultimately the planning process should help mobilize and align management. Budget proposers should feel a sense of ownership over the plan, rather than accepting it as something that has been handed down to them by functionaries and managers. And senior managers should have a better understanding of the challenges and opportunities that each business or department faces.

Power games

You suffer them as a junior manager. It's only fair you should enjoy them when you become a senior manager. Pass the misery on from one generation of managers to the next. If you haven't made it yet, use this checklist to score all the great panjandrums. Give the winner a power Oscar at the next big conference. A statue of Napoleon should do the trick.

Meeting power

- Always be the last to arrive: keep them waiting.
- Never read documents ahead of the meeting. Read them in the meeting. This shows you are very busy, and very smart because you can absorb 100-page documents in five minutes while chairing a meeting.
- When people come to meet you, keep them waiting outside your door. Ideally, the door should be open and they should see you are looking at e-mail. This shows the visitors how unimportant they are, and gives you the chance to complain about the 200 e-mails you receive every day. This shows you are important.
- Interrupt the meeting to take a call or to step outside and talk to someone. Tell everyone they can carry on: it shows that their agenda item is unimportant and leaves them trying to double guess your point of view.

Travel power

- Whatever your travel arrangements are, change them at the last minute. Show you are busy and maximize disruption for staff.

- Travel with junior bag carriers. Changing travel plans should mess them up. And when you board the plane you turn left, they turn right. Let them know their place.

- Never pay for the taxi. Either put it on account (a weak position) or make a junior pay and make the junior sit in the backward-facing sickie seat (emphasizing your strong position).

Office power

- Make sure you have the plum office. A separate executive floor, with separate reception, a separate lift and ideally separate security protects you from the riff-raff and spells power.

- You should have the most up-to-date computer. Never use it, except for e-mail.

- Doctor photographs to show you with various presidents or prime ministers, and leave them where they can be seen. Alternatively, a picture of a grand country house or vintage car will help.

Communication power

- Always make your secretary receive and make phone calls for you; then keep the other person waiting on the line for a while.

- Internal newsletters are there to carry your picture on as many pages as possible. You should either be seen awarding prizes, doing a 'royal visit' to a factory, or making speeches about the future.

- Only communicate to other managers through your staff. You are too busy to deal with them directly. And it makes it harder for them to argue with you.

- Write either with an antique fountain pen (conveying tradition and expensive) or with a red biro (which is good for commenting on papers: it makes recipients of your comments feel as if they are back at school).

Conference power

- At public conferences, turn up only for your speech and then leave immediately afterwards. This shows you are busy.

- At in-house conferences, make the big speech. In coffee breaks only ever talk to people at your level or above. Do not talk to underlings.

- Give people the impression that you are deciding their fate, even if you are only arranging the afternoon golf match.

Eating power

- Have a special diet. It should be very awkward to cater for. Force people to offer some sympathy about your allergy, but don't be too cranky (such as opting for a vegan diet). A gluten-free diet is perfect.

- Be the big host. Always go to an exclusive place, where you will see some celebrity that you can talk about later (use Christian names, implying that you regularly meet him or her). This is the one occasion when you do pick up the bill so that everyone knows how generous you are.

- Maintain the private dining room for entertaining guests. Eating in the office is good. It shows you are busy. But the sandwiches must be on proper china, be high quality, well presented and come with a bowl of fresh fruit (uneaten) every day.

Pastime power

- Your pastimes should show you have money and mix in the right circles: **opera and shooting are good, but not at the same time**.

- Active sports where you can claim some talent are good. By taking part in these you can irritate everyone else who has not got the time to be superfit and is one up against your more sedentary peer group. Skiing in exotic locations is good. It combines the illusion of health with conspicuous consumption.

- Bad pastimes include soccer (because it's common) and anorak pastimes (such as stamp collecting or bird watching).

- Involvement with charities is good. It shows compassion, implies wealth, and helps you meet other power people.

Dress power

- Bespoke is expensive, discreet and good.
- Designer is trashy.
- Cufflinks are a must.

- If you are forced to wear casual, make sure it is expensive, new and very crisply turned out. This shows that you maintain high standards and keeps some distance between you and the junior staff.

PowerPoint points

Death by a hundred bullet points to the head is an ugly way to die. And yet this is the fate that many presenters are determined to inflict on their audiences. Here is how to make the most of PowerPoint. Throw it away. When was the last time you saw CEOs or presidents persuading each other with a PowerPoint presentation? People in power make their point without PowerPoint. And the best public speakers do not need the crutch of PowerPoint. With PowerPoint, you are a slave to the logic of the slides you prepared; without PowerPoint you can change and react to events.

Minimize PowerPoint if you must use it. Seeing a presenter has reached page 7 of 85 after 30 minutes brings out the inner axe-wielding maniac in the most docile audience. Your presentation is not complete when you can say no more, it is complete when you can say no less. Being short and concise is harder than rambling on.

Having a smart presenter and dumb slides is better than having smart slides with a dumb presenter. Your job is not to read aloud densely packed prose on each slide: your audience can read faster than you can speak. Have slides with a few words on them to anchor your talk, and then bring the words to life with your wit, wisdom and insight.

Presentation heaven and hell

Try this exercise. First, talk about the most interesting and exciting (legal and decent) thing you have done in the last year. Second, try describing the cost allocation system in your company. If you fall asleep before your audience does, you have failed.

In the first exercise you probably showed you have the natural talent to be a great presenter. You probably displayed the three 'Es' of any good presentation:

- energy;
- enthusiasm;
- excitement.

Sadly, **in many organizations, enthusiasm is regarded as a certifiable mental disorder**. Put this to your advantage. Audiences that are not used to enthusiasm will enjoy the difference. As a rule, if you are not energetic and enthusiastic, then the members of your audience will not be energetic and enthusiastic for you. You have to generate their interest.

Now think back to some great presentations you have been to (if any). The chances are that you remember little of the content, but you can remember the presenter. If you remember any of the content, it is likely to be a story. You will be remembered the same way: you will be remembered for how you performed, and perhaps for a story, much more than for what you said. Do you really want to be remembered as the King of the Mumblers who sent everyone into a catatonic stupor?

To tell people to be energetic, enthusiastic and excited is a bit like telling people to be happy. The goal may be clear, but the means are elusive. Here, in practice, are 10 things you can do to help your cause:

- *Prepare well.* The more you rehearse, the more confident you will feel and appear. It will become easier for you to enjoy rather than endure the event.

- *Script your start and your end.* Remember the first 30 seconds of your talk: ensure you get a fast start and get over any early nerves. And have a memorable finish: avoid the limp 'Any questions?'

- *Script key phrases.* These can be memorable phrases that can anchor your talk and give you structure and direction.

- *Tell a story, which will have three parts.* This is where we are; this is where we are going, this is how we will get there. Start, middle and end. And then let people know where you are so that they do not get lost on the journey you are taking them on.

- *Keep it simple:* tell people what they need to hear, not what you want to say. If necessary, focus on the one or two most important people in the room. Once you understand what they need to hear, you can radically reduce the scale and scope of your talk.

- *Focus on your audience.* Don't talk to your slides. Talk to your audience. Hold eye contact with one person at a time: you can be sure that once people know that you may talk to them personally, they will pay attention.

- *Visualize success, like all good sportspeople do.* Imagine what good looks like, sounds like, feels like and then make it happen. If you

visualize failure, you will find it is a self-fulfilling prophecy as all your
demons come to haunt you.

- *Stand well.* Stand so that a slip of paper could pass beneath your heel.
  This will give you good posture and keep your energy levels up. When
  your body slumps, your energy slumps and you send out all the wrong
  signals to your audience.

- *Look the part.* People will remember you much more than they
  remember what you say. If you look like a tramp, you will be
  remembered as a tramp. If you look confident, positive and relaxed
  then that is how they will see you and that is how they will remember
  your message.

- *Arrive early.* There are always logistical problems: room layout,
  computer connections, microphones, etc. If you are early, you have
  time to deal with these problems calmly, and still have time to meet
  other people as they arrive and to do some last minute preparation.
  Arrive late and you will be tense and have no time to sort out any last
  minute hitches.

Pricing

Chaos and confusion

Controlled pricing chaos is profitable. Uncontrolled pricing chaos destroys
profitability.

Controlled chaos

Controlled pricing chaos takes advantage of consumers who lack the time
or inclination to understand pricing choices completely. In reality, no one has
the time to shop around for good prices on everything they buy. Instead,
consumers want reassurance that they are getting good value, and that they
are not getting ripped off.

The reassurance comes in two forms. The first form of reassurance is the
brand. No one who goes grocery shopping checks the price on every item in
the basket before deciding which retailer to use. Shoppers choose one retailer,
and then rely on that brand to let them fill the grocery basket at reasonable
cost. Even after the shopping is completed, customers are unable to recall
individual product prices accurately, and have little notion of whether the
shopping would have been cheaper elsewhere. But the sting in the tail is that

if the customers do sense that they have been overcharged, the trust in the brand is lost, and the loyalty and the customer go.

The second form of reassurance comes from pricing chaos. Customers want to know that they have got a good deal, that they are not stupid buyers and that they have not been ripped off. Pricing chaos helps provide this reassurance, while giving the business the chance to price profitably. Essentially pricing chaos and segmentation go together.

Here are two examples. First, let's take telephones. It should be possible to compare prices on the humble phone call. In practice, it is not. There are several thousand tariffs. By mixing line rental, call charges, volume discounts, free minutes, differential tariffs for different times of day to different types of phone at different destinations, phone companies have made price comparisons between carriers an arcane art.

Calls from the UK to Japan can cost anything from 1p a minute to £1 per minute. This allows carriers to make profit. Industry pricing has disguised the essential commodity nature of the product. But it also allows customers to believe that they are getting a good deal: they can always find some package that suits their particular usage patterns. Customers can always create a good story, or post-rationalization, as to why their deal is the best: because they don't pay any line rental; or they get a lot of free minutes every month; or calls are cheap at peak periods or at off-peak periods. Chaos allows consumers to create in their mind the story that reassures them they have done the right thing.

Second, let's look at electrical goods retailing. Everyone wants to believe they have driven the best bargain on a new computer. The evidence of how people shop is that the belief of getting the good deal is more important than the reality. After a little shopping around consumers get totally confused about all the different makes and models, the different options in terms of delivery, installation, service, guarantees. After a while, they give up. They want a salesperson to give them some decent guidance, and to reassure them that they have made a good decision. This allows the manufacturer to price for profit, and it allows consumers to be given some rationale for why they have made a good decision.

Uncontrolled chaos

This is familiar in business-to-business selling. There is the price list, on which profit assumptions are made. But then, one fast-moving consumer goods (FMCG) firm offered its retailers the following:

- prompt payment discounts;
- new store stock allowances;
- featuring and advertising allowances;
- occasional promotional allowances;
- returned goods allowances;
- coupon handling rebates;
- volume discounts.

By the time the list price had cascaded through all these discounts and allowances, the achieved price could be 25 per cent lower than the list price. Given the net margin was about 8 per cent, this was a recipe for disaster. Control over the discounts and allowances was split between the finance, sales and marketing departments. And the information systems could not track clearly the achieved price and profitability by product and customer. Essentially, profit was being eroded in an uncontrolled way for unknown benefit.

Pricing for profit

Profit is a function of margin and volume. The perils of overpricing and losing volume are acutely seen and felt. The perils of underpricing are just as acute. Raising margins from 8 per cent to 10 per cent has the same effect as a 25 per cent volume increase. The way pricing is set is central to profitability, and is often poor. The pricing questions that are asked are often the wrong questions. **Asking the wrong question is a good way of getting the wrong answer**. The wrong questions focus on margins. The right questions focus on value. Typically, there are two sorts of margin-driven question. First, cost plus calculation. The aim is to sustain margins by setting a target margin. Second, the historic price plus calculation. This is a minor variation on the cost plus equation. It takes last year's prices and tries to adjust them up by inflation or better.

The margin-driven approach has internal logic. And it is extremely easy to apply. There are simple, visible metrics that drive the pricing decision. It is a relatively simple process. It keeps the accountants happy: it is a rational way of keeping the financial ratios whole. As a way of setting pricing tactics day to day it is fine.

But in many industries it is fatally flawed as a logic. It ignores the customers' point of view, until customers start voting with their feet and deserting the business. That is the only signal that the business gets that it is overpricing. It gets no signal that it is underpricing. As an incrementalist approach it does nothing to attack some of the broader risks and opportunities of the business. The day-to-day pricing tactics need to be set within the context of a clear customer- and competitor-focused pricing strategy.

Pricing and value questions are externally focused, and harder but more profitable and sustainable to answer than internally focused margin discussions. The ideal pricing strategy is customer-focused. It asks: what value are we adding to the customer? The answer is normally messy. Different customers give different answers, and it is difficult to pin a price on both the tangible and intangible value of the offering. The effective pricing strategy has four major elements:

- It clearly focuses on value, not just price. Value is about product performance versus price and expectations. So the pricing decision is part of the broader product and positioning question. It will also force the discussion about how value and price can be differentiated to different customer segments.

- The market logic and financial logic should marry. The market logic should force difficult questions about how to achieve superior product and cost performance. The financial demands for profitability should force the awkward questions about how to go to market effectively.

- The pricing discussion should be based on aggression, not incrementalism. There are two forms of aggression. The Japan Inc version typically looked at rapid volume and share growth supported by pricing down the learning curve: lowering prices in expectation of future scale cost reductions, which are achieved by lower prices. The alternative is to look at aggressive price increases to maximize profitability.

- Pricing will look at competitive logic. Aggressive pricing upwards can send strong signals to competition and help industry pricing and profitability rise. Downwards pricing either destroys industry profitability and is self-defeating, or simply leaves one winner in place.

Pricing strategy in action: the launch of Ariel Automatic

Detergents are seen by many as close to being a commodity. Even the industry began to fall into the trap of treating them as a commodity. The pricing strategies of the leading brands all called for prices within 3 per cent of the market leader. This was the classic incrementalist approach to pricing that was generating unacceptable profit. Competitively, there was no escape.

Then P&G decided to launch a new flagship detergent: Ariel Automatic. Everything was set, and on the day of the launch the salespeople gathered to see the dry ice, dancing girls and detergent. They were disappointed. The launch was pulled, at the last moment.

Those at head office had had second thoughts about the pricing strategy, which had been to stay within 3 per cent of the market leader. Given the trade would accept lower margins on the market leader, this meant that the price to the public would be about the same as the competitor's market leader. The economics sucked. One week later, the salespeople got to see the dry ice, dancing girls and detergent. But the real eye-opener was the price: a full 7 per cent above that of the market leader. This was busting the commodity mindset big time. The implications of this decision were huge:

- The economics of Ariel Automatic were transformed, enabling it to double the advertising spend and get the message across that it was a truly better product. The high price justified the advertising and vice versa.

- The economics of the industry were transformed: competition got a signal that it was safe to price up occasionally, not always to price down. Ariel Automatic gave the industry pricing cover.

- A high price/high value position denied the market leader the traditional response to a new entrant. Normally it would lead a short sharp price war. The biggest brand with the most trade power and lowest costs would always win. A price war would be financially painful against the higher margin Ariel Automatic. It would also reinforce in the customer's mind the perceived quality gap between the brands.

- Strategically, Ariel Automatic outflanked the market leader. The market leader was caught between the low price products on one hand and the high price products on the other. It could not fight on both fronts and had to concede share somewhere. Pricing had created different market segments.

Other examples demonstrate the potential of pricing for value. In none of these cases would a cost plus logic reach the pricing or profit potential that value pricing achieves:

- Mineral water has minimal product costs, but can retail for US $3 per litre. The value is in the convenience, perceived taste and health benefit, and status.

- Airlines charge anything from US $300 to US $10,000 to cross the Atlantic on the same plane at the same time. The difference is space, a low-cost investment in some food and wine, and status.

- Consulting firms will hire a new graduate for US $50,000 and charge the graduate out at US $250,000. The value is not in the individual consultant, but in the solution that the consultant promises to bring to the client's business.

Pricing, profits and prison

Making a 10 per cent price rise stick is a lot more pleasant than trying to find another 10 per cent off the cost base. And it has more instant gratification than hoping to double sales volume, which would have the same effect if margins are at 10 per cent currently in a variable cost business.

The problem, of course, is making the pricing stick without being crushed in the stampede of customers heading for the exit to your nearest competitor. Some industries are consistently better at making price rise stick than others. There are, broadly, six ways of making a price rise stick. Some of them are legal.

Create a cartel

This is strictly illegal, unless you are OPEC, in which case it is strictly politics. Some industries still operate effective cartels. In one industry I found that no one spoke of competition. They only referred to their co-producers. Presumably, they used different language to the anti-trust authorities.

There are all sorts of ways of signalling intentions across competition without the cartel having to meet in shady motels or Viennese palaces (OPEC). One cartel contracting for government services used the phases of the moon. Depending on the phase, three competitors would put in very high bids, one would put in a good bid and win. They were caught. In an auction for telecoms licences different competitors used the last three digits of each bid to signal which licence they most wanted. There was no actual collusion or agreement, and the authorities were left frustrated.

The problem with a cartel is that it is illegal. Prison does not get to be more fun the older you get. It is hard to maintain cartel discipline. OPEC has had occasional success and years of failure. It invites new entrants into a market it sees as being profitable and inefficient.

Use pricing signals

It helps if all the competitors have explicit pricing strategies. Unilever and P&G have explicit pricing strategies, and over the years have evolved rules of the game without ever colluding. Price lists inevitably leak from the trade to the competition. Far from damaging commercial confidence, this is helpful. It is a way of checking that pricing strategies remain in place. When one of the price leaders raises prices, all the other brands can follow. When one brand cuts prices, the competition can see whether it is a temporary price reduction for a promotion (retaliation is not normally necessary) or whether it is a permanent reduction (retaliation is absolutely necessary). By reading and respecting the pricing signals, the two competitors can still slug out their brand wars without destroying the pricing structure of the industry. Competition remains, but it is not focused on price. Price discipline is enforced by the retailers' own brands at the bottom end of the market.

Create pricing chaos

In fragmented, competitive markets, pricing signals and disciplines cannot be maintained. If the product is also a commodity, such as a telephone call, potentially prices are driven down to the marginal costs of the weakest competitor. This is not a recipe for profit.

The response of the telephone companies has been to create pricing chaos. There are well over a thousand pricing tariffs in the UK alone, all of which are changing frequently. No one can keep track of all the tariffs, know which is best and keep switching to the best one. The result is that the intensity of pricing competition is reduced, especially as there are switching costs in terms of effort from the telephone user's point of view.

Segment the market

Flying across the Atlantic can cost anything from US $300 to US $10,000 on the same plane. There are some people who will happily pay the US $10,000 (provided the company picks up the tab). For others, the choice will be made on the basis of US $2 difference between the lowest-cost carriers. In between there is a range of trade-offs in terms of convenience, comfort, flexibility. Effective yield management optimizes the revenue from these segments.

Focus on non-price competition

In the retail market, this is the purpose of brands. They promise the customer non-price value, in the form of product performance, values or lifestyle.

The professional services market is profitable because it is based on non-price competition. For instance, in a takeover the predator and the prey do not choose their advisers on the basis of who is cheapest, but on who will maximize their chances of success.

Other business-to-business markets are more susceptible to price competition, especially where there is a price-driven purchasing department intermediating the purchase. As long as the suppliers are unable to deliver value beyond price, they are likely to be locked into a price war. Unless they have a cartel.

The radical alternative: declare an all-out price war

Price wars tend towards death or glory. The glory version is akin to the entry of Japan Inc into autos and consumer electronics in the 1980s. By pricing ahead of the learning curve the company undercut competition, which allowed it to build scale, go further down the learning curve, reduce prices further and enjoy a virtuous circle: low prices to more volume to lower costs to lower prices. Meanwhile the firms in competition were forced into the death spiral of smaller volumes, higher unit costs and higher prices. Eventually, the Japanese turned to non-price competition that has enabled them to sustain scale and profitability.

The price war can backfire. It can attract justified or unjustified anti-trust and government action, such as the imposition of anti-dumping duties on imported steel. It also drives profitability out of the market and makes it difficult for any of the competitors to thrive, as in the global glass industry. It structurally builds low profitability into the industry until the industry is restructured and enough capacity is taken out of the market.

Problems versus solutions

We have all learned the very sensible lesson that we should be solution-focused, not problem-focused. But, like Mars Bars, beer and Morris dancing, you can have too much of a good thing.

One CEO of a leading bank was obsessed with being solution-focused. He gave great speeches about how his bank was going to be the one that always brought solutions, not problems to the table; his management team would be positive, drive to action and get results unlike the wimps in other banks who always find problems. It all sounded very macho and no one dared argue against him.

The CEO's favourite phrase was 'Don't bring me problems, bring me solutions!' So that is what happened: no one dared bring him any problems. They knew that would be a career limiting move. Most of the time this worked: they found solutions and got on with the job. But some problems just grew and grew. The mortgage book, for instance, looked sicker by the day as the economy turned down. Of course, no one told the CEO. And no one stopped selling the dodgy mortgages, because that would mean missing targets and that would be a problem: problems were not allowed. So the bad debt problem spiralled out of control.

Eventually, the inevitable happened: the bank went bust for more billions than you or I can imagine and the CEO was fired with a great big pension to compensate him for destroying a long-established, major bank.

Strong managers are, of course, solution- and action-focused. But they are not blind to problems. Problems happen all the time, because that is the nature of the world: suppliers mess up, the economy hits a bump, technology changes, the competition does something unexpected. Occasionally, we might even mess up ourselves. Stuff happens. The solution is not to stick your head in the sand or to go round making macho speeches about bringing solutions not problems. Don't create fear around raising problems. You need to hear about problems early so you can act on them fast and contain them. **You cannot deal with a problem you do not know about.**

Processed to death

Programme management is, in theory, a very good discipline. In practice, it has become a way for more unscrupulous consultants and contractors to rip off the risk-averse public sector. In the toxic public–private sector interface, programme management is no longer the means to an end: it has become an end in its own right.

Programme management has the veneer of professional management. It sounds sophisticated. It is certainly complicated by the time the consultants and contractors have got hold of it. In one case I saw the consultants produce risk logs, issue logs, progress logs, meeting logs and master logs. They had project initiation documents and work packages all of which had to be designed, reviewed and approved through a programme structure going up to a programme board. There were escalation procedures, review procedures and monitoring procedures. It was a field day for the lawyers who had to draw up the contractual arrangements.

This programme management took up a huge amount of time and effort: over 35 per cent of the programme budget was devoted to it. There was one tiny problem with all this programme management: it did not actually do anything. It led to no results and no action on the ground. It was just administrative overhead. We removed the entire programme management work stream and the result was that the programme worked better.

The fallacy of programme management is to believe that if you control the process you control the outcome. In practice, a good process leads to a good process and nothing else. To be effective, programme management has to focus on outcomes, not just on process. Knowing the difference between process, outputs and outcomes is vital:

- Process focus involves risk logs, issue logs, progress logs, review procedures, monitoring and assessment, governance.
- Output focus reveals, for example, number of people trained; number of phone calls made; lines of code written.
- Outcome focus is concerned with, for example, grades achieved at school; prisoners who no longer reoffend; profits made.

Effective managers in the private sector focus on outcomes relentlessly, and are often highly flexible about how they get there. Being slaves to a process is often unhelpful. When Whitehall becomes more outcome-focused, we will all benefit.

Professionals and pyramids

Professional service firms are pyramid structures. They are also pyramid selling schemes. The **partners take all the financial gain while junior staff do all the work**. As with all pyramid selling schemes, this only works as long as the pyramid keeps growing. As soon as the pyramid stops growing, disaster strikes. It is possible to argue about the morality of this. It is more profitable to argue about the career implications of this. In essence it means that a small partnership has a better chance of sustaining fast growth and creating more partnership opportunities than a large partnership. Do the maths.

Let's say two consulting firms maintain a ratio of 15 staff to 1 partner. The average time it takes to become a partner is eight years. Both firms grow at 20 per cent per annum. Firm A has 100 people. Firm B has 60,000 people.

In both firms, the chances of becoming partner, provided they promote 100 per cent from within, are about 3.5 to 1. If the time to partner is extended to 10 years the chances become 2.5 to 1, but no one wants to wait that long. So the pressure is on to promote people faster. That can only be done if people are also weeded out faster, or if the growth rate is faster.

Small firm A only has to grow to 429 staff to sustain a 20 per cent annual growth rate. Big firm B will have to grow to be a mega-firm with over 250,000 staff to achieve 20 per cent annual growth for eight years. That is not a partnership, it is a bureaucracy. It is not based on having the best talent, but having the best machine with average talent. And it also faces a big challenge in growing to 250,000 staff. The chances are its growth will be slow, while the small firm can grow fast.

Different growth rates dramatically affect the potential to become a partner. If the growth rate slows, in the conditions described above, to 15 per cent annually only 1 in 5 new recruits can expect to become a partner. Smaller firm B, if it grows at 25 per cent annually, can expect to make 1 in 2.5 recruits into a partner. Arguably, if recruits cannot do the maths and cannot figure out the risks, then they deserve to end up in the wrong firm. The trade-off is between business risk (the smaller partnership could fail) and promotion risk (the larger partnership will not fail so badly, but its growth prospects are not so great either). Even the maths may not help. The temptation for the partners to sell out before you get there is just too great.

Professors and the one night stand

Good business school professors are great for a one night stand. They are very smart, entertaining and they normally have one great insight and one great speech in them. After one night you have got the insight and got the speech from them, and they have done the job of energizing and enthusing the team with a new perspective.

The temptation is to then ask them back again for some more of the magic. Don't ask them back. You will simply see the same trick again, or a pedestrian imitation of someone else's trick. The magic will be gone and you will be disappointed. (A few world-class professors stretch to two tricks, one stretches to three.)

Remember that their magic is essentially a solution looking for a problem. It is the same solution, the same insight that they bring to every company. If you have their problem, great. If not, they are still worthwhile for the entertainment value and the different perspective. Just don't expect to get your problem solved.

Also, the stories and the cases they give you in immense detail are not true. They are not trying to recount history. They are trying to make a point. Nowadays, professors have got smart about this. Working with one professor in Europe, I was astounded by the range and depth of cases he was able to draw on from Asia. Working with him in Asia, he told all the same stories but with all his cases drawn on European companies. I knew they were detailed works of fiction, but the audience had no chance of catching him out.

Project management

The four horsemen of the apocalypse

There are four ways to destroy a project. Savvy consultants and managers know this instinctively and respond accordingly.

The wrong problem

The best way to focus on the wrong problem is to focus on the latest fad or solution, and to decide to implement it. Many consulting firms will happily aid and abet you. They need to sell something to keep the revenues flowing and they probably have teams that can do the fad. The partner gets no reward for not selling, or selling something that you need and the partner cannot deliver.

You may have the right problem if you can clearly see some significant benefits from fixing it. Size the prize: the prize does not have to be all financial. If the solution being offered does not yield a big prize, it may well be that it is a solution to a problem that does not really exist.

It does not matter how well you do everything else, if you have the wrong problem, you have the wrong result.

The wrong team

Worthwhile projects are normally tough projects. This means they need great people working on them. So the right people are probably the ones you can least afford. This gets down to priorities. But if the project does not merit the best people, then it probably is not a very significant project. Go back to the problem, size the prize again and work out where it is on the list of corporate priorities.

Surefire losing teams are ones that come from staff functions, or from just one department. The project needs to be embedded in the line and owned by the people that will be responsible for producing the results. This is not the consultants, nor the staff, nor one department alone. It will be cross-functional, and line-led.

The wrong client

The client is the godfather, godmother or sponsor of the project. He or she will be powerful and will have resources and the power to work across the business. Critically, the individual will also have enough time to be a sponsor and to make things happen when they need to.

A sponsor from a staff function, too low in the organization, with no direct stake in the outcome of the project and too busy to sponsor the project, would be a good way of killing the effort.

The right process

Provided you have the right problem and the right team, you will probably find the right process (quality, re-engineering, change management, etc). Select the wrong process and the team will go charging down the wrong road, and will be very difficult to recover.

These four horsemen of the apocalypse will strike before the project has even started. Effectively, by the time the project has started, it is already destined for success or failure. Like most battles, it is won or lost before it starts. This means that over-investing in the right project set-up pays huge dividends later on. The actual management of the project represents 90 per cent of the effort, but influences perhaps 30 per cent of the outcome. And most project management can done by managers, without consultants.

Punks, hippies, experts and the future

In early 1977 I left my hippie friends behind in England. I hit the hippie trail through Afghanistan to Nepal. Six months later I floated back to what I hoped would be a summer of love, only to find that my friends had in fact been punks for at least the last three years. I was baffled: neither they nor I had ever heard of punk until then.

In 1987 re-engineering hit the management world. We had never heard of it before. But this was OK because managers told us that all our projects for the last three years had in fact been re-engineering. We were therefore experts and could go and sell more re-engineering work.

In 1997, I returned to my colleagues in New York after a six-month absence. I suddenly found that they were all internet experts, and had been for the last three years. I had never heard the word before.

In 2007 we had all become convinced that capitalism had found the elixir of eternal growth and prosperity, fuelled by the pixie dust of endless credit. Then we got the hangover with the crash of 2008.

There are some patterns in here somewhere:

- Big change happens in arbitrary 10-year intervals. Beware 2018.

- People lie. At least, they are creative about past reality. They regard past reality as thermoplastic: it can be moulded to the needs of today.

- The future is genuinely unpredictable. You must move with the times. If you don't move you will land up like the managerial equivalent of a superannuated hippie lost in a time warp. This is not a recipe for managerial success.

- Expertise is relative. Use relative expertise to your advantage. If you have seen part of a re-engineering project and no one else has, you are the expert. And despite most of the consulting jargon and bluff that surrounds these fads, at heart most fads are simple. With a little experience, a good reference book and good judgement, you can lead one of these fads. This is what consultants do.

For instance, in late 1996 I returned to the UK. I decided to build a business helping banks prepare for the euro. At the time most banks did not know what EMU stood for. I did. I was the expert. I was probably never more than one step ahead of my clients, but what I learned from one client would help me keep ahead of other clients. We acquired 26 new clients in 18 months, which was exceptional. Never be intimidated by the professed expertise of consultants or others, especially if they are talking about a new fad.

Qualifying quality

Which is higher quality: dinner at a three-star Michelin restaurant such as the Fat Duck at Bray, or a Big Mac at McDonalds? As a consumer, the obvious answer is the dinner at the three-star restaurant. It has quality the same way a Rolls Royce car has quality: it is prestigious, high cost and exclusive. But as you eat your snail mousse you may wonder whether that is what you really expected out of quality.

As a manager, quality is not about making everything expensive and exclusive. **Quality is about consistency.** The Big Mac I bought today in London should taste the same as the Big Mac I bought last month in New York. I do not want to be surprised by finding some very exclusive snail in my Big Mac. If I order a million integrated circuits, I want every one to perform in precisely the same way: I don't want any creative differences in every tenth chip.

The quality movement has done very well in the world of manufacturing, whether you are making micro chips or chips (French fries) to go with the Big Mac. To succeed, the quality movement needs a stable and predictable product: that allows for the creation of a stable and predictable process to make the product. But the management world is never stable or predictable. It is more like the three-star restaurant, where customers come in and suddenly decide to start ordering off menu: you have to be prepared for anything at any time. There is always ambiguity and uncertainty. If you are asked to prepare a report, it could be one page or 100 pages: as a manager you never know when enough is enough, so your work is never done. There is always one more fact to check, one more section to write, one more number to find.

So it is no surprise that the quality movement has made great strides on the shop floor, but virtually no progress in the offices above the shop floor. Instead, managers are gravitating to the next best solution: specialization and scale. The more specialized each role becomes, the more predictable the work becomes and the greater the expertise of each manager becomes, albeit in an increasingly narrow area of expertise.

For instance, consultants used to be general consultants: the same person would work across industries, functions and geographies. Now you have consultants who only build business cases for IT work in the life insurance industry in the UK. Quality is driven by the expertise that comes from focus. In turn, that means that the consulting firms have to be huge to harbour so many different specialists. Law, accounting and the professional services are going the same way.

Outsourcing means that specialists take on jobs that used to be done in house. Most things can be outsourced: accounts payable, IT, receivables, employee benefits, cleaning services. Again, quality comes from having specialist firms who build experience and scale.

This leaves managers in an awkward position. Managers make things happen through other people: they learn the art of motivation, dealing with people and politics, delegation and the challenges of corporate life. You do not learn all of this by writing business cases for IT projects in the UK life assurance industry. Quality encourages you to build deep functional expertise; your career says you must build a broader set of management skills.

Quality zealots

These are dangerous. The mantra is that quality is free, but the price is that you have to sign up to the faith. This means documenting in great detail exactly how you meet voluminous quality standards that are arbitrarily set by a standards body that may or may not know your business.

The consequence of signing up is that all your management time and attention will be devoted to fulfilling these quality standards. Even worse, you will need to prove that you are maintaining these standards through endless documentation.

This is a favourite of government departments. They can use quality certification to show that they are doing a good job. By selecting suppliers that meet these standards, no one can accuse them of doing a bad job. **Quality certificates and manuals are a risk-free substitute for management judgement.**

Quality bureaucracy could be tolerable if it was relevant. But the quality process becomes an end in its own right. Certification becomes the goal, not making a profit or serving the business. In its extreme form it is a way of ensuring that you take far too long to get exactly the wrong product out to the wrong market at the wrong time. But at least you will know that you were wrong in exactly the right way. You should be able to buy the quality certificates from your liquidators at a knock-down price. Quality should be a servant of the business, not the master.

Quick fix fixation

We see the snake oil salespeople coming. We know they are going to con us. We know that they will pitch up with the promise of some corporate quack medicine that will cure everything from a flagging share price, unhappy customers, demotivated staff, to personal and corporate health and happiness. We know it's rubbish. And yet we go on buying it.

We get our fix of each new cure-all: total quality, re-engineering, kaizen, portfolio management, time-based competition. We've been there and we've got the holiday snaps to show it. And of course, the cures never quite deliver what they promise.

We still have flagging share prices, unhappy customers and demotivated staff. So we are all set up for the next snake oil salesperson who comes cruising into town. Either we are all terminally stupid, or there is something else going on. The real questions we should ask are:

- Why do we always fall for the snake oil salesperson?
- Why are the quick fixes destined not to meet expectations?
- What can we do about it?

Why do we always fall for the snake oil salesman?

Managers are rationally making the right choice when they sign up for the latest snake oil, even if they know it will not deliver what it promises. Consider the possible outcomes for managers. If a manager adopts a new fad, he or she cannot lose. If he or she opposes it, he or she cannot win.

The snake oil might actually do some good. Any corporate initiative that gets people together to work out how to improve things is likely to have some benefit. Each new fad gives a structure and focus for getting people together constructively. So if the manager brings in the latest fad, he or she has a chance of winning. He or she may be able to show some progress.

If the initiative does not succeed, the manager is unlikely to lose out. First, most of these initiatives are anchored at the top of the business. Once a CEO has signed up to a programme and has devoted people and money to it, the CEO will not let it fail. The CEO will make sure something comes out of it. Even if the reality is poor, managers will simply declare victory and move on.

If managers do not try the new snake oil, then they are exposed. If things start to go wrong in the business, then the finger can be pointed at the manager who failed to implement a re-engineering effort or a quality programme. Even CEOs do not want to be seen resisting change and best practices. If things go along well without adopting the fad, then there is absolutely no news.

We may be cynical about the fads, but for risk-averse managers adopting the fad is lower risk than opposing it. The greater the marketplace momentum of a fad, the greater the visibility and risk of not adopting it. This is why fads tend to snowball and then die away. As momentum builds, fewer and fewer people want to be left off the bandwagon. Once everyone has been through their re-engineering programme, managers tick that off the list and wait for the next bandwagon to come rolling round the corner.

Why are the quick fixes destined not to meet expectations?

Here's why quick fix fads are destined to fail:

- *They are non-replicable.* The fad is normally built on some case studies where it has had spectacular success. But the cases cannot be replicated accurately, because:
  - The best talent led the spectacular cases: your version of the quick fix will be led by people who have learned about it second- or third-hand. They do not have the same level of skill as the creators of the fad.
  - The fad may be a great solution to someone else's problem.
  - Your conditions are different from the original's. Kaizen may work in Japan, but it is part of a broader system that includes just-in-time production, life-time employment (sometimes), quality, unique corporate relationships and culture and eating sushi. There is not much sushi in West Virginia.
- *The fad is a zero-sum game.* Once everyone has re-engineered and dropped their cost base by 20 per cent, you are no better off in a

relative way than you were before you started. At least operational fads are zero-sum games. Strategy fads are negative-sum games. To the extent that everyone adopts the same strategy prescriptions and analyses at the same time, they will all be attracted to the same markets. This competitive conformity is also competitive suicide, destroying industry profitability until there is an industry consolidation.

- *The fad represents at best a partial solution.* Quality, knowledge management, time-based competition, re-engineering, are all great ideas in their own right. But they are not stand-alone solutions. They need to be integrated into the way the business works.

- *There is poor execution.* This is common, and there are a thousand ways to mess up the execution. Most businesses are quite creative about finding new ways to mess it up. The fundamental problem is that managers are by definition trying something new where they do not have experience. This dramatically increases the chance of failure. The consultants do not help. They will throw in junior staff who have as little knowledge as managers; or the partner has picked his or her knowledge up second-hand. Your only hope is that in the middle there is someone managing the project who actually knows what he or she is doing.

These factors are more or less hard-wired into any quick-fix implementation, and guarantee that the results will not live up to the hype. So this raises a big question: What are we meant to do about it? The solution is not magic. It is common sense.

- *Focus on the problem, not the solution.* When you understand the problem, you have a chance of finding the right solution that may or may not include the fad.

- *Go for a full solution, not a partial solution.* The fad by itself is more or less certainly not the whole solution. Going for the full solution is high effort. Low effort is probably just wasted effort. You may need to implement not just the fad, but much more besides.

- *Put the right people in place.* The right people are probably the people you can least afford. This is about priorities. If the problem does not offer a big prize when fixed, then you probably should not be bothering with the solution or the fad. If it is worthwhile, it will need talent to make it happen. Getting the right people also requires giving the project the right political sponsorship, and finding the right external support if required.

- *Size the prize*. Know how big the opportunity is. Measure and track performance against the prize. The prize is not just financial. If it is a purely financial prize, then you will have people running round cutting budgets for the short term rather than trying to build the long-term capability you need. Ultimately, **if we buy snake oil and it does not work, we know who to blame: ourselves.**

Recruiting

The most intense competition between firms is in the marketplace: the marketplace for customers and the marketplace for talent. The best talent and resources of the firm focus on the customers. Functionaries within HR focus on the marketplace for talent.

Put the best talent onto the talent hunt: this is the future survival of the business. Those who are the best talent can easily be spotted: they are the ones who are not available. Most big professional service firms have it about right. They send out a mix of recent graduates who have credibility and relevance to the campus recruits, together with some senior managers. Choose the senior managers with care. Do not just send the person with the biggest title. Students are unaware of all the fine nuances of your hierarchy, and are not impressed by it anyway. The test for the senior manager is whether the students would aspire to be like that person in 20 years' time. A heavyweight, crusty old fart does not meet the bill.

Every firm sells the same pitch, so no one believes it: we are the fastest growing; we are the biggest and most individualistic; we are entrepreneurial but risk-free; we are hard-working and family-friendly. Students do sometimes appear marginally cynical because of this. Find a distinctive message that is true to what you are. It is possible to be both positive and honest.

Do not let recruiting professionals do the interviewing selection and follow-up tasks. This is your decision, and you need to show your commitment to the recruits. The only question that flushes out the true opinion of fellow interviewers is the acid test for managers: 'Will you take this person on your team for next year?' Let them know that if they say yes, they are likely to get the person. Make managers live with their decisions.

Re-engineering re-engineering

Re-engineering is in urgent need of re-engineering. **Re-engineering** as sold by consultants is a deeply perverted form of re-engineering as it was conceived. It **has become little more than cost cutting with a smile. And**

the smile is optional. There are three distinct forms of re-engineering being touted in the marketplace.

IT-enabled re-engineering

This provides a technology fix to inefficient operational processes that wind through the business like a cow path through a field. The technology may not straighten or simplify cow paths, it may simply pave them over. High fixed-cost technology replaces high variable-cost labour. The system remains inherently inefficient, but now it is also inherently inflexible; adapting the processes to future requirements takes a significant technology cost.

Process re-engineering

In its traditional form, this is a charter for the consultants to go in and map out all the process flows of the business. It is simple, high-margin, high-leverage work for the consultancies. They like to sell it. If they do it well, they will straighten out the cow paths, and the business will reduce its costs and increase its speed of operation. It looks successful. But it is based on a purely internal view of the world that assumes that the existing processes are the right processes delivering the right products and services to the right customers. If any of these implicit assumptions are wrong, process re-engineering simply takes the business up a blind alley. Process re-engineering focuses on doing things efficiently. This is useless if it enables the business to do the wrong things efficiently.

Business re-engineering

This is closer to the original vision of re-engineering spelt out in *Reengineering the Corporation* by Champy and Hammer (1993). Business re-engineering starts with the marketplace. It is forward-looking and asks the basic questions about what is the very best way to go to market. It does not start with the status quo of today. It does not require hoards of analysts mapping what you already know. It requires the best brains thinking about how to design a business for tomorrow. It is less re-engineering; it is more about creating the zero-based business. It is what the successful dot.coms like Amazon have done. It simply blows away the old way of doing things. It presumes that businesses do not shrink their way to success, but should grow their way to success. From the consulting point of view, this is high-risk, low-revenue and low-leverage work. Do not expect to see much of it being sold.

Re-engineering: sheep and wolves

Consultants and senior managers sell re-engineering as transformation. Others, when they hear the sales pitch, hear rightsizing, downsizing, redeploying, cutting and firing staff. Re-engineering has earned itself a bad name. When you hear re-engineering is around, there are four possible survival strategies. These are common to all threatening initiatives, and threatening bosses:

- *Ignore it and hide.* This is called the 'get lucky' strategy. It is the strategy of sheep: they hope that the wolf will pick another sheep. The sheep strategy identifies you as a potential victim. You are likely to land up as dead meat.

- *Fight it.* **Sheep do not have a good track record of killing wolves.** But at least it is a more spectacular way to go. Re-engineering is normally driven top–down. Resistance is tough.

- *Run.* Find another shepherd, another department or firm where there are no re-engineering wolves, or you can be protected. Good survival chances, but everyone else is also going to be running, so you need to run fastest.

- *Join the wolves.* Sheep in wolves' clothing are not always convincing. But it is the safest place to be. You get to pick who the victims will be. Unless you have a strong death wish, you will not pick yourself.

Resisting insanity

You do not have to succumb to the latest hare-brained initiative oozing its way out of the executive suite. There are plenty of ways of stopping it, without resisting it:

- *Ignore it.* Hopefully the executive achieves a moment of sanity and quietly kills the initiative. Or the executive will be promoted or moved, or you will get moved in the next reorganization before anything happens.

- *Reinvent reality.* If all commerce in your organization has to be e-based, show how all your work is now e-based. If you use a computer, then it must be e-based. This keeps everyone happy that the targets have been met without doing anything.

- *Pass the buck*. Agree it is a great idea that would be ideal for the people in marketing or sales or engineering or whoever. Make sure they are too busy to deal with the idea.

- *Agree with the idea*. Set up a team to look at how to implement it. Come back enthusiastically with the recommendations that require doubling your budget, reallocating resources away from the bosses' other pet projects and that will cause maximum harm and disruption.

- *Delay, obfuscate and confuse*. Muddy the waters about who has to do what, when, where and why. By the time this is sorted out, the idea should be past its sell-by date.

Whatever you do, don't resist openly. You will no longer be a team player. You will be a problem. Worse, it will force the issue into the open and bring about exactly the actions you want to stop. Apathy is the best resistance: it puts all the pressure on managers to create the momentum. They probably lack the time, focus, resources or energy to overcome corporate apathy. If they don't, then it is probably worth getting on board the bandwagon.

The respect agenda

I was in the Highlands of Papua New Guinea working with a tribe that had survived wars, famine and disaster with minimal help or resources. I had been asking members of the tribe about their culture, so they asked me what was important about ours.

'Respect for the individual' I replied, without thinking. Respect people for who they are and what they do, regardless of their faith, colour or sex. The tribal elders looked aghast at this revolutionary concept. They saw it as a recipe for individualism, competition, politics and conflict. **Any tribe that fights itself will not last long.**

'There is something much more important than respect for the individual' said the elder. I looked blankly at him and wondered what he was getting at. 'Respect for the community – without that we all die.' Looking at some of the strongest organizations that last the longest, they have the same assumption: respect for the community trumps respect for the individual. The armed forces put this to an extreme, and religious orders are not far behind. The Catholic church has survived for much longer than the great businesses of today by following this principle.

Every organization and every team can build respect for the community: show that you have a worthwhile goal; live but do not preach good values; celebrate successes together and fix problems together; be loyal to each other. These things will help your team members work not just for themselves, but for the organization as a whole.

Responsibility

Part 1

Responsibility is the one thing managers cannot delegate away. Ultimately, we are always responsible for the performance and outcomes of our teams and our business. When you try shifting the blame, you look weak and defensive and you set up toxic tensions in your team: everyone starts playing the politics of the blame game.

Part 2

But there is one other thing all managers are responsible for: our own feelings. We can choose how we feel. If we want to feel angry, frustrated and depressed, we will feel that way. No one will tell us to feel that way. We can then watch as our little cloud of gloom spreads like a major depression across the whole office. We should not then be surprised by the storms that follow, and are unlikely to lighten our mood.

But we can also choose to feel positive, enthusiastic and energetic. And most of our teams will mirror our feelings: they will act more positively and enthusiastically. You create a virtuous circle for yourself and your team.

When the slings and arrows of outrageous fortune rain down on us, it is easy to fall into a foul mood. But we do not have to: we can choose how we want to react to all the bad stuff. Effective leaders learn to **wear the mask of leadership**: they project the character they want to project. You can choose to be angry or positive, authoritarian or inclusive, defensive or open, depressed or enthusiastic. There are endless masks for you to wear. Choose well.

Revenge

From time to time, we all get stiffed. Sometimes the other person has been a miserable, malicious, Machiavellian mismanager. Other times the person has been plain incompetent, and you have been left holding the baby. It is tempting to seek revenge. It is not worth it, and it does not work.

If you try to get revenge, everyone sees what you are doing and all the individual and institutional defences go up. You just discredit yourself. If you stay aloof, it is possible that days, months or years later the chance for quiet revenge comes along. Take it if you want. But do not bother to wait for the opportunity. Revenge is immediate and at hand. It is called happiness.

Happiness is the ultimate revenge, because no one can take it away from you. And this will infuriate your detractors: the more they see you are calm, collected, confident and happy, the more frustrated they will become that they have not got to you. Their behaviour will become more dysfunctional, while you will continue to look professional: you win, they lose. You only lose when you sink to their level.

Churchill was once accused of being drunk at dinner. He turned to his accuser and said: 'I may be drunk, but you are ugly. At least in the morning, I will be sober.' Leave the ugly feelings and behaviour to others: that is the way they are today and the way they will be tomorrow.

Reviewing documents: the art of reading

This is when the reviewer gets reviewed. Members of a team fix a time to review a document or a presentation they are preparing. They expect you to be smart, constructive and add some value. You may quietly be judging whether they are any good. But they will certainly be judging whether you are any good, and will have no hesitation in telling each other what their verdicts are. Your competence as a manager is about to be assessed by the toughest group of all: your team.

Some people are naturally smart and brilliant and can look at the document in real time and add great insight. This is also a managers' ego trip: it shows that they are so busy, smart and important they do not have the time or need to do any preparation. For many of us, this is not a clever option.

Others ask for the papers in advance and carefully prepare lots of comments. Sometimes this just does not work logistically. And teams do not like it: it slows them down and then you cease to be their coach; you become their examiner. So, you may well land up having to do the review in real time.

The key to success is not to rely on having to react to what is in front of you. This simply lets you get trapped in the internal logic, which may or may not be great. Instead, prepare your own criteria ready for looking at what is produced. At this point, four minutes' preparation makes all the difference. Quickly jot down four things:

- Your argument or point of view on the subject the team members are seeing you about. This will give you something against which to test their ideas.
- The content headings you expect to see covered in the document. This lets you see the invisible: the items that are missing.
- What next steps you expect to see to ensure momentum is maintained.
- Any coaching items you want to cover with the team on either substance or style.

With this is in your mind you have a proactive agenda to work with them, a distinct point of view to offer, and a yardstick against which to measure what the members of the team have done. Even if the document is sent to you in advance, it is still worth going through the four-minute test before opening the document and getting sucked into its logic. Do this, and you are in danger of looking naturally smart. Your office reputation might actually survive.

Reading for pleasure is reactive: you are taken on a journey by the author. Reading for business is different. It is about reading for a purpose. **To read well, read with prejudice and purpose**: know what you are looking for.

A similar method can be used in any meeting or at any presentation. Do not simply react to what is being discussed or presented. Jot down your own point of view and expectations before the presentation contaminates your mind. You will be able to make a much better intervention.

Risk and marzipan

People hate losing. Humans are risk-averse animals. And the more we have, the more risk averse we are, because we have more to lose. The great risk takers, the entrepreneurs, tend not to be people in big management positions with big titles and big salaries. They do not give it all up to do some start-up in a garage, unless they suddenly lose their job anyway. The start-ups in garages are for dropouts. Bill Gates and Steve Jobs gambled when they had little to lose: no mortgage, no school fees, no family to feed. Managerial risk has real-life complications and opportunities:

- *Where there is risk, there is resistance.* The resistance is to the risk of loss. Managing resistance is often about managing risk.

- *Resistance to big change often comes from the 'marzipan' layer of management.* The 'icing layer' (top managers) are in control of change. Since they are leading change they are reasonably confident they will be safe. The 'sponge' layer (junior managers) have less to lose, and more to gain from a shake-up of the business. Those at the marzipan layer have most to lose, least to gain, and lack control. Changing the loss, gain and control equation is important.

- *Risk is personal.* Managers have no difficulty taking risks on behalf of the organization. That is what they are paid to do. It can be rationally managed. Personal risk is emotional, and theoretically off-limits as a management issue. Unless the emotion of personal risk is managed, resistance will appear under all sorts of rational guises. Trying to deal with the rational objections will miss the point and result in frustration all round.

- *Risk is unequal.* People have different risk appetites, and what is safe for one person is risky for another. Again, this means that risk management has to be customized to the individual.

There are four ways of dealing with risk:

- Take away or reduce the risk.

- Increase the reward relative to the risk; given people's risk aversion, an exponential increase in rewards equates to a linear reduction in the risk side of the equation.

- Increase the individual's control over the situation. Most perceived risk comes from fear of the unknown. If you give people control, the fear reduces and the perceived risk reduces.

- Increase the perceived risk of all other options. People will do nothing until doing nothing becomes the riskiest option. Create the crisis: show that the status quo will lead to the sky falling down and people will start to move.

Risk is not absolute and not logical, it is relative and personal.

Rushing and relaxing

One of the smartest people I ever knew believed that if he did not miss at least 1 flight in 10, he was wasting too much time. He was always running from meeting to meeting at top speed, to fit everything in. He was a very stressed person. He smoked too much, drank too much and died too young.

The best salesperson I know is not that smart. Whenever he goes to a big new client he goes outrageously early. Even if the plane is delayed, the taxi gets lost and he has been given the wrong address, he still has enough time to get there.

This is not just about avoiding missing the meeting. It is about being relaxed and prepared. Because he knows he will be early, he concentrates on preparing for the meeting, not on how he will get there. When the meeting starts he is 100 per cent ready and focused. He does not go to many client meetings, but each one is a knockout. **The tortoise that moves with purpose beats the hare running round in circles.**

Of course, he also drinks too much and smokes too much. But he is much less stressed, and he is still alive.

Salaries and secrets

There is an obsession with secrecy. Secrecy just encourages rumour, gossip and misinformation. Blow it away. There should be a presumption of openness, not of secrecy. Secrecy belongs to the old command and control environment of the traditional hierarchy.

Salary is a sacred cow when it comes to secrecy. Kill it. Publish the salary information. It stops all the salary rumour and gossip, and gives staff useful information. It shows them clearly who is perceived as successful. It is a clear way for managers to indicate who the successful role models are. You would hope that it gives staff some aspirations in terms of their earnings potential. **Dumb staff ask 'How can I earn 10 per cent more?' Smart staff ask 'How can I earn 10 times as much?'** The 10 per cent crowd are focused on winning small in this year's salary negotiation. The 10 times crowd want to win big by getting their career right, rather than worrying about small amounts this year.

Publishing the salary information puts pressure on all the right people. Individuals who achieve a big salary increase will be under real peer pressure to show that they are worth it. Senior managers will have to show that they are worth it to the most demanding critics: their teams. Managers will be under pressure to get the results right.

Publishing the salary data also brings true market forces into play. The competition and headhunters may find out. If they can poach the lower-paid staff, no problem. Provided managers have rightly judged the capability of the lower-paid staff. If the higher-paid staff are being poached, that's a signal that managers are underpaying the key talent.

Seagull management

This is the preferred form of management for 'big bananas' from other offices. They want to show they are pressing the flesh, in touch with the business and they are adding value. So they fly by and drop guano. The fly-by is the one- or two-day visit. They say they want to add value, so instead of having some internal meetings they demand to see all your most senior clients and add some value to them. They do not know the clients or the businesses, but have a simple faith that their innate brilliance will somehow rub off on the clients.

As they leave, they drop their guano. This is in the form of some gratuitous advice that they will expect to see followed up. They will also leave you with a big post-dated cheque. They will tell you what a wonderful opportunity you now have at client X. The implication is that they have created the opportunity. So if the sale comes through, they get the credit. If it does not, you're a turkey.

Shooting seagulls is tempting. I prefer slowly boiling them. In Japan we always had big bananas coming through, normally with their family, on a company-sponsored holiday. We had a simple routine:

- From the moment the big banana stepped off the plane after a 14-hour journey, the diary would be filled for 16 hours a day with meetings, briefings and dinners. Big bananas are normally macho, so a busy diary is a Good Thing. And they do not want to show weakness in front of their underlings. We, meanwhile, covered the big banana in shifts to stay fresh.

- Most of the external meetings would be with Japanese clients. They do not speak English. This minimizes the chances for gratuitous advice, and adds to the sense of confusion, culture shock and jet lag the big banana is feeling.

- One or two meetings would be set up with tame Western clients. They all have the same big banana problem, and would know exactly what script was required. They would focus on how difficult and expensive business was in Japan, and what a wonderful job we were doing. We would return the favour later.

- We would let the big bananas pay for dinner. The big bananas would probably think they were buying the restaurant, not the dinner. Expenses did not get questioned again.

- We let them go from one meeting to another unaccompanied, just once. They would get lost, freaked out and spend a fortune. And they would learn to respect the challenges of doing business in Japan.

- At the end of the allotted 48 hours, we would take them to the airport and ask for their advice. One big banana looked at me in despair and said: 'They don't speak English!' At least he had learned something.

In every business there are similar defensive routines to deal with the big bananas who come flying through.

Sell-by dates: when to move on

We all have a sell-by date, which is when it is time to move on. There is an ultimate sell-by date, which is beyond our control. It's the same date that will appear after 'best before...' on our gravestones. It's worth knowing when you are reaching your professional sell-by date. There are five warning signs:

- The job is boring or unenjoyable. You know this as you struggle into work each day. Listen to your instincts.

- You are not learning or developing any more. Ideally, the job would always be stretching. There should be moments when you feel that you are outside your comfort zone. If the whole job is well within your comfort zone, you are going nowhere. This drift can carry on a long time, until you wake up one day and find the world has passed you by.

- You cannot see clear progression ahead. I use a simple benchmark: can I see a way of earning 10 times as much in 10 years' time? If I can, I know I can see a way of stretching and developing: I will be doing something totally different and more challenging at the end of the 10 years. I started at 50p an hour. It's worked since then. Everyone will have a different way of looking at progress.

- How will I remember the next one or two years when I retire? This is the test of are you doing something that is intrinsically memorable and exciting today. **Life should be led with the record button on, and in full technicolour.** Don't let the years slip away in monochrome before deleting them from memory. It helps if you feel that you would not only remember the next two years, but that talking about them would be of interest to other people. Going into the office and having meetings fails this test.

- Performance is declining and the politics are moving against you. These may well go hand in hand, and are probably a sign of burnout and demotivation. Read the signals early and act on them before you go into a death spiral in the current job. You do not want to become damaged goods on the market. The stress and excitement of a new start in a new environment will be energizing.

Selling

One-to-one tactics

Managers do not like to be called salespeople. But good managers are always selling. They are in the business of selling ideas to bosses, peers and staff. They are trying to motivate, enlist support and get action. Bad managers do not see the need to sell. They hope that traditional command and control is enough to tell people what to do. Command and control is for administrators seeking compliance, not for managers seeking commitment.

Perhaps the most important thing for salespeople to remember is that **we were born with two ears and one mouth, and we should use them in that proportion**. Effective selling is not about making a pitch. It is about listening intently, and understanding the expectations, prejudices and concerns of the other side. Once you really understand that, you have some chance of communicating in a way that will be well received. The blind pitch is an invitation to disaster.

Having said that, it is worth having a model of how to sell. I was taught a method of selling soap in Northern Scotland. I also used it to sell nappies to chemists in Birmingham. And I used it to sell multi-million dollar projects to CEOs in the United States, Japan and Europe. And I have used it to sell my bosses and staff on ideas for the business. The principles are the same the world over. The most important steps of the seven-step model are the first and last. The steps are:

1 *Agree the problem or situation.* You cannot do this unless you understand it from the buyer's point of view. That means preparing and listening. If you both totally agree on the problem, the chances are that the solution will pop out easily. The rest of the sale is easy. And you cannot sell a solution to a problem that does not exist.

2 *Agree the benefits fixing the problem:* they should be tangible, relevant and credible. Benefits are not simply financial and business-focused. They are sometimes intangible, non-measurable and personal. Removing risk can be a huge benefit to individuals. From the start you want buyers excited about some good outcomes they can expect to enjoy. This will put any concerns they may have into perspective.

3 *Suggest the solution.* This should be short, sharp and simple.

4 *Explain how it works.* Show the suggestion is practical. This should address the questions you know will be asked. Avoid unnecessary

detail. The more detail you give, the more likely you are to get bogged down in discussion about the detail, not about the big idea. Brevity is good.

5 *Pre-empt any big concerns*. You should know what they are, especially if you have been listening. By pre-empting buyers' concerns you show that you are positive, you understand their situation and you are responsive to their needs. Handling objections reactively always appears defensive and can degenerate into an unnecessary conflict.

6 *Reinforce the benefits of the suggestion*. This is the time you want the buyer focused on the prize.

7 *Close*. This is crucial. It is where you get the buyer's agreement. A good close is not an open question such as 'What do you think?' Open questions invite the buyer to start acting as judge and jury, and he or she may come up with the wrong verdict. You want the buyer to be moving into action with you. A good close focuses on action. Typical examples could include: the alternate close: 'Shall we start this week, or would you prefer for us to start next week?' or the action close: 'Would you like me to draft the memo announcing this?'

The close can be brought forward. If the buyer is ready to buy, close and stop selling. You will only frustrate the buyer and you create the risk of unselling the sale.

This sales process can take place over weeks for the more complicated and risky sale where you need to build trust and intimacy. The longer it takes, the more listening you probably have to do. It can also take place over a few seconds for an easy sale to people you know. For example, when getting your team to the pub at the end of a long day:

- State the problem: 'Tough day today.'
- Preview the benefits: 'We should relax.'
- Make a suggestion: 'Let's go to the pub.'
- State how it works: 'It's just next door, we can talk things over there.'
- Pre-empt objections: 'Just a pint and we can still get the last train home, I'm buying.'
- Reinforce the benefits: 'It's better than sticking round here getting more frustrated.'
- Close: 'Last one out, turn off the lights' (action close).

If you are getting nowhere with a sale, go right back to step one. If there are objections, listen and listen again. Show you understand the objections by paraphrasing them back. If the objection is simple, it will go away. Do not get into a conflict trying to handle objections. The conflict will only destroy trust and make the sale harder.

Disagreement over the problem or the situation is probably at the root of your difficulties. And the nature of the problem may well be personal: how the individual will be affected by what you are suggesting. It does not matter that the person's fears appear to be irrational, they have to be overcome. Only when you have shown that you understand and respect the other person's situation will you have the trust to start the sales process over again. And you have the knowledge about how to pre-empt the person's concerns. When you first use this, it will feel awkward and clumsy. Eventually it is as easy as breathing air.

The big complex sale

As a junior manager, selling can be simple. You only need to persuade the boss and maybe one or two other people that your idea is good, and you have succeeded. As managers gain seniority, the selling task becomes much more complicated. There are multiple constituencies with different agendas, over whom you have no power, that need to agree with what you want to do. These sales always take longer and are much tougher.

But at heart, the same principles apply as one-to-one selling. You are applying the same selling skills, not just one to one, but to a whole network of people in one-to-one situations. The big sales meeting may happen at the end, but that simply confirms the outcomes of all the one-to-one sales you have already done. To identify the network you need to sell to, spot the following:

- *The authorizer of your initiative*. This will probably be a senior executive who is above all the constituencies you need to align. The authorizer will rely on the views of all the different constituencies, and may not be deeply involved. Opposition from the authorizer is fatal. Access to the authorizer can be difficult and intimidating. Get access early to understand his or her agenda. Align your proposal with that agenda, and your conversations with the rest of the network will be transformed.

- *User buyers*. These are the people who day to day will live with the consequences of your proposal and may have to implement it. This could include you. Users should be turned into the champions of the proposal. The benefits to the users are not just rational business benefits. They must also be personal benefits, where the career opportunities are great and the risks are neutralized in your proposal. It is an emotional and political sale to the users, not just rational.

- *Economic buyers*. This will largely be a rational sale to bean counters in finance or accounting. Give them the chance and they like to act as judge and jury. Do not let this happen: it is a game where you are guilty until proved innocent. Remember the mafia saying: **keep your friends close and keep your enemies closer**. Co-opt the economic buyers early: seek their input and get them to build the business case with you. Then, when the user or authorizer asks the statutory awkward financial question, let the economic buyers respond. The economic credibility of your proposal will not be questioned again.

- *Technical buyers*. These are people who have special technical expertise, who will need to be convinced that the proposal hangs together. The group may also include a purchaser or buyer who is desperately keen to see that lots of little forms are filled in neatly. It is a cross to bear, unless you have a good relationship with the CEO. Then the functionary will get back into his or her box and do as he or she is told. Do not let technical buyers take over: they can unravel any deal through death by detail. Make sure that the decision remains a management decision, not a bureaucratic decision.

- *Key influencers*. These people are hard to spot. They have no formal role in the decision. But often they are the people whom the CEO or other executives will turn to for informal advice. They might be in planning, a staff function, non-executive position, or might be old friends from a previous job. Find them. They are a great way of informally selling, and normally they are delighted that someone else is taking the time and trouble to speak to them.

- *Coaches*. Among this network, you should find some coaches. The ideal is to position each of these people as coaches. In other words, do not go to them trying to sell them, go to them asking for advice on your idea. Seek their help. This turns potential adversaries (such as the finance department) into advocates. Generally, people love being coaches. It plays to their sense of self-worth and importance to be consulted. It also establishes the right, mutually supportive relationship in which you sell by listening, not talking. Good coaches will knock down technical obstacles for you, give good advice and give you access to constituencies you are finding hard to reach.

- *Gatekeepers*. These can be dangerous. Some people appear as coaches, promising to get you access to other key people. Then you find they are simply acting as gatekeepers preventing access other than on their terms. This is their way of gaining control over your initiative. Bypass them as gently as you can.

As you build your network, monitor it. Keep tabs on each person. The key things to note are:

- *The basics*. Have you noted each person's name, title, location, contact numbers, secretary's name and number?
- *Role*. What is each person's role in the buying process?
- *Hot buttons*. What turns the individuals on? What do they like and dislike about the proposal? These are not just their rational hot buttons, but their personal ones as well. Understand their ambitions and fears and how your proposal may affect them.
- *Key relationships*. Who does each person appear to influence, and is this a risk or opportunity?
- *Contact history*. What happened when?
- *Personal style*. For each person, is he or she a people person, a numbers person, an assertive talker or more of a thinker and listener? Adapt the tone of your approach to suit his or her style.
- *Next steps*. What promises have been made? When is your next meeting? etc.

People often try to keep all this in their heads. For a small simple sale this is possible. For a big complex sale with lots of moving parts, this is not possible. If you have a small team helping you build this network sale, then keeping tabs on where you all have got to with different parts of the network is essential.

Sex and drugs and rock and roll

- *Sex*. In the office, it's not worth it. It may be fun at the time, but it just leads to endless complications and always ends in tears.

- *Drugs*. These are compulsory in some businesses. Power is addictive and should be classified as a Class A drug, but we all get hooked on it anyway. Otherwise, Just Say No.

- *Rock and roll.* Grow up and get out of your time warp. As managers age, most of them get stuck in a time warp. It can happen when they are 20 or 60 or any age in between. In private, their tastes in music and fashion, their sporting heroes, the films and celebrities they admire all get frozen around a certain time. They talk about the 'good old days'. They lose interest in new stuff, which always seems to pale by what happened before. This personal ossification is matched by professional ossification. The rules of the game they learned at that time are the rules of the game they stick by. The old dog will not learn new tricks. Even if the new is shocking, successful managers maintain a lively interest in it and always learn and adapt.

Sex and drugs offer a short cut to ruin. Rock and roll is the slow and easy road to ruin.

Shakespeare and management

Shakespeare wrote three sorts of play: comedies, histories and tragedies. Most management reports, management time and managers fall into one of those three categories. It is worth knowing which sort of play you are in, and to act your part appropriately. But whichever type of play it is, it is drama and it is the stuff of life. So enjoy it.

Sheriffs and cowboys

Accountants and auditors are the sheriffs of the corporate world. It pays to have them on your side, especially if you are a cowboy. Instinctively, it's easy to hate the sheriffs. They spoil all the fun, stop you doing what you want to do and generally get in the way. Unfortunately, they have authority on their side. Because so many people get frustrated by the accountants, it is easy to make them into allies; they are not used to being well treated.

Look at the world through their eyes. They are meant to keep everything in order, often with recalcitrant and uncooperative managers. At the end of the month, they need to get all their numbers to balance out, and they have to spot any risks, fraud or potential problems. If there are any banana skins out there, they have to spot them. They hate surprises.

The worst accountants get into pettifogging detail and believe that the business is there to serve them, not vice versa. But many accountants will help you, if you help them. Bringing them on side is basic stuff:

- Talk to them at the earliest stage of new proposals. Find out how the idea will be assessed, and what the rules of the game are going to be. You give them a feeling of control. They will be grateful.

- Co-opt them into helping draft or at least validate your proposal and its numbers. Let them avoid surprises. Let them look in control and let them be seen to be doing a good job by their boss.

- Make their life easy: if they need certain data at a certain time, give it to them ahead of time packaged the way they need it. They will return the compliment when it is their turn.

- Never pick a fight over numbers with them in public. Even if you are right, they will use enough smoke and mirrors to confuse everyone, delay everything and knock you off course. You will have an unnecessary battle and enemy on your hands. Preview data with them in private and sort out disagreements then.

Once the cowboys get the sheriffs on their side, they can really go to town.

Skills: stuff and people

Most people start their careers learning technical skills. It may be cutting code, balancing books, doing pricing analyses or designing promotions. If you are still cutting code, balancing books (etc) 20 years later, you have probably failed.

Narrow technical and functional skills become proportionately less important over time. People skills and general management skills become more and more important with seniority. But as people get more senior, they retain the bias of their original functional training. CEOs with accounting backgrounds always look to the financial ratios and performance figures first. Marketing-bred CEOs look to the marketplace, customers and market share performance first. Engineers look to the product first. This has some basic implications:

- Personal development depends on building people skills and general management skills. Business schools help with the general management perspective. They offer no preparation for the messy reality of people management.

- **Too much functional excellence** and enthusiasm **is career limiting**. People who are functionally excellent are often asked to do more and more of their functionally excellent work. They are typecast as the expert for designing promotions or doing pricing analyses. And this is a box from which it becomes ever harder to escape. The company wants you to do your excellent work. You increasingly become seen as a bit of an anorak in your specialist area, and will not be trusted with broader responsibilities.

- Choice of leader is not just about managerial excellence: it is about fit. A growth company may need a growth-focused marketing CEO. A company in a declining market may need a more control and accounting-led CEO. The leadership team as a whole need balance between these skills.

Sorry and sympathy

Sorry is a powerful word. Said early enough and with honesty, it draws the anger and emotion out of a situation. People can move on from blame to action. Some people seem to be pathologically incapable of saying this word. Some of them may be so perfect that they are never wrong and never need to say sorry. Others would rather fight tooth and nail to protect their dignity by redirecting the blame. Saying sorry is good business sense.

Spend, spend, spend

Make your accountants weep. Ignore the cost savings and go on a spending spree. Here are the 10 top cost savings to ignore:

- cheap chairs for secretaries who need them all day: executives only get fancy chairs; maintain the caste system;

- poor quality coffee machine: make it a pay machine, not free, real coffee, china cups for executives only;

- cheap office party to show you don't care about the staff;

- lights and air-conditioning that turn off automatically at 6 pm to make sure no one works hard;
- second-class post: show your suppliers and customers how much you care;
- cheap stationery to project the right company image;
- no hot water in the toilets: stop people cleaning their hands;
- cheap fluorescent lighting: make sure no one gets too comfortable;
- skimp on the cleaning and maintenance contracts: show you care about costs, not quality;
- replace the canteen with a vending machine: watch everyone leave for lunch and take longer – the smart ones never come back again.

Staff and the masters of the universe

Two hundred years ago business survived without many staff. Goodbye consultants, lawyers, investment bankers, accountants, PR and marketing people, recruiting and HR departments and goodbye to the high priests of IT.

Now, they represent the corporate life support systems of any large business. Managers only discover how important the staff are when they leave the firm and are denied the oxygen of all the support services. But the servants of the business are acting above their station. In the 21st century they want to be the masters of the house. Sack them, shoot them, stuff them. Never let them take over. **Staff functions make wonderful servants, terrible masters.** When they take over disaster looms:

- The business becomes internally focused, not focused on the marketplace. Managers spend time on getting budget codes for paper clips and worrying about the ensuing variance analysis of paper clips.
- Decision making is slowed down. Decisions are vetted, previewed, reworked and analysed by all the worthy staff in finance, strategy, HR, IT and elsewhere. They all need to add value, so they all add comments and questions that need to be dealt with. The goal should not be to jump through staff hurdles, but to make the right decision.
- The wrong decisions are made. An IT implementation designed by IT may be technically exquisite. A simpler but less technically beautiful solution is often what the business needs.

- Responsibility is diffused. Once staff start to get involved in decision making, it takes away responsibility from line managers. There are more people to blame. Politics escalate.

- Reporting and coordination costs increase. More people need more information on more subjects. And when they get the information, they want to do something about it, so there are more meetings and more discussions and more internal focus.

- Costs escalate. More staff cost money and cause more indirect costs as a result of all the extra internal work they create.

- Morale drops. By this stage the business is in the death spiral as it becomes ever more internally focused; everyone is blaming everyone else for problems. Instead of putting out the fire, they argue about who started it and who is responsible for filling the water buckets.

- The competition wins.

Good staff functions are worth their weight in gold. They understand that they are there to serve the business. They give the business leverage and help managers focus on what is important by taking away from them the routine and the complicated.

Status

Everyone craves status. But the more senior you are, the less it is necessary. For junior managers, every little sign of status is another way of giving them some recognition, giving them some confidence that they are advancing. It costs little and does more good than harm.

But status is as addictive as crack. Managers cannot kick the habit. Every year the office and the desk must be bigger, but the PC and mobile phone must be smaller. And then there are the demands for golf club memberships, boxes at all the big sporting events, first-class travel and ultimately the chauffeur-driven car and corporate jet. All this is justified on the basis of meeting clients and saving time. And it is all self-serving garbage.

Focus on status is in inverse proportion to focus on the business. And it serves to alienate managers from the rest of the business: it creates a 'them and us' situation. It reinforces the strongly hierarchical nature of the business. Not that senior managers will notice: they will be cocooned in their first-class cabin, their big corner office and their executive box. They will not be in touch with the reality of their organization. There are three solutions to the status problem:

- *Get rid of the status symbols.* Share an open office, perhaps with the rest of the leadership team. These are the people you need to talk to most often, and with no walls in the way, talking is easier. Make it easy for staff to visit. Most of them are not stupid: they will not seek to waste time. With less status but better communications and faster decision making it is easier to stay in touch with the business.

- *Monetize the status.* Work out how much all the perks cost, and offer 50 per cent of the value in cash instead. The business saves a fortune, and the executives land up with greatly increased income. Curiously, when it is their own money they will not have quite the same need to spend it on first-class travel.

- *Give everyone a uniform.* Have a five-star general's outfit for the CEO through to sergeant's stripes for the front-line supervisor. At least the status and the hierarchy is now clear for everyone to see. And you can even start awarding medals for good conduct and bravery in the face of the competition.

Stewardship and values

Stewardship is for success and failure. Stewardship should mean leaving something in better condition than you found it. Stewardship applies as much to the two or three years that managers spend in each job as it does to the two or three hours managers spend each day on helping staff, going to meetings or any of the other daily activities of management. As a value, it is powerful.

In some businesses the idea of stewardship is corrupted. It means being seen to leave things in better condition that you found them in. This is the survivalist approach to stewardship. It requires careful positioning and expectation setting more than performance. Here are some examples of the survivalist approach to stewardship:

- On taking a new job show that you have inherited a disaster. Things can only look better when you leave.

- On leaving a job paint a picture of imminent victory. If your successor wins, claim the credit. If he or she fails, it's because he or she screwed up.

- On new initiatives offer lots of advice, take no responsibility. If the initiative succeeds, jump on the bandwagon and claim the glory. If it fails, let the turkeys roast.

The corporate version of stewardship is a powerful driver of performance and of making the parts of the organization work together. The survivalist version is a recipe for politicking, internal strife and poor performance. The values of the business are not in the values statement. They are in the daily rules of survival and behaviour of managers, starting with the leaders.

Storytelling

You are with some friends. You start comparing mobile phones and you want to see who got the best deal. All of them will have a story about why they got the best deal: more free minutes, unlimited downloads, cheap foreign roaming, free insurance. And the same happens when we buy a car. We all have a story to tell about why we got a great deal: free alloy wheels, a great trade-in, free insurance or servicing, extended warranty. No one wants to be seen as the klutz that got ripped off. So we construct a story to persuade ourselves and others that we drove a great bargain. But you can be sure that the dealer on the other end was not out of pocket either.

At work, the same thing happens. No one wants to be the fool who made a dumb decision. So we all create simple stories about why we made a great decision on the photocopier, or the new recruit, or the sale we made to a customer.

Now turn the conversation around. You are no longer the buyer, you are the seller: you are selling the photocopier or you are selling yourself for promotion or to be hired. Now you know that the buyer who will hire you, promote you or buy your photocopier is going to want a story that makes him or her look good. But the person does not know what the story should be. So you should give the buyer the script. The best script is very short and simple: 'I bought the car because it came with five years' free servicing' or whatever.

So what is the script your boss will use to persuade the powers above that you should be promoted? It will have to be much better than 'this employee is a very good worker who works very hard', because that is a story that everyone will tell. You need to have something different: you need to have the free alloy wheels that no one else has. You need a claim to fame.

And what is the script your colleagues will use when they give approval to your latest and greatest new project? You may be able to wax lyrical for hours about your idea, but ultimately people need a short script they can repeat to anyone else who asks them. This is the classic elevator pitch: what will they say about your idea on a short elevator ride?

A good script has three basic elements:

- It is short, very short.
- It is relevant: it addresses a need, problem or opportunity.
- It is distinctive: no one else could credibly claim the same thing.

Make it easy for your colleagues and bosses. Do not assume that they will work out the right script from your brilliant 45-minute presentation. Give them the script, and then hang all your presentations and arguments around that short and simple message. **Smart people make things complicated; really smart people make complicated things very simple.**

Strategy: war and peace

Part 1: war

Strategy is very important. But no one knows what it means. Every professor in the world has a different version of what strategy means. This keeps the professors in business but does not help managers. In answer to the professorial question 'What is strategy?', there is only one universally accurate answer: 'It means exactly what you want it to mean to make your point.'

There are broadly two schools of thought that battle it out on the bookshelves and conference circuit. First, there are people from the intellectual and analytical school, led by Michael Porter. They are the ones that come up with lots of diagrams and analytical tools that only brainy people like them can really understand. This means you have to pay them lots of money to take your data and rearrange it insightfully for you. The good news is that they can come up with good insight, and using facts is better than blind guesswork. The challenges are that much of what they do is either not useful, or positively dangerous:

- Data only exists about the past, not about the future. Strategy is about the future. **Looking into the rear mirror to drive forward is rarely smart.**

- Most strategy tools are prescriptive: they tell you what you should do. But everyone has the same tools, which means that much strategy leads to everyone settling on similar strategies. This is competitive suicide. You cannot build advantages by being the same as everyone else: competitive advantage involves being different.

- The analytical focus ignores the importance of creativity in seeking original solutions and the importance of engaging and mobilizing the organization behind a new way of thinking. Most strategy reports wind up as expensive door stoppers. They may have provided some comfort to senior managers and the board, but they are not living, actionable documents.

On the other hand, the process school created by Hamel and Prahalad is the revolt against the intellectuals. The essential argument is that good strategy is about stretching the organization and leveraging its resources to achieve the unachievable. It is a call to arms for the organization. It emphasizes ambition, stretch, creativity and mobilization of the business. This is all good stuff. And it is extremely dangerous if misapplied.

There is a fine line between goals that stretch and goals that break the organization. For every case they cite of businesses that have set outrageous goals and achieved them, there are many more for whom the ambition has been pie in the sky.

Ambition that is not rooted in an understanding of the market, which lacks the fact base of the intellectual school, is free from constraints in terms of ambition. It may also be free from reality. All of this would not matter if it was simply a matter of business school professors arguing over abstract theory. Unfortunately, it matters hugely. The methods of these two schools of thought permeate senior management and consulting firms. In practice, this means that strategy is not built around the needs of the business. **Strategy is determined by who you ask and the approach they use.** Ask the wrong person, get the wrong strategy.

Part 2: peace

Given the cacophony of noise from all the experts on strategy, managers are on their own in terms of working out what strategy is and how they build and implement it. Ask five different experts for advice, get six different replies.

There are no prescriptive answers. But there are questions that will let you know whether you have got there. And by answering the questions, you have a fighting chance of getting something that works:

- Is the strategy distinctive? If it is the same as your competition or it is easily copied you are heading either for competitive stalemate or a game of never-catch-up.

- Is the strategy stretching? A strategy that is essentially an extrapolation of past financial performance is not a strategy. In most firms, **the best predictor of next year's strategy is this year's strategy** plus or minus a bit: most firms drift strategically. A stretchy strategy will force the business to find new ways of doing things, new ways of competing and new ways of using limited resources. Business as usual is a criminal waste of internal capabilities and external opportunities. Strategy should match the capabilities to the opportunities.

- Is the strategy relevant to everyone in the business? The test of relevance is whether it helps people make choices and focus on the right things. Each part of the business may have wonky-sounding things like a floor-space strategy, or customer-satisfaction strategy, or euro-conversion strategy. Purists are appalled by this use of the strategy word. But provided people are developing their local and departmental strategies in line with the corporate one, it is helping focus priorities and resources the right way.

- Is the strategy reality-based? This is not the same as having it proven 300 different ways in some big strategy report. It may be based on some insight about how the market or competition are inefficient, or customers are dissatisfied. The insight should have some justification, but it should be future-focused, not backward-looking. Unless you have a good crystal ball, do not bet on getting too much data about the future.

- Is the strategy actionable? It should be owned by all managers, not just the executive committee. Everyone will have to live with it and implement it. A process that involves managers in developing the strategy is more likely to engage managers than a process that simply informs them after the event.

Stress tests

Decide where you work best:

- *the chill-out zone:* easy hours, easy bosses, whale music in the subsidized cafeteria;

- *the workout zone:* high pressure, high but clear demands, constant stretch;

- *the stress-out zone:* bosses who shout and demean; internal competition and politics; uncertain and changing demands.

Most people find they perform best in the work-out zone. The chill-out zone is fine if you are a monopoly or an organization that suffers no competition. It does not matter how dysfunctional the organization may become, it will survive.

The problem comes when pressure turns into stress. **The difference between pressure and stress is control.** If you face tough deadlines, but you are in control of your destiny then you will feel pressure but you will not feel too much stress. Now take away the control. You have tough deadlines, but you depend on other people delivering, and the goals may change at any moment: and the consequences of failure are too horrible to contemplate. Suddenly, your pressure has turned into stress.

When stress comes, erratic behaviour follows shortly behind. And that only makes the stress worse because your colleagues will start to react negatively to your erratic behaviour. The spiral of stress is hard to escape.

Here is how you can cope with stress at work:

- *Recognize what is happening.* Don't freak out: stress is a normal human reaction.

- *Find out what you can control.* You cannot control everything, so focus on what you can do rather than worry about what you cannot do. Even small steps will help you regain balance.

- *Find help for the things you cannot control.* If you take on the whole burden yourself, it will crush you.

Finally, find a chance to relax. Holidays and weekends are a wonderful chance to decompress after a stressful time. If you let the stress invade even these times, you will find yourself burning out fast. Relaxation is not a guilty pleasure: it is a way of helping you sustain performance for years instead of weeks.

Sweet shop economics

When I was young I had an aunt who owned a sweet shop. When you are six years old, things do not get better than that. Aunt Hatty was my very favourite aunt in the whole wide world. I learned much from her – such as how to get rotten teeth and zits; how to become manically overactive; and how to get fat. But it was a great way to go.

Hatty was also smart. She was always reading stuff and improving herself. She keenly felt her lack of formal education and wanted to make up for it. She decided to teach me applied and behavioural economics, at the age of six. She probably taught me many things I promptly forgot or never worked out in the first place. But two lessons remain with me to this day.

Lesson 1

Whenever I visited Hatty, she would give me a choice between two sorts of sweet: I could pick either. I knew those were the rules, and she always picked pretty good sweets. She made the choosing easy for me. Then one day she changed the rules. I could pick any one type of sweet from the entire shop. Brilliant! My eyes grew as large as saucers as I contemplated the cornucopia of options. I must have taken ages to decide, because I could sense Hatty was becoming a little impatient. Eventually, I picked a sweet and immediately regretted my choice. I was sure that I must have missed the best choice somewhere. I had missed out. I had lost. It was a disaster.

I had discovered the principle of restricted choice and regret. If we have too much choice, we will always fear that we have not made the best choice. With a restricted choice it is much simpler to decide which of two is the better option. To this day when I am selling, I use the principle of restricted choice. Give the buyer a simple, but limited choice. The more choice buyers have, the harder they will find it to make a decision and they often fail to make any decision at all. **Less choice is better than more.**

Lesson 2

On one trip to her shop in Newark, she said I could have as much of any one type of chocolate bar I could eat. I had learned from lesson 1 and was prepared. I knew what I wanted. I wanted to eat her shop clean of Milky Bars, because the Milky Bar kid was really cool (despite his spots). The first two or three Milky Bars went down so fast I could have won a speed-eating competition. By the fourth I was slowing down. Somewhere around the sixth or seventh Milky Bar I was wondering whether I had had enough. The heretical concept of 'too many' began to trace its way across my consciousness. I banished the thought: I was not going to be defeated by the Milky Bar kid. No way, never.

To this day, there are family arguments about how many Milky Bars it took to defeat me. With each passing year, the total mysteriously seems to increase. All I know is that by the end of the day, I never wanted to see another Milky Bar again. And I really hated the snotty Milky Bar kid. Hatty had very successfully introduced me to the ideas of utility and scarcity. We value the scarce over the common; **and the marginal value of extra anything decreases**. Our first £20,000 of income or spending is highly valued and well used. Adding £20,000 to a £1 million budget or to an executive earning £1 million a year, and the money simply disappears down a black hole. Once again, less is more.

T

Team players

There are three sorts of team player.

Team players

These people actually play for the team, rather than for personal glory. Provided they are good, they are invaluable team members. But they rarely get the recognition. Other people are better at claiming the credit. They are not alpha males and females who lead from the front and get all the best pickings, they are the beta category who are always the second in command.

Flat organizations depend on team players who are prepared to work 'outside their box' and support other people. Reward and measurement systems are rarely geared up to recognizing this sort of effort. Annual evaluations often come down to the boss looking at what each individual has done for him or her, not for the business as a whole.

Non-team players

These players were useful in the traditional hierarchy. They could accept their own area of responsibility and get on with it. But with more and more business requirements crossing functional requirements, the non-team player is an endangered beast. Except at CEO level, where the focus is on captaincy and leading the team, not being a team player is unhelpful.

'My team' players

These people abound in flat organizations, and claim to be great team players. Their basic premise is that either you are on their team, or you are not a team player. In this context, disagreeing with them or failing to follow their instructions without question is taken as proof positive that you are not a team player. This is the traditional hierarchy disguised as team playing. Under these circumstances the traditional hierarchy has greater honesty and clarity.

Teflon-coated management: turning losses into investment

Investment is good, spending is OK, and losses are bad. This is a problem when you are given a hospital pass: a loss-making business. The art is to turn losses into investment. Do this and you turn from a leper into an Olympian.

In tough times, **manage expectations and perceptions, and show that you are in control. You will fast acquire a thick coat of Teflon**.

For example, let's say you get to run the business in Japan. You arrive to find it has no sales, no income and no prospects of any sales. But it does have an expensive office and expensive staff. You could close it down, but you have been sent to build the Japanese business, not kill it. And you know that you are heading for big losses. Here are the six rules you must follow:

1 *Take control.* Do not let the corporate functionaries get ahead of you with the bad news. Their spin on the bad news is unlikely to be helpful. This means you have to get to corporate managers before they do; do not try to hide. They will find out, and then you will appear not to be in control of the situation.

2 *Get all the bad news out.* You do not want bad news to keep on trickling out. If there is bad news, get it all out. If necessary, overestimate the extent of the financial damage. This gives you some leeway later, and managers might even be relieved that you pull the projected loss back from US $6 million to a mere US $5 million. If you have set their expectations that they will only lose US $4 million, then US $5 million looks like a failure. Same financial result, different expectations, and different career result.

3 *Have the solution.* Do not go to corporate managers with only the problem: you then become part of the problem. Come with the solution. This then shows you are in control. And corporates are unlikely to have a better idea than you about what should happen.

4 *Find a positive spin.* The losses need not be losses. Instead, propose a three-year investment programme to build a successful business in Japan. Be clear about the great outcomes: skilled staff, profitable business, and happy clients. The investment simply represents the excess of costs over revenues for the first three years. Corporate managers may underwrite your investment plan, even if they do not tolerate losses. They are, of course, the same thing.

5   *Build a coalition.* You know who the key decision makers are. Get them on board as soon as possible, and in private. Try to co-opt one or two of them into being your coaches. You are certain to come under fire. Identify the potential problem makers, and try to pre-empt them personally, or through your coaches.

6   *Deliver on your new plan.* You have just used up several of your corporate lives. Do not risk disappointing people again; they will not be so generous next time round.

Teleworking: myth and reality

Reports of the death of the office are premature. Technology allows us to do more on the move, but we will remain anchored to an office. Teleworking was a reality for hundreds of years through to the industrial revolution. The cloth trade was based on putting work out: individuals would be paid a piece rate for working the wool in stages from the sheep to the shirt. The work would be done at home to supplement the income from farming.

Teleworking in the 18th-century succeeded because the teleworkers needed no human interaction, there was no complex coordination required, and the output measurements and rewards were transparent. Teleworking did not require broadband telecommunications and high technology. It required the right sort of work.

All the technology for teleworking is in place. But teleworking will remain an 18th-century, not a 21st-century way of doing things. The 21st century may be high tech relative to the 18th century, but it becomes ever more high touch. Work in the 21st century needs personal contact and:

- *Trust.* We need to trust the people we work with. So far, human nature has not changed enough for us to be satisfied with a purely remote contact. Air travel grows even as e-mail and voice mail grow. We need to be able to see our colleagues, clients and business partners in person.

- *Complexity.* Business is becoming more, not less complicated. This means that the depth and frequency of coordination efforts are rising. It also means that it is becoming harder to measure the contribution of many management jobs. The 18th-century piece worker needed little coordination. The task was to produce the goods by a certain day. In a more complicated world, direct high touch contact helps blow away some of the ambiguities of business, coordination and performance contribution. Seeing is believing.

- *Motivation.* The basic discipline of turning up for work, free from domestic transactions, makes a huge difference to productivity.
- *Communication.* The water cooler and the open office door remain the best tools for communication. E-mail and voice mail help, but cannot replace the immediacy and intimacy of office contact.

Teleworking will arrive as fast as the paperless office has arrived.

Thank you

This is nice to receive. It's easy to give. It's much underused.

Thinking

Thinking and responsibility: the outsourcing options

Thinking is painful and risky. It's painful because it is about making choices. It is risky because choices lead to actions, which may be wrong. This is why management avoids serious thinking. Continuing the current status quo, the current trajectory is the safe option. Even if the trajectory leads to disaster, the failure is absolute, not relative. In other words, everyone has failed, not just the person who stepped out of line with some fresh thinking and a new perspective.

Ultimately, thinking is about responsibility and dealing with reality. Managers have four choices when it comes to thinking and responsibility. They can:

- outsource their thinking and their responsibility;
- outsource their responsibility, but keep the thinking;
- outsource their thinking, but keep the responsibility;
- keep both the thinking and the responsibility.

Outsource thinking and responsibility

This is the pass the buck game. It is also consistent with the follow the herd game. You do not think, you follow. It is the course that most managers follow most of the time. It is easy and low risk, it makes for a quiet life for both the business and the individual. It keeps the wheels of the business turning, without moving the business forward.

This is a sustainable approach in the civil service and other risk-averse monopolies where doing nothing (and not making any mistakes) is preferable to doing something. In businesses that are intended to compete and move forward, it puts all the pressure on the leaders to come up with the great ideas that move the business forward. This approach is consistent with that of junior managers in traditional hierarchies.

Outsource responsibility, but keep the thinking

This is the classic role of the staff function. Staff go away and analyse, criticize and recommend. But they have no responsibility for doing anything. And the line managers have no responsibility for thinking. This sets up a classic blame game.

Staff can show that managers are messing it up and recommend changes. If managers then succeed, staff can claim the credit. If managers fail it was because they did not follow the recommendations, or they implemented them poorly. Either way, the staff cannot lose and managers cannot win.

Outsource the thinking, but retain the responsibility

This is an unusual, but potentially high-performance choice. It can be done well or badly. At worst, this is the management version of pass the buck and avoiding doing anything. Set up a task force or a committee, hire in consultants and then managers have someone to blame if things go wrong.

If the manager truly retains responsibility, then he or she may still set up a task force or committee. But this is in pursuit of both getting the best ideas, and of building the commitment across the organization to make something happen. The manager retains responsibility, but personally commits moving the business forward, not just to spinning wheels.

Retain the thinking and the responsibility

This is a trap. It appears to be what managers should do, but it is not. It is the paradigm of leadership in the traditional hierarchy where leaders did the thinking and workers did the working, with managers in the middle doing the communicating.

This paradigm is still strong. Organizations like to think that the leaders have all the answers. They delegate the thinking upwards. And some leaders like to be seen as all-powerful and all-wise, so they go along with this paradigm. These are the downsides of this:

- The thinking is rarely as good as it could be: one leader cannot be expected to have all the answers.
- There is a gap between the thinking and the action: apathy and resistance are more common than committed enthusiasm to someone else's idea. The leader has a job to do to sell the idea.
- Decision making gets slowed down as it filters its way through the hierarchy, and this creates a low-empowerment, low-commitment culture.

Thinking versus doing

In an ideal world managers think, then do. Some think and do nothing; they are called staff. A few try neither thinking nor doing. Many prefer to do without thinking. This is the easy way of simply following orders. But it leads to wheel spinning, not progress.

Clear thinking normally depends on good questions. The easiest question to ask is: 'Why?' Keep on asking it until everyone gets sick of trying to answer it. By about the sixth answer to the question 'Why?', you may be getting to a real answer. Asking why is a luxury for consultants, staff and senior managers who wish to interrogate hapless line managers.

The way for managers to help themselves is to have a very clear model of how their business or department works. The model should not produce prescriptive dumb answers that all your competition will have. The model should help ask all the right, pertinent questions that will lead you to the right answers. These models tend to be highly context-specific, which is what makes them useful. If you are sick of the why question, think of the model of how your business makes money.

The simplest model is the pyramid of ratios, which accountants use to understand financial performance of the business. It does not give answers, but it helps highlight where some of the problems and opportunities lie. Every part of the business can have its own model. The following is a case study of a sales organization.

CASE STUDY   Sales: thinking versus doing

Sales were slack. People thought it might be a sales productivity problem rather than a product or advertising problem. So the sales business went into overdrive: there were bonuses, competitions, promotions, hiring and firing of staff, new campaigns and pep talks. Each effort produced a small peak in a downwards sloping sales graph. The harder they tried, the less each effort had an impact in the noise of all the other initiatives.

After lots of doing, they decided to start thinking. They realized that their sales were the function of a very simple formula, which could show them where there might be opportunities.

The formula is: $VS = NS \times CD \times HR \times CS$.

The equation says that there are four management levers that can affect the value of sales. The issue for managers was to see which could yield the best results:

- VS = Value of sales.
- NS = Number of salespeople. This asked the basic question of coverage density. A further look at coverage patterns showed that some parts of the country were inadequately covered relative to market potential, others were covered too densely which led to low productivity per salesperson. The higher the density of coverage, the higher the total sales and the lower sales per salesperson. Obvious, but rebalancing coverage helped raise both total sales and productivity per salesperson.
- CD = Number of calls per day per salesperson. This is a function of how the salesperson spends the day and how the business supports the sales effort. We found that on average, under 10 per cent of the salespeople's time was spent face to face with the customer. This would be fine if each call was effective and the rest of the time was spent preparing for the call. But the rest of the time was spent largely on administrative activities and client-servicing activities that other staff could handle. Doubling the amount of client-facing time transformed productivity, and raised morale of salespeople. They had less administrative rubbish to deal with and were earning more by selling more.
- HR = Hit rate or conversion rate of calls into sales. Further analysis showed this was driven by three factors:
  - Salespeople's effectiveness varied by a factor of 5 overall, and by a factor of 12 for individual products. Some salespeople were beyond hope. The broad mass were good at something, and were able to raise productivity by learning best practices, or tips of the trade, of the best salesperson in each category through a structured programme.
  - Client targeting had a large impact: some customer groups were three times as likely to buy as others.
  - Warm versus cold selling had a huge impact. The cold sales had a hit rate of about 1 in 20. Warm leads converted at closer to 1 in 3.

- CR = Contribution per sale. The size and margins of each sale varied widely by product. This is a function both of the product strategy and the sales force compensation and measurement system. Salespeople are rational. They will sell what yields the most benefit for the least effort. The incentive scheme was realigned with the economics of the business, and some products were dropped altogether.

Clearly, none of what the case study outlines is magic. It is not even clever. It is simply about driving clear thinking into clear action. It is about achieving forward motion without spinning wheels.

Time: activity, efficiency and effectiveness

Time is not on our side. We do not even know how much our allotted time on earth is. We have to make the most of what we have. Basically, there are three ways of making the most of our time.

Run round ever faster in ever-decreasing circles

This is the most popular form of time management. Senior managers are addicted to it. They tend to believe that a full diary, 200 e-mails a day and business dinners every evening show that they are important and busy. Being late for each appointment is a way of reinforcing the point that they are busy and important. This is not time management; it is an ego trip where activity is a substitute for efficiency or effectiveness. Because senior managers do this, junior managers copy them and the office is full of people chasing each others' tails.

A standard study is to look at what managers do during the day. This is old-fashioned time and motion. It is worth doing to yourself. In one case I found a middle manager who was well respected as someone who got things done and sorted things out. Over the course of eight hours he had the following profile:

- *Eighty-two phone calls.* Seventy-four of them were either inbound calls, or outbound calls to fix the issues raised by the inbound calls.
- *Sixty-three face-to-face interactions.* Fifty-nine were fixing inbound issues (fire fighting). Four were arranging travel for the following week.

- Three formal meetings, which were not his. They were other people's agendas. He was late for each.

- He never had more than two minutes between phone calls, a face-to-face interaction or a meeting. This time was used to read or respond to some of the 70-plus e-mails he received.

At the end of the day, the wheels had not fallen off the business, but it had not moved forward. The question for managers is: '**Are you simply stopping the wheels coming off or are you moving the business forward?**' The danger signs that managers are not moving the business forward are:

- fragmentation of time: lack of focus on a few things;
- reactive not proactive agendas;
- internal versus external focus;
- reporting and fixing versus proposing and doing.

Test your own time against these four criteria.

Efficiency

This ranges from the trite to the useful. Anyone who has been one-minute managed knows how irritating it is. The trite and insincere morning compliment, which is meant to be your one-minute motivation for the day, is a small example. The concept of quality time is a fiction: spending 15 minutes showing a three-year-old flash cards is not a substitute for parenthood. Some things demand time if they are to be done well.

Other efficiency savers make sense. For the individual some basic rules help. Handling each piece of paper once, doing things right first time, saves time. But there is a trap here: **doing the wrong thing with stunning efficiency will not help you**. Even more important than time efficiency is time effectiveness. That means knowing what you should and should not be doing.

Effectiveness

An old friend from California visited President Reagan at the White House. They had a leisurely lunch. They played golf. The President then invited the friend back for the evening. The visitor was astonished: 'Don't you need to get to any meetings? Don't you need to be running the nation?' he asked. The

President looked surprised and said, 'No, I've plenty of good people doing all that for me.'

Working all day and all night is not a prerequisite for success. We all know of someone who is apparently lazy and still successful. The lazy way to success depends on three things:

- Being very good at something (Reagan, the great communicator). This requires real focus, effort and commitment.

- Delegating like crazy. Know what you are not good at, and let other people do it. Give them the glory. The business will be better for it, and so will you.

- Focusing on what is important. Have clear personal objectives, which will help you prioritize what you will do.

Time management is 10 per cent about being efficient in what you do, 90 per cent about knowing what you will not do.

Businesses have a duty to help staff manage their time properly. At a trivial level, this can mean things like a concierge service to stop staff being distracted by the administrivia of home life. At a more fundamental level, it is about organizing work well.

A standard study I do on sales forces looks at how salespeople spend their time. Rarely do salespeople spend more than 10 per cent of their time face to face with a client. If the other 90 per cent of the time was well spent on call preparation and prospecting, this might be justifiable. Normally the other 90 per cent of the time is spent on internal meetings and reports, travel and client administration activities. Salespeople often go along with this. It is not as tough as the key job, which is selling. Most non-sales activity can be eliminated or reassigned to administrative staff.

Titles

Titles are about human dignity and vanity. At junior levels, titles are about dignity. Salespeople hate being called salespeople. They want to be known as account managers, relationship managers, business or market development executives or managers. Anything but salespeople. This is a cheap way of giving people dignity and status. Give it. A little title inflation can go a long way.

Further up the organization, titles are about vanity and power. Everyone is a vice-president (VP). The real competition is to become a senior vice-president (SVP) or executive vice-president (EVP). Title inflation may be fine at the bottom of the organization. It is not acceptable at the top of the organization.

Always keep a gold standard title, which everyone can aspire to. The VP must want to become an SVP, and the SVP must want to become an EVP. Outsiders probably neither know the difference nor care. Internally, people care passionately. At some level, the title signals that the manager has finally arrived in corporate Valhalla. This is in the land of the gods. Give this title out sparingly: keep people hungry. Make sure that the few that get into Valhalla really do represent the role models for the business. **If vanity counts so much, make it work for the business.**

Training versus experience

There are three sorts of formal, off-the-job, training:

- technical training;
- people training;
- the training you want, but never get.

Technical training

This is useful. Most of the technical training that people actually use is professional training such as in law or accounting. This provides the fundamental skills and frameworks of the profession.

Formal off-the job technical training rarely achieves as much as it should. It is not normally customized enough to the needs of the individual, and it arrives at the wrong time. To be effective, training needs to be of immediate relevance, so that the new skills can be applied in practice at once. The best sort of just-in-time training that can be customized to individual needs is always going to be on the job, not off the job.

People training

People training suffers for many reasons:

- Too much training is not very good: a facilitator with a franchised theory and a flip chart, where you are meant to guess what is meant to be written on the flip chart, is not a happy way to spend a day.

- Like technical training, it often lacks immediate relevance.
- People training suffers from deficit syndrome: going on a motivation or interpersonal skills course implies that you are no good at motivation or interpersonal skills. At least no one feels demeaned if given the chance to brush up on his or her marketing, accounting or IT skills.
- Most people do not like to change and even if they do, it takes them years not days. In practice, however, task-driven people remain task-driven and assertive people remain assertive. They cannot be transformed into tree huggers.

At best, people training gives people a bit more self-awareness, a bit of insight into other people and a temporary high fuelled by the conference drinks bar and freedom from the office.

The training you want but never get

What people really want to know is how to succeed in their own organization. This is not a manual that any organization writes. And people want to learn it not from some training functionaries, but from successful people they admire and trust. This sort of training is possible.

Basically, success training is about sharing best practices. Most people are successful at one aspect of their job, and want to learn more about other aspects. Everyone has part of the answer to the question of how to succeed. Everyone can contribute to, and learn from, best practices. Most people have enough vanity to enjoy being seen as a best practitioner and are willing to give time and effort to sharing their experience.

Delivering a best practices programme takes effort from the training functionaries as well. They cannot simply buy an off-the-peg training programme and send everyone the diskette or book the conference centre. They have to build a programme that systematically codifies the learning in a structure that makes sense, and create a programme in which knowledge is consistently shared, spread and codified. The knowledge has to be made a living beast.

Then the training has to be delivered by the most credible people at the right time. In other words, it needs to be provided on a just-in-time basis by the best practitioners themselves. This takes time and effort.

The choice is between an expensive but good training programme, which is used, versus a cheap off-the-peg training programme, which is not used. Most companies prefer to invest less and lose the value of the whole investment, than to invest more and get a return.

The trust equation

Trust goes to the heart of all the decisions we make. Budgets and business plans are worth only as much as the people standing behind them; if we trust the authors, we trust the plan. We only go into new departments or businesses if we trust the managers that will lead them. We will accept change if the change is being led by someone we trust. The extent of trust between two people can be assessed through the trust equation

$$T = (S \times C)/R \text{ where:}$$

- **T = Trust.**
- **S = Shared goals.** If both of us have common goals, common interests, we are more likely to want to work together and succeed together. If we have different interests, the art of trust building is to find those areas of common interest where we can work together.
- **C = Credibility.** It's no use having common goals if one of the parties can never deliver on promises and can never make the awkward decisions and compromises needed to succeed. People have to walk the talk.
- **R = Risk.** This is the great test of trust. You may trust me to post a letter, but will you trust me with a million-dollar discretionary budget?

In business, the greatest risk that anyone faces is career risk. This makes the relationship between an individual and his or her manager critical. The risk to the individual of a bad or unsympathetic manager is huge. The challenge to both sides is to build trust. This is not just about results (credibility) it is about listening and understanding and establishing truly shared goals.

Shared goals are not a formal document. They are a psychological contract in which there are implicit expectations on both sides. That contract exists from day one in any relationship. The problem is that both sides may have totally different understanding of what is in the contract. Make sure you understand what the other person thinks is in that contract.

Understanding and paraphrasing

How often do you hear people say something like 'I hear you'? You know that is a shorthand code for: 'I can hear your babble, and I wish you would just shut up, but I can't say so because I need to show that I am being kind, considerate and that I understand your point of view.' They are hearing but not listening.

Of course, if you really can understand the other person, see the world through their eyes, you are in a powerful position. You can start to speak a language they understand and respect, you build trust and you build cooperation. But **understanding is more than saying 'I hear you'**. It takes effort. The best way to achieve understanding, and to show you understand, is to paraphrase. When someone says something that you think is important, paraphrase it back to them in your own words. This has several advantages:

- It demonstrates to the other person that you are really listening. This encourages the person to open up more.
- If you get it wrong, you get immediate feedback. You then find the correct message, and future misunderstanding is avoided.
- If you get it right, the other person will be delighted: you are building trust and the basis for cooperation.
- Paraphrasing forces you into active listening. You will become a much more alert, better listener. You will pick up much more information than through passive listening.
- Paraphrasing helps you remember what happened in the conversation much better. With passive listening the substance of any conversation is easily and quickly forgotten.

Paraphrasing is simple, low cost, low effort and has a big impact.

Unfair competition

The competition is only unfair if it is winning. If we are winning, it is because we are smarter then them. Managers will never say they are losing because they are no good. It is always someone else's fault. Denial is natural. But it stands in the way of reality and recovery.

In 1995, the big three US auto companies launched a huge campaign to build their presence in Japan. Most companies seeking to build market share worry about things like product, pricing, promotion, service and quality. This was irrelevant to the Big Three. Instead, they argued that the Japanese government should arrange to give them more dealerships across Japan, to counteract the unfair competition of the Japanese.

The evidence that the Japanese were unfair was the very low sales of the Big Three in Japan. At the time, the Big Three were selling cars with the steering wheels on the wrong side of the car. The cars were totally outsized for Japanese roads. They cost twice as much as Japanese cars. Quality sucked. Even the British Mini, produced by one of the world's smallest and worst auto manufacturers, had sales in Japan greater than the combined sales of Ford, GM and Chrysler. The Mini filled a niche. But the US manufacturers could not conceive that the solution lay with them. They were losing. It had to be someone else's fault.

If the Japanese had gone to the US government and demanded that the US government arrange for them to be given extra dealerships to sell cars with steering wheels on the wrong side of the car at high prices and low quality and in the wrong size, they would have been laughed out of town.

But **government intervention is a legitimate business tool**. As long as there are politicians desperate enough for popularity, there will be opportunities to get a free lunch: the extra subsidy, soft loans, start-up grants, import protection, sanctions on competition. If governments are dumb enough to give all this, businesses should be smart enough to take it. It may be bad economics, but as long as it is good politics, it may as well be good business as well.

Unreasonable management

Reasonable management is dangerous. Good managers are not reasonable. They are, selectively, unreasonable. Reasonable management would have told Virgin that they were crazy to take on British Airways. Toyota and Honda were insane to take on the Big Three US auto manufacturers. President Kennedy was way out on a limb when he promised to send a man to the moon within 10 years, and bring him back again alive.

Reasonable managers listen to all the logical, rational reasons why a 20 per cent cut in costs and working capital while maintaining revenues cannot be achieved. They then cut the targets back to more reasonable goals for each business.

The **reasonable managers** are the ones that **land up in the quiet backwaters of underachievement**. They are weak. The unreasonable managers are the ones that demand, and enable, an organization to stretch and achieve previously unthinkable goals.

Somewhere, there is a dividing line between stretching and breaking a business, between unreasonable and insane management. Goals that are not backed up by a real focus of corporate effort are simple daydreaming. In setting the unreasonable goals, managers should:

- build a coalition in support of the goals;
- make the goals an inescapable reality for all managers;
- line up all the rewards and measures behind the goal;
- focus the resources of the organization behind the goal;
- be flexible about how the goal is achieved, and inflexible about the goal itself.

But having done that, they will not hear excuses. Any setbacks simply represent another challenge to be overcome on the way to success. **We remember Alexander the Great, not Alexander the Reasonable.**

Upwards management

Careers depend on upwards management. Flat organizations make upwards management a minefield of ambiguity and contradictions. In the traditional command and control organization, the rules of engagement are clear. The boss said what needed to be done, and the underling went away and fulfilled those obligations. Everyone knew where they stood, even if they did not like it. There was no ambiguity. And in many organizations, this remains the case today.

In the flat organization, the culture is that everyone acts as a peer to everyone else. Culturally this is attractive. It encourages openness, communication, flexibility and responsibility. But the rules of the game are totally ambiguous.

Three hundred and sixty degrees of ambiguity

The evaluation process is at the heart of the ambiguity. In a command and control environment, the boss rates you, and that's it. Flat organizations encourage the 360-degree evaluation. But this 360-degree circle is a mathematical mystery. It is a circle with distinct and uneven sides. The boss's evaluation will still determine your bonus, pay and promotion prospects. Your evaluation will be useful feedback to the boss, but will at best have limited impact on your prospects.

So how honest should you be? The boss sucks. If you tell the boss, will he or she extract revenge? The organization may be flat, but there is a distinct slope to it at evaluation time. This nagging awareness of the power and decision-making hierarchy affects the day-to-day behaviour of everyone in the flat organization. To make it worse, there are no clear rules of behaviour.

Flat organizations and rules of engagement

The first thing to do is to find out what the rules of engagement are. Every boss has different rules and different expectations, which even they may find hard to articulate. Some rules of upwards management are universal, others will be specific to the style of the boss. Universal rules of upwards management include:

- Understand the rules of engagement: the behaviours that do and do not work with the boss.
- Focus on what is of most value to the boss: understand the boss's agenda.
- Always, always, always keep promises and avoid surprises. This is central to building trust.
- Deliver the results.

Other rules of upwards management will vary according to the boss:

- *Initiative.* How much initiative are you really meant to take? Control freaks want everyone on a short leash; elsewhere failure to lead and take the initiative is terminal for careers.
- *Debate.* Some bosses want their ideas to be tested and challenged, others want them obeyed.

- *Formality.* Do you drop by the boss's office when you need or do you have to make an appointment?
- *Risk.* Is this a risk-taking, high-performance environment, or is it a no-errors, compliance environment?

A decent boss in a flat organization will go out of the way to make these rules of engagement clear. Setting or asking for an expectations discussion at an early stage is a useful start. The expectations are not about performance. They are about behaviours and what both individuals want to achieve personally. Requesting an expectations meeting quickly gets the boss to reveal the informal rules of engagement:

- Defensive command and control types will avoid the request.
- Traditional bosses struggling to get into the new world will have the meeting, and use it to focus on performance goals, not on mutual rules of engagement.
- Some bosses may actually contribute to a useful discussion about rules of engagement.

V

Venting: the art of getting the shits out

This is an art I learned from Professor Chan Kim, a great professor at INSEAD. The message is simple and powerful. In a crisis, managers have long political and emotional agendas that stop progress. These agendas are about denial of the problem and spreading the blame for the problem. Any amount of rational argument is doomed to failure. In a crisis, managers get very creative and eloquent in putting forward rational arguments to deny the problem and spread the blame. You may not be convinced, but they will be. People need to 'get the shits out' before they can start dealing with reality. It is a painful process for everyone.

Getting the shits out in practice

We were responsible for leading three-day workshops for a major multinational in crisis. And the managers hated being there. They suspected the workshops would either be irrelevant, or a vehicle for forcing them into making unwise performance promises. And there was deep antagonism between departments, countries and layers of management. Managers were all gathered together for the first time and they all felt the problems were caused by the others. Of course, collectively they were the others: there was no one else.

Leading these sessions can be suicidal. Managers may hate each other, but they are not going to declare warfare in front of 50 of their most senior colleagues. There was an obvious outlet for all their anger and frustration: the outsiders leading the programme.

The solution was to let them 'get the shits out' in the words of Chan Kim. They would do this over the first day, into the evening and through to the early hours of the morning. Getting the shits out was about letting their anger and frustration surface, and about listening, not preaching. For consultants, academics and CEOs, this much **listening tends to lead to blood blisters on the tongue**. Talking and challenging the baloney is tempting, but fatal. The managers needed to talk themselves into submission.

At about 2.00 am there was a valley of death where everyone was in total despair. At around this time they made several discoveries:

- The business was in real crisis: denial was no longer an option.
- They were the enemy: spreading the blame would not work. Between them, they were the management team and there was no one else for them to blame.
- They needed to start dealing with reality.

After passing through the valley of death, there was a catharsis, and enthusiasm for tackling the road to recovery. In practice, getting the shits out is good daily management exercise. The more creative rational arguments become, the more they are likely to hide political and emotional issues that do not lend themselves to rational argument.

Victimless crimes

The best crimes are those where the victims do not know that they have been victims. If no one knows there has been a crime, the criminal can never get caught.

Businesses are full of criminals who have got away with appalling crimes. The worst of these is missing market opportunities. No one can be pinned with the blame. The only sign of missed opportunities is when new competitors suddenly emerge out of the ether to challenge traditional industry players.

Canon entered Xerox's market through distributed, non-leased copying; Apple created the PC market, not IBM; CNN, not the established networks nor the BBC, created 24-hour news broadcasting; Microsoft created and owned the operating system business; the Japanese redefined the market for motorcycles and small cars in the United States, displacing incumbent US firms; FedEx, not the long-established UPS, created the overnight delivery business. The list is endless.

Innovation within an established company is risky. If you get it wrong, you're fired. Naturally, managers shy away from big risk, and play the percentage game instead. The incremental improvements to existing products bring visible results and recognition at low risk. No one at Xerox got fired for missing the distributed copying market; no one at IBM got fired for missing the PC market.

This logic can be turned on its head. If businesses have the courage to take risk and innovate they can commit the perfect crime: they can take a market before it is contested. This takes a notion of strategy, risk and organization that is wholly alien to most businesses. The traditional solution of the corporate skunk works is valid: give it money, a powerful political patron, good talent, and an office far away from head office out of reach of all the corporate functionaries who may help it to death.

Vision statements

These are excellent for dysfunctional managers. Give them the challenge of writing a vision statement and it should keep them happily occupied for months, and out of harm's way. The end product will use up some space in the annual report, and otherwise be quite harmless.

Vision statements can be created through the original vision machine. All you need to do is put the following statements into a random number generator, and then assemble the vision statement in the order the numbers come up. Here are the statements you need:

1 We will be the best at what we do.

2 We will be the market leader in all the markets we serve.

3 Staff/customers/our values are our most important asset.

4 Our business is built on respect for the individual.

5 We aim to exceed the expectation of all the constituencies we serve: our customers, shareholders, employees and their families, government and the local community.

6 We will never compromise our ethical standards.

7 Diversity is where it's at, man.

8 We care passionately about caring passionately.

9 We care particularly passionately for the environment.

10 We seek to make above average returns for our shareholders over time.

11 We are global and local.

12 We will all live happily ever after.

Note that this is a non-discriminatory vision statement. You can use it for any industry in any country, in any order. Should your dysfunctional managers produce the vision statement too fast, confuse them by asking them to produce a values statement to go alongside the vision statement. There will then be long discussion about vision versus values and what values really are, and is it culturally biased to have the same values across the world. Don't worry. The same statements used in the original vision machine can also be used for the values statement.

Visions and values are not about crafting elegant statements for the annual report. They are about guiding the daily business and behaviour of the firm. They are about what people do, not say. It is about the walk, not the talk.

Visions with value

Visionaries are dangerous. **For every visionary who takes you to the Promised Land, there are another 12 who march you straight back into the desert.** Visionaries never lack self-belief, even if they lack competence.

And yet visions can be powerful. Remember Kennedy: 'We will put a man on the moon and bring him back alive again within 10 years.' It sounded impossible, but it galvanized a nation and the United States achieved it. Since the vision was realized NASA has had successes (Hubble) and failure (Challenger) but has never quite risen to the heights it achieved with the moon shot.

Clearly, not all of us can be visionary in the office. We are not like Martin Luther King and 'I have a dream...' If you have dreams in the office, keep them to yourself. But we do not need to be like Martin Luther King or President Kennedy to be visionary. We just need to tell a story about our part of the organization in three parts:

- This is where we are.
- This is where we are going.
- This is how we will get there.

Most of us can do this. A simple story like that is a vision: it gives clarity, direction and purpose. And the shorter the story is, the better it is: it becomes clearer, simpler and more memorable.

If you want to make your vision really motivational, you add a fourth part to it: 'This is your very important role in helping us get there.' In other words, personalize your vision to each person on your team. The janitor may not feel wildly passionate about globalizing your product or service. But if your global customers visit you from far away, will they be impressed by filthy toilet facilities? Suddenly, you have a story to tell about how your janitor has a vital role to play in fulfilling your global vision.

Wake up!

We are often told to wake up. But no one teaches us how to wake up. For a long time I woke up in the middle of wars, famine, disasters, corruption, lying politicians and greedy businessmen. It was called waking up to the news, and it was not a good way to wake up.

After a very hard trip in Africa, I returned to the edge of civilization and found a hotel with a corrugated iron roof and barbed wire for a fence. Bliss. I woke up in the morning and a miracle happened: I turned on a tap and cold, clear water came out. I was assured it was drinkable. I did not have to walk 3 kilometres to a muddy, crocodile-infested river to get my water. And then another miracle happened. I turned on another tap and hot water came out. I did not have to gather brushwood to light a fire and heat the water. So nowadays I wake up to two miracles in two minutes: cold and hot running water. **It is pretty hard to have a bad day when you start with two miracles.**

We can all choose how we want to wake up. We can wake up with the media gloominaries. We can leave for work at the last minute so that every minor delay sends our blood pressure soaring. Or we can wake up to the miracles of modern life, and give ourselves enough time to relax on the way to work. Choose well.

Well-being: be happy or die

Nuns are a very useful group to do human experiments on: they all live the same sort of lifestyle and have the same sort of routine. And one nunnery inadvertently set up a great test of longevity: the nuns there asked all their applicants to write letters saying why they wanted to become nuns at the age of 18. The nuns fell into two sorts of groups: 'duty' nuns talked about their calling and duty; 'joy' nuns talked about how lucky they were to have the chance of doing something they really wanted to do.

By the age of 90, over half the top 'joy' nuns were still alive, but only 11 per cent of the 'duty' nuns were still alive. The stark conclusion of the study seemed to be: 'be happy or die.'

The study gives you two ways of living longer. The first is to give up your job and become a nun. The alternative is to do things that you really enjoy and that engage you. The well-being industry is rapidly becoming inhabited by smug charlatans who claim to have found the meaning of life, which they will share with you for an immodest fee. But behind the charlatans there is some serious research that shows consistently what will make you live better and live longer:

- Find meaning in what you do. Most people find time is elastic. When you have nothing to do, time drags on. When you are totally engaged in something, time flies. Find work that is genuinely engaging for you. That does not mean taking the easy route. Find work that stretches you, develops you.

- Have interests beyond work. Work drudges are just that: they are drudges, even if they are highly paid drudges.

- Riches will not make you happier, but poverty will grind you down. The poor die earlier than the rich. But the rich do not report any greater happiness than the comfortably off. Relative wealth is important: the poorest person on the street feels worse than the richest person on the street. The green-eyed monster of jealousy will not help you.

- Diet and physical activity help both body and mind: the old and tedious adage of 'a healthy body for a healthy mind' might just have some substance to it.

- Friends help.

- **Take responsibility for the hardest thing to take responsibility for: your own feelings.** Research shows that beyond a few exceptional circumstances, people pretty much feel how they choose to feel. As someone who can always find the cloud to any silver lining, this was a surprise.

- Count your blessings, which helps with taking responsibility for your feelings. As a test, recall all the bad things you heard about or encountered today. You should find a little cloud of gloom forming over your head. Now recall all the things that went right, or that managed to not go wrong today. The sunshine should break through your cloud of gloom.

What do you do?

Answers to this question are normally inaccurate and revealing in equal proportions. The dull but truthful answer for many managers should be: 'I sit in meetings, talk to people, write e-mails and answer the telephone all day.' This is not an inspiring vision of a life. The most inspiring and accurate answer is when people say something like 'I am setting up a new widget business.' Even 'I sell nappies to chemists in Birmingham' is at least accurate and revealing. Most people answer the question 'What do you do?' in one of three ways:

- *The status seeker's answer:* 'I am a partner, vice-president, big banana at Megacorp.' This may impress underlings, but cannot impress outsiders. It says nothing about what the person does: it simply shows an interest in status.

- *The professional's answer:* 'I am an accountant, lawyer, doctor, consultant, etc.' Again, this does not say what the person does. What do consultants really do? But it shows that the person's first loyalty is to their profession, not to their company.

- *The company person's answer:* 'I work for Megacorp.' This is now rare in the West, but is still standard in Japan. It shows that the person is less concerned about what he or she currently does. Instead, loyalty is to the business.

Why work?

If work was so wonderful, the rich would have found a way of monopolizing it. For most of us, work is not so wonderful. Listening to another boring presentation, writing yet another report, dealing with the daily grind of management is not wholly uplifting.

The most basic answer is that we work to eat. This may be why young professionals are prepared to work all night and all day as they build their careers. This impressive display of passion and commitment is totally unconnected to passion and commitment to the employer. High staff turnover rates give the lie to that assumption.

The passion and commitment is more about instant gratification. Working hard has two immediate benefits. First, it allows for the work-hard, play-hard lifestyle in the short term. Second, it holds out the hope that within a few years the staff can acquire enough money to no longer have to work to eat. They can then move on and set up their own business, become artists, raise a family or whatever their dream is.

The passion and commitment is to themselves, not to the business. The underlying proposition of most businesses is that employees work hard to make someone else richer. The most highly committed workforces are those where there is a strong link between the performance and rewards of the individual. There are exceptions in the voluntary sector and arts where people are not working to eat. But for the majority of managers in the majority of businesses, working to eat remains a powerful motivation. This is perhaps cynical, but it is healthy for the individual and the business. The individual has a clear focus. The business gets a hard-working workforce. High attrition allows for flexibility.

Wishful thinking

The smarter people are, the more likely they are to indulge in wishful thinking in more catastrophic ways. **The smartest people are capable of the dumbest judgements.** Because they are smart, they trust their judgement, and believe that they will win. We all like to think of ourselves as winners; we do want to be seen or act as losers.

Nowhere is this wishful thinking more dangerous than in career choice and managing money, financially the two most important decisions people make.

Wishful thinking career choices

Professional service firms and banks suck up most of the best talent from universities. Recruits are smart people. And because they are smart, they think they will win. They believe that they will get to the top, get to be a partner. Typically, about 10 per cent of them will succeed. They have a 90 per cent chance of failure. And yet they always believe that the 90 per cent are the other people. Objectively, they could look around and see that their peer group is exactly that: their peers are their equals and they are more likely to be part of the 90 per cent than the 10 per cent. It is probably this mindset that encourages young men to go to war or drive fast: it is the other person that will get killed.

By the time it comes for the 90 per cent to leave a company, they have normally rationalized in their own minds why they did not want to be part of that firm anyway, and would rather compete to win elsewhere. But the disappointment in their faces as they reach that conclusion over months or years is always visible.

Wishful thinking investors

As smart people, we like to think that we are smart with our money. We are all smart investors. We like to think we can beat the market. By definition, not everyone can beat the market, especially after trading costs.

One private bank offered its clients an options and futures trading facility. This private bank had a minimum investment of US $1 million, so its customers were wealthy and presumably fairly comfortable handling money. And because of this, they thought they were smart. Options and futures represent a great way to back your judgement against the market and make money fast, or to lose it fast if your judgement is poor.

Eighty-six clients signed up for this service. We decided to look at how many of them made money, and how many of them lost money on this service. We found that all of them lost money. And the more they traded, the more they lost. They were not stupid, but spreads and dealing costs are stacked against the private investor as surely as the roulette wheel is stacked against the gambler. The more you play, the more the house wins. Wisely, the bank withdrew the service. It was making money, but losing customers.

Ultimately, everyone has to take risks. But when wishful thinking blinds smart people to a cool assessment of the odds, disappointment follows.

Working hours

For the manager, working hours should be an irrelevance. The issue is not about time put in, but about results that come out. So, if people want to turn up late, and need to disappear in the middle of the day, that's fine. As long as there is clarity about what needs to be achieved, by whom and by when. Most people, when trusted, will respect this. The working hours may be unusual, but they will go out of their way to repay the trust and get the results. In return, they get the flexibility to manage their personal lives as they need. There will be some who abuse the system. But they will not get the results either. The normal evaluation system will catch them.

The fly in the ointment of this flexible approach is regulation. This creates an environment long on rights and short on responsibilities. Regulating working hours and family-friendly policies puts the focus on time and rights, not results and responsibilities. It also fosters resentment from non-family types who have to fill in for family types. Eventually, the dead hand of bureaucracy will take over. Until then, smash the office clock and make sure it is not repaired.

Work–life balance

When was the last time you heard a work–life guru advocate that you work longer and harder?

Work–life balance has become a euphemism for working less. As a result, it is a toxic discussion to start in any high-flying group: no one wants to be seen as the wimp that wants less work. But everyone struggles with this to some extent. Part of the problem is about expectations: the media push images of people with perfect bodies, perfect smiles and perfect lives. And then we turn away from the poster and find that life is not like that at all: we are faced with stroppy customers, unreasonable bosses, ambiguous work, the train is running late again and we have 55 e-mails in our inbox.

The first step is to work out what your work–life balance is in reality. The evidence shows that we are the idlest generation in history: we work fewer hours per week, and fewer years and have more holidays than any generation before us. But it does not feel that way: we all feel more overworked than ever. So what is your reality? First, check how long you really work.

- When was the last time you got caught in the 7.45 am rush hour on a Sunday?
- How many meetings are scheduled to start before 7.00 am or after 7.00 pm, or on Saturday?
- How many work e-mails do you receive after 8.00 pm?

Whatever the reality: we feel more pressured. We may leave the office, but the office never leaves us. We wear our electronic ball and chains with pride as we show off our latest smartphones, tablets and computers. In contrast, when our parents left the office, they really left it. The only things in the briefcase were the leftover sandwiches from lunch. And perhaps we can learn from them: compartmentalize our lives better. Work time is work time and leisure time is leisure time. Don't mix them up. And if you are addicted to e-mail, set aside one time each evening to satisfy your craving. Last thing at night and first thing in the morning will give your e-mails time stamps to impress everyone.

The second check on work–life balance is to check the work element of it. If our main concern is to figure out how to work less, maybe we are doing the wrong sort of work. If work is drudgery, then perhaps it is time to find work that is more engaging. Top sportspeople and artists train like crazy, but do not complain of overwork: they are engaged in what they do. We only succeed at what we enjoy, so find work that you enjoy.

Finally, check the 'life' element of work–life balance. Media pressure tells us we can have it all and have it now. We cannot. We have to make choices, and yet many people don't make real choices: they drift along trying to have the best of all worlds and becoming frustrated that the ideal is always just out of reach. If setting up a vegan farm, or surfboarding, or raising a family is what is most important to you, then act accordingly. There will be compromises, but know what you want and act on it.

Write right

None of us can be Shakespeare. But we should spare our colleagues the standard jargon-filled drivel that passes as writing in too many organizations.

The best editor I ever had distilled effective writing down to five principles:

- *Write for the reader.* Understand who you are writing for and why the person needs to read your memo. This will focus your story, and help to keep it short and relevant.

- *Tell a story.* A good memo does not include everything that may be relevant. It corrals all the facts and figures, and then presents only those that tell the story, that make the point you need to make. This makes reading the memo easy, avoids diluting the key message and minimizes the chances of misinterpretation.

- *Keep it short.* Churchill once wrote a long letter to his wife, Clementine. At the bottom he added a note: 'I am sorry I wrote such a long letter, I did not have time to write you a short one.' Writing short is difficult. It means clear focus on the key messages only. It also means using short words, avoiding jargon. Finally, it means using short sentences. Short words and sentences are easier to understand than long ones. A busy executive probably does not have the time or inclination to wade through a long-winded document. A good average is 12 words per sentence.

- *Make it active.* Avoid the passive tense, avoid the impersonal. It sounds dull and bureaucratic. Dull may be fine for the civil service and insurance companies, but is not so great for other businesses.

- *Support assertions with facts.* Just because you believe something is right, don't assume that everyone else will make the same assumption. Make sure the facts are there. This also implies that you should make few, not many assertions to keep the writing short. That means focus on the key messages by telling a story.

Finally, where appropriate, make use of visuals: use diagrams, charts and pictures. People are much better at remembering pictures than they are at remembering words. A well-judged cartoon will be better remembered and more persuasive than reams of prose, even at CEO level.

To make this simple, write out the five principles on a piece of card and put it on your desk. Use it when writing, editing, reviewing or coaching other people. It works. It remains a standard to which I always aspire, and always fall short.

Writing and editing skills

1 *Write for the reader.*
2 *Tell a story.*
3 *Keep it short.*
4 *Make it active.*
5 *Support assertions with facts.*

Theories X, Y and Z

Theory X has three underlying assumptions, which lead to a strong command and control business:

- People hate work.
- Formal rewards (bonus, promotions) and sanctions (firing, withholding bonuses) are required to make people perform.
- People hate risk and like security. This implies they like to be led and directed, even if they grumble about it.

Theory Y takes the contrary view, which focuses on building a high-commitment workplace:

- People like work: it gives structure and purpose to their lives.
- People need more than money: they need recognition. They have egos that need to be fed, as well as bellies. They will work for a higher purpose.
- People will be flexible and take risks to the extent that it is worthwhile (for money, ego, vision).

Most organizations display deep schizophrenia over which model of human motivation and management they believe in. They want to believe that theory Y is correct, and this is what all the gurus urge in talking about high-commitment, passionate organizations. The 21st century is meant to be about theory Y. But theory X is going to be around. Ultimately, we probably end up with a fusion of theory X and Y, call it theory Z:

- People need money both for today (to eat) and for their egos (big pay means big car means big ego; big pay means retire early and do your own thing). Formal rewards and sanctions are powerful motivators and demotivators.

- **People crave recognition and status.** They want to be valued as individuals both formally (through titles) and informally (for example when their boss shows that he or she cares about them personally).

- People are schizophrenic about responsibility: they want freedom and power, but like security. Security tends to come from leadership and direction.

To make matters more interesting, businesses and individuals vary widely in character from theory X to theory Y. It helps to know what sort of business and manager you have got.

Ygwyd

Ygwyd is a Welsh word. It is an important one for managers to understand. Next time things go wrong, use it. In English, it means: **'You get what you deserve.'**

If you work for a lousy, dispiriting business with bad management and no prospects, ygwyd. You can complain. Or you can do something about it: leave. If you run a lousy business, the staff are lousy, the consultants are lousy, the information systems are lousy and the results are lousy, ygwyd. You can make excuses, or you can do something about it. Ygwyd is about management responsibility and taking control. If we do not accept responsibility and we are not in control, we are not managers.

The yogi and the commissar

The great manager is an impossible creature: a combination of the yogi and the commissar. The yogi has deep insight. The greatest yogi understands all of human nature, understands the world, sees the future and can provide solutions to even the deepest problem. Such is the yogi's wisdom that he or she attracts devotees that will follow the yogi with enthusiasm to the end of the world. The yogi probably lives on a mountain in Shangri-La rather than in the office next to you.

The commissar is the paragon of efficiency. He or she can equip, supply and move an army overnight. Everything happens where and when and how it is meant to happen. Nothing is left to chance. The commissar makes good decisions fast and gets them obeyed. No one dares to disobey. The troops have learned to follow the commissar wherever he or she goes. Every office is full of aspiring commissars who lack only the military uniform to go with their aspirations, if not their capabilities.

Most of us struggle to be anything like a yogi or a commissar. But the assumption is that we can be both at the same time. Like being Buddha and Genghis Khan, or Plato and Alexander the Great all rolled into one. We cannot do it.

Luckily, everyone else is as deficient as we are, more or less. The trick is not to try to be a yogi if you are a commissar, or vice versa. The trick is to make sure that yogis are in yogi positions and commissars are in commissar positions. If you are in a position that requires both talents, get someone else to support you in the other role. The managerial yogi needs a commissar and vice versa. Like Marx and Lenin.

Z

Zones of comfort and discomfort

Everyone has a comfort zone. And no one should operate completely within it. Within your comfort zone, you know that you are capable of doing all the tasks for which you are responsible. This is efficient and leads to a secure and easy life. It is comfortable. It also means that you are not stretching yourself, not building new skills and capabilities, not achieving all that you can for either yourself or your business. Long term, operating inside the comfort zone alone is unsustainable.

The results of operating in the comfort zone can be seen throughout any organization: they are the grey people sitting in corners doing the same dead-end jobs that they have had for the last 10 or 20 years. If new technology or new skills come along, they are dead meat.

Long term, taking controlled risks by developing new skills and taking on new challenges is a lot less risky than sitting on your hands and hoping the status quo survives. There are typically four stages of competence:

1 *Unconscious incompetence.* Most of us are terrible at most things: it's only when we try them we discover just how bad we are. Try a simple task, for example juggling. Luckily, we do not need to be good at most things, such as juggling.

2 *Conscious incompetence.* This occurs when we actually try a new task, such as juggling. It is far better to be aware of how bad we are, than unaware. At least we can then make the decision about whether we want to acquire that particular skill.

3 *Conscious competence.* This is where we are learning and it tends to be where people get most frustrated and give up. It's like speaking a foreign language: every word and phrase has to be thought about and it is very tiring to sustain. Having a good coach at this point helps.

4 *Unconscious competence.* By this stage we have mastered the new skill and no longer have to think about it. At this point, we no longer think about the foreign language we are speaking: it comes naturally to us.

As an exercise, identify all the skills you need and want. Then identify your capabilities in those areas against the categories above. If the portfolio consists purely of skills where you are consciously incompetent, you are in trouble. You are probably drowning in your current position. If all your skills are in the unconscious competence category, you are complacent and going backwards in your career. Time to wake up. Ideally, you will have a balanced portfolio: have some strong skills that allow you to excel in your current role, and other embryonic skills that allow you to grow in the future.

References

Hammer, M and Champy, J A (1993) *Reengineering the Corporation: A manifesto for business revolution*, Harper Business Books, New York

Parkinson, C N (1958) *Parkinson's Law*, John Murray, London

Porter, T and Waterman, R (1982) *In Search of Excellence: Lessons from America's best run companies*, Harper & Row, New York

Wiseman, R (2004) *The Luck Factor: The scientific study of a lucky mind*, Arrow Books, London